NORSE MYTHOLOGY

A FIREFLY BOOK

Published by Firefly Books Ltd. 2024

First printing

Library of Congress Control Number: 2024935771

Library and Archive Canada Cataloguing in Publication
Title: Norse mythology : the gods, heroes, monsters, and legends of Viking culture / Finn D. Moore.
Names: Moore, Finn D., author.
Description: Previously published: Irvington, New York: Moseley Road Inc, 2021.
Identifiers: Canadiana 20240359216 | ISBN 9780228105046 (hardcover)
Subjects: LCSH: Mythology, Norse. | LCSH: Scandinavia—Religion. | LCGFT: Illustrated works.
Classification: LCC BL860 .M66 2024 | DDC 293/.13—dc23

Published in the United States by
Firefly Books (U.S.) Inc.
P.O. Box 1338, Ellicott Station
Buffalo, New York 14205

Published in Canada by
Firefly Books Inc.
50 Staples Avenue, Unit 1
Richmond Hill, Ontario L4B 0A7

President: Sean Moore
International Rights: Karen Prince (kprince@moseleyroad.com)
Author: Finn D. Moore | Features by Finn D. Moore, Duncan Youel, David Edgell
Series Management: Oiloften.co.uk
Editors: Duncan Youel and Fiona Baile
Book design: Stuart Jones
Series art direction and covers: Duncan Youel
Picture research: Stuart Jones, David Edgell

Printed in China | E

NORSE MYTHOLOGY

THE GODS, HEROES, MONSTERS AND LEGENDS OF VIKING CULTURE

FINN D. MOORE

FIREFLY BOOKS

CONTENTS

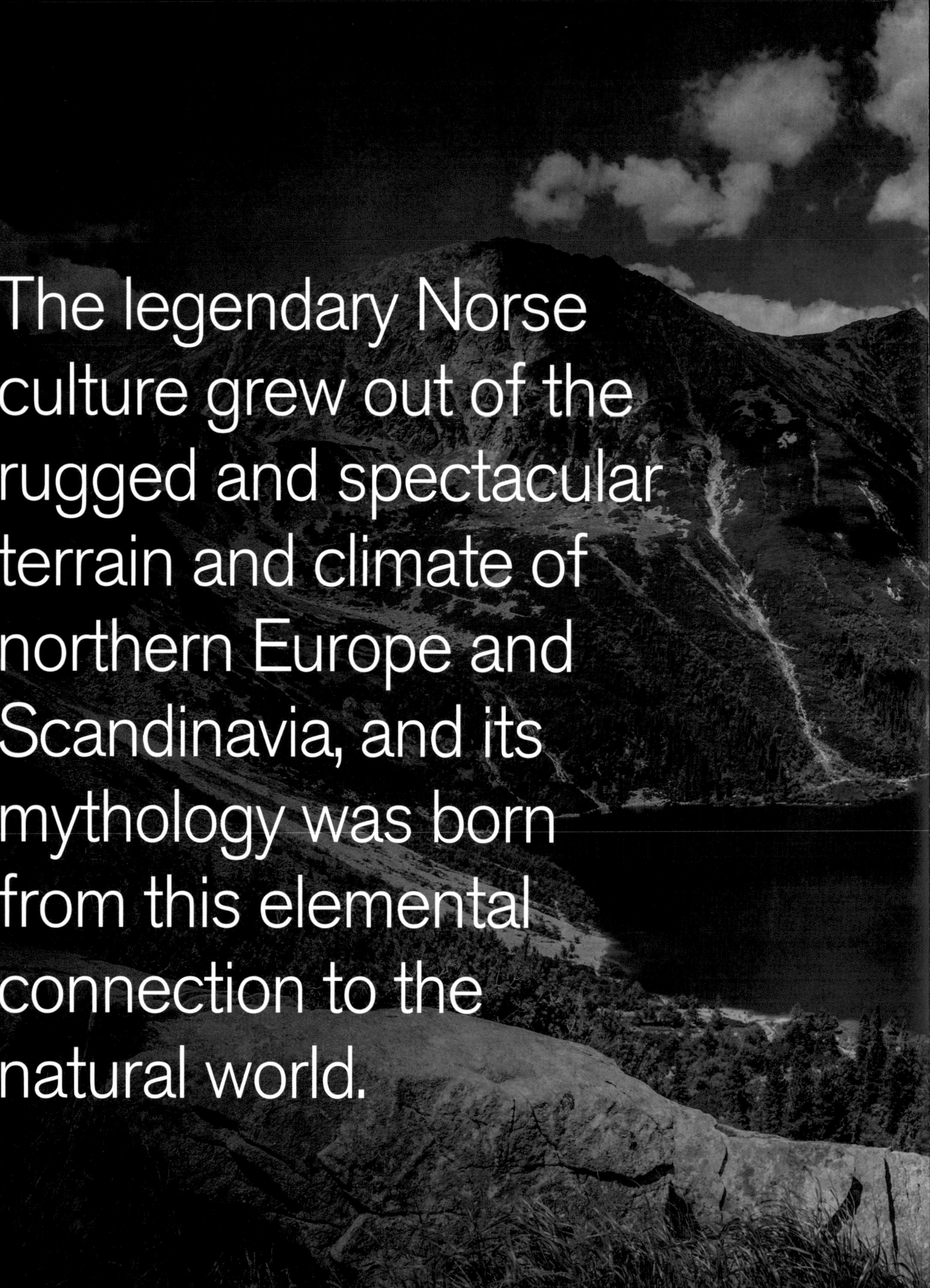

The legendary Norse culture grew out of the rugged and spectacular terrain and climate of northern Europe and Scandinavia, and its mythology was born from this elemental connection to the natural world.

NORSE CULTURE

ISLANDE
Skalholt
Hekla
Is. de Feroe
Isles Schetland
LES BRITANNIQUES
Isles Westernes
I. Orcades
Wick
Inverness
Elgin
New Aberdeen
ECOSSE
Edenbourg
Glascow
Londonderry
Down Patrick
Armagh
Galloway
IRLANDE
Dublin
Wexford
Cork
Cap Clear
Lancaster
York
Chester
Caernarvon
Lincoln
Montgomery
Norwich
Pembroke
Glocester
Oxford
Bristol
ANGLETERRE
Londres
Canterbury
Launceston
Cap Lizard
Grenesey
Gersey
Dieppe
Dunkerque
Bruxelle
Lille
Amiens
Rouen
Soissons
Caen
Reims
Alencon
Paris
Chaalons
Rennes
Orleans
Troyes
Metz
Nancy
Nantes
Tours
Bourges
Dijon
la Haye
Amsterdam
Embden
Groningue
Munster
Cassel
Cologne
Liege
Francfort
Mayence
Manheim
Bremen
Hanover
Brunswick
Leipsick
Hambourg
Wiborg
DANNEMARCK
Bergen
Christiania
Stavanger
NORVEGE

LAPONIE
Kola
Kandalax
Ponoi
Mer Blanche
Mezen
Archangel
Kewrol
Cholmogorod
Dwina R.
Kargapol
Totma
Wologda
Tornea
Kimi
Lulea
Pitea
Ulea
Golfe de Botnie
Cajaneborg
Carlby
Umea
Wasa
Hernosand
SUE
DE
FINLANDE
Biorneborg
Hudwik
Tawast
Wyborg
Kexholm
Olonek
Ladoga
Falun
Giafle
Abo
Borgo
G de Finlande
Petersbourg
Biel-Ozero
Upsal
Stokholm
Narva
Rewel
R U S S
Pernow
Weliki
Nowogorod
Tuer
Pskow
Livonie
Luki
Gottland
Riga
Calmar
Witepsk
B A L T I Q U E
Courlande
Rosienne
Polock
Smolensko
Carlscron
MER
Konigsberg
Wilna
Mscislaw
LITUANIE
Dantzik
Marienbourg
Minsk
D'E
Colberg
Stettin
PRUSSE
Nowogradek
Grodno
Thorn
Inowroclaw
Bielsk
Nowogorod Siewerski
Posna
Plock
Brzese
Guesna
Warsovie
Batorin
Glogaw
Kalisz
Rawa
Zitomirz
Kiow
Breslaw
POLOGNE
Lublin
Luck
UK
Schweidnitz
Sandomirz
Woladimirz
Cracovie
Przemysl
Leopol
Olmutz
Kaminieck
Braclaw
Halicz
Vienne
Presbourg

INTRODUCTION

The Norsemen of old Scandinavia were a tough, and hardy people, perhaps known best today for their prowess in both bloody combat, and storytelling.

ABOVE: A late 19th century work depicts Odin, sitting on his high throne above Asgard, with his two ravens Hugin and Munin close by, and his wolves Geri and Freki at his feet. *Geri* and *Freki* are Old Norse words, both meaning "the greedy one." Hugin means *Thought*, and Munin translates as *Memory*; **OPPOSITE:** An early 20th century woodcut depicts viking longships sailing up the River Humber in Yorkshire.

The legend of the Norse vikings—the fierce, fearless warriors who ravaged much of Europe for centuries—has made them infamous, but many other aspects of Norse culture have been overlooked or lost to time altogether. The Norsemen had a rich and vibrant culture that thrived in spite of—or perhaps because of—the violence, hardship, and hostile conditions that were intrinsic facts of life in their time.

For thousands of years, ancient cultures all over the world have relied on mythology and religion to help explain and understand the phenomena of the natural world around them, and Norse culture was no different: The home of the Norsemen was one of long, dark nights, constant warfare, and the bitter ice and snow of their harsh winters. Norse mythology, by extension, is flush with much of that same violence, darkness, and hardship; it helped the Norsemen to understand the world they lived in, to guide their lives and their morality, and to give them hope of a better life in Valhalla after death. In this way, Norse mythology was a source of both entertainment, comfort, and history; it included the origins of the universe and explained the natural world, enriched culture and tradition through storytelling, and cast the ever-present threat of violent death in a more acceptable light.

It is important to remember that the myths of the Norse gods, the nine realms, and the inevitable coming of Ragnarök were not simply works of fiction to the Norsemen. These stories are tied inextricably to the religion of Old Norse paganism; they were a core part of the Norse belief system, and figures such as Thor and Odin were as real to the Norsemen as any other aspect of the natural world.

Sadly, what few recordings of the Norse myths we have access to today are only a tiny fraction of the originals. The original tellings of these myths were not recorded but passed down orally, and it was not until the end of the Viking Age that the first written compilations of Norse myths were put down on paper. As such, there are no surviving manuscripts of Norse myths that were written by Norsemen of the time.

In this book you will find a collection of some of the most significant Norse myths, compiled largely from the *Prose Edda* and *Poetic Edda*, the two earliest and most faithful recordings of Norse mythology. As the source material is now centuries old, there have been countless adaptations, retellings, and evolutions of these stories over time; some inconsistencies with the modern understanding of the Norse gods and their stories are to be expected, and the fluid nature of Norse mythology also allows for a good deal of inconsistency between the original myths themselves. Still, the core aspects of these immortal figures—Thor, the hammer-wielding, giant-slaying god of thunder, Odin, the wise All-Father and king of the gods—have remained recognizable and iconic to this day.

NORSE HISTORY

TOP AND CENTER: An artist's impression of hunter-gatherers during a reindeer hunt in the Stone Age, c. 12,000 BC; **ABOVE:** Impressions of a Bronze Age settlement in northern Europe, c. 2000 BC.

There is no one country that holds a claim to the culture and traditions of Norse mythology and religion. The word "Norse" in this context generally refers to the early North Germanic tribes of Scandinavia, particularly from around 2000 BC to the end of the Viking Age in the 11th century AD. There are many terms for the people of early Scandinavia, including North Germanic people, Norsemen, and Vikings, although it should be noted that the term "Viking" refers specifically to the seafaring Scandinavian war parties that were prevalent from the 8th to 11th centuries.

The earliest Scandinavian tribes lived over 10,000 years ago, originally as nomadic hunter-gatherers before later building permanent settlements. Little is known about these prehistoric tribes beyond archeological findings such as burial mounds and the remnants of stone tools. The first settlements were established around 5000 BC, when farming and cattle-raising began to replace the earlier hunter-gatherer lifestyle. By the time Scandinavia entered the Bronze Age in 1700 BC, civilization had advanced by leaps and bounds; Bronze-Age Scandinavians relied heavily on shipbuilding by this point, and trade with other cultures was common. Written language was not yet in use, however, leading to a dearth of information about the culture and religion of the time, but many surviving artifacts hint at the values and rituals of the time period. A notable warrior culture—a value system that placed emphasis on combat and warfare—is signified in many carvings, and some artifacts depict an early sun-worshiping religious system that died out around 500 BC. It is believed that many aspects of the earliest Germanic religions were preserved in the more well-known Old Norse religion, established at the dawn of Scandinavia's Iron Age.

Scandinavia entered the Iron age around 500 BC, bringing a period of thriving wealth and expansion. Trade of amber, slaves, and iron and leather products increased drastically, particularly with the Roman Empire, and the

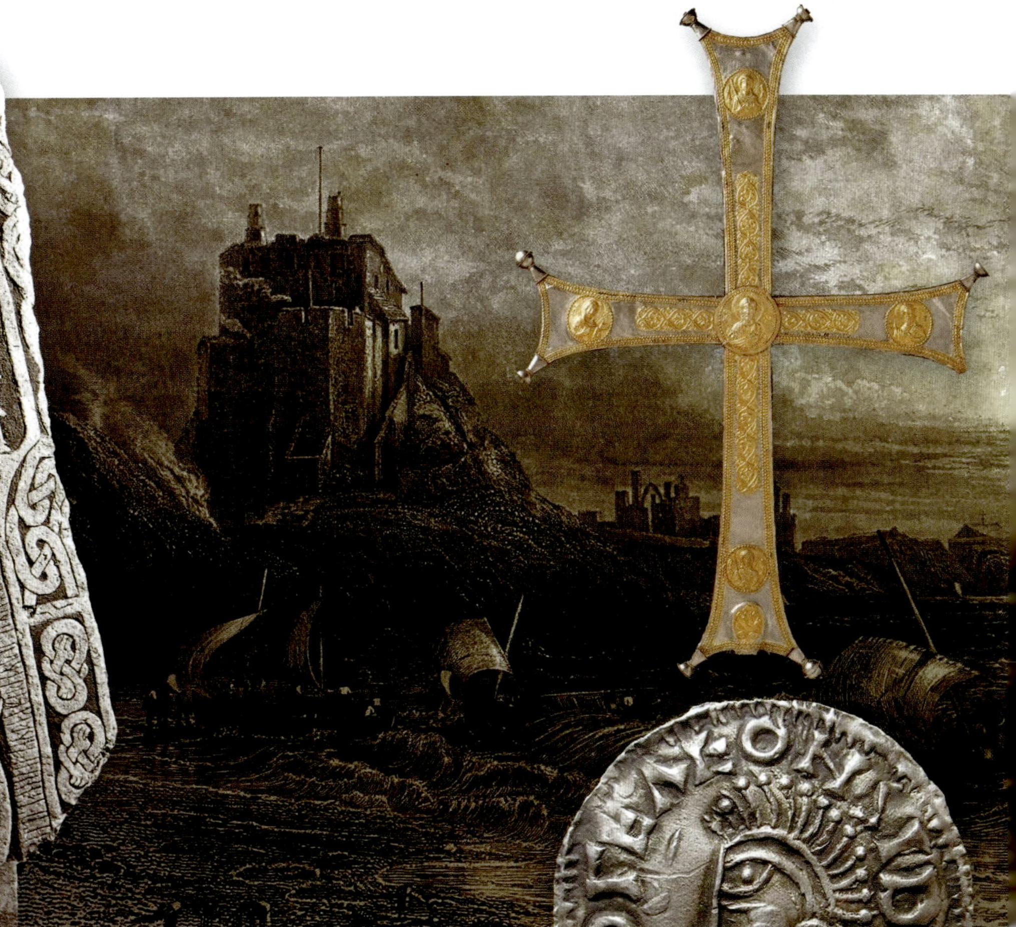

many tribes began to conglomerate into larger settlements and villages. At the same time, legal systems and normalized class structures were further developed. The Elder Futhark, the first system of written language in Scandinavia, was established around 200–100 BC, and Old Norse religion—also called Norse paganism, heathenism, or North Germanic religion—expanded, giving rise to the stories that are remembered today in Norse mythology.

By 300 AD, Scandinavia's warrior culture had become even more prevalent; the development of advanced shipbuilding techniques, the consolidation of disparate tribes into powerful strongholds, and the high value placed on talented warriors all contributed to the reputation of early Scandinavians as fearsome warriors. By 500 AD, the first Scandinavian raiding parties had begun plundering small European settlements. This practice grew, with raids becoming bolder and more frequent, until the Viking Age began in Britain with the raid of Lindisfarne Abbey in 793 AD.

The Viking age was a period of massive expansion, warfare, raiding, and conquest by the Norsemen (the common term for medieval Scandinavians) that spanned from 793–1066 AD. During this period, Viking raiders were feared throughout Europe for their sudden, devastating attacks; their seamanship and combat prowess allowed them to appear without warning, raze a town to the ground, and disappear with their plunder before any soldiers arrived.

The Viking Age ended in the early 11th century; around this time, most of the pagan tribes of Scandinavia had been converted to Christianity, and the practice of Viking raids began to ebb. The last Scandinavian king to adopt Christianity was Olof Skötkonung, who reigned from 995–1020 AD. Although Norse pagan religious beliefs persisted at least until the 12th century, the rising influence of Christianity combined with the steady decline of Norse beliefs marked an end to the Viking Age, and to the era of the Norsemen.

MAIN IMAGE, ABOVE: An 1843 engraving of Lindisfarne, the Holy Island on the Northumbrian coast; **ABOVE, LEFT INSET:** The Runic Stone, from Tjängvide, Götland, depicts Odin (riding his eight-legged steed, Sleipnir) and Frigga; and longship. c. 700 AD; **INSET, TOP:** Byzantine Processional Cross, c. 1000 AD; **INSET, ABOVE:** Coin depicting Olof Skötkonung, the last Scandinavian king to convert to Christianity; **BELOW:** St. Boniface fells the sacred Jove's Oak by an apparent miracle, thereby converting the people of the Germanic region to Christianity.

VIKINGS

The etymology of the word "viking" is uncertain, but one of the most likely origins of the word indicates that it is derived from an Old Norse word referring to a long voyage by sea.

TOP, LEFT: Depiction of a viking raid on the English coast. Hand-colored engraving, 1879; **TOP, RIGHT:** A 1950s recreation of a viking voyage; **ABOVE:** Viking metalwork depicting "berserker" warriors.

The word "viking" would have described the voyage vikings undertook when setting out on raids; in this case, the word "vikingr" would likely have been the word used to describe the actual person doing the raiding.

The vikings were feared throughout Europe, particularly coastal towns and monasteries, for their devastating hit-and-run tactics of warfare. Instead of using their advanced shipbuilding techniques to wage naval war or relying on numbers to march armies inland, the vikings used their long, narrow ships to sail up rivers and along coasts; their mobile warships were able to land almost anywhere there was water, which allowed them to appear as if out of nowhere in small, well-trained groups, raze a town to the ground, and be back on their ships with their stolen treasure and captured slaves before the local militia could arrive.

The vikings came from a culture that valued combat prowess, bravery, and the accumulation of personal wealth. They were also uniformly unafraid of death, as to die in battle was seen as the only honorable way to die. A death in battle would ensure that one's soul was taken to Valhalla for eternal glory after death, according to Norse beliefs of the time. This mentality, combined with their advanced ships and combat strategies, gave them a huge advantage over the relatively small and poorly-defended settlements they preferred to attack. Their reputation as fierce, almost demonic, warriors also worked to their advantage,

as well as the fact that the social norms of Europe held no sway over them. Vikings frequently raided churches and monasteries, attacked at night and without warning, and generally showed complete disregard for the conventions of warfare "etiquette" of the time. Many sources also state that vikings were known to enter a state of frenzied battle-rage called *berserkergang*, allowing them to fight with reckless abandon, which led them to be known as "berserkers."

Later in the Viking Age, as the raiding parties provided more and more wealth and resources the vikings began to expand further, transitioning from earlier hit-and-run tactics into more long-term conquests and permanent settlements. This, along with the many Christian slaves the they brought back to their homeland, had the unintended side effect of bringing them into contact with aspects of many other cultures and belief systems. As a result, the vikings slowly began to be converted to Christianity by the various missionaries, priests, and holy people that they interacted with, a cultural shift that played a major role in the decline of the Viking Age.

One popular misconception about the vikings is that they were barbaric, lawless savages; this is far from the truth. They were certainly brutal and efficient warriors when they went out on their raids, but this was only one aspect of Norse culture—albeit one that was highly valued. Not every Norseman was a viking, and most vikings were also farmers, builders, blacksmiths, and craftsmen for most of the year when they returned home with their plunder.

The Norsemen were also much cleaner and more hygienic than most modern depictions imply. Archaeologists have recovered several artifacts—notably several hundred hand-carved combs—that indicate cleanliness was an important part of Norse culture. Bathing and taking care of one's personal hygiene and appearance was a common practice in Norse culture, which allowed for greater control over disease and infection.

According to custom, all free Norse men were permitted, if not obligated, to carry weapons at all times. Weapons were such an integral part of Norse culture that even *thralls*, or slaves, were expected to carry a knife for utility and personal protection. Weapons were a distinct status symbol in Norse culture; the quantity, craftsmanship, and quality of a Norseman's weapons would have been the best way to determine their class and social standing. Most carried an ax or a spear as their primary weapon, usually paired with a *seax*—a kind of machete-like knife—as a tool and secondary weapon. Swords, which were less durable and more expensive to make, were usually owned by wealthier vikings, although they were likely not often used in battle. Bows were occasionally used at the onset of a battle or during (extremely rare) ship-to-ship combat.

TOP: Children's book illustration of vikings in a somewhat improbable longship clash in a fjord. Early four-color litho reproduction from 1925, of a painting by Manning de V. Lee.

LONGSHIPS

The vikings voyaged across the North Sea to the British Isles, south into France, around the Iberian Peninsula into the Mediterranean, and westwards across the North Atlantic to Greenland, finally to the American continent.

Archaeological evidence dating back thousands of years reveals that shipbuilding was an important part of Norse culture long before the first viking raids began; and the first longships may have been constructed as early as 300 BC—well before the Norsemen had developed a written language. One of the key factors contributing to viking success in battle was the quality and craftsmanship of their vessels. Their advanced shipbuilding techniques and deep understanding of sailing and navigation gave them a huge advantage during their attacks on coastal settlements. Their longships were the epitome of viking innovation. Specialized vessels that were designed to transport small, highly-trained groups of warriors quickly and quietly. The crafts were long, narrow, and designed to be as light and as maneuverable as possible. Driven by several rows of oars, and an additional mainsail, they could travel long distances across open ocean at high speeds, while still remaining light and low-profile. Because of the mobile, narrow design, they could safely navigate waters as shallow as one meter. They were also symmetrically designed with no designated front or back, allowing the ships to quickly reverse course and row in the opposite direction without having to execute slow turns. The ships were compact and fast enough so that they could be sailed along even the smallest of rivers, traveling miles inland to attack places no other ship could reach. One Viking expedition in the 9th century navigated the course of the Seine river all the way to Paris. Although most coastal settlements were at least

somewhat prepared for attack by sea, those areas further inland were often unguarded. Their most common tactic was to sail a longship silently up the coast either at night or on an especially misty day, so that the warriors could appear as if out of nowhere. From the late 700s AD the vikings were able to terrorize many parts of northern Europe, before settling and colonizing in Britain, Ireland, and northern France. Huge swathes of Saxon Britain fell to the Vikings, and their culture and language had a profound effect on British history through the Danelaw. In France their settlements were eventually formalized into the region of Normandy, its name deriving from the Latin *Nortmanni*—the Norsemen, and giving rise to the Normans, by then Christian, who in 1066 successfully invaded and conquered the whole of England and the Welsh provinces. Viking outposts and settlements were established in much of Iceland, then further west in Greenland, and the Norse chieftain, Leifr Eriksson, and his clan, voyaged as far as the American continent, settling in Newfoundland in c. 1020 AD.

TOP RIGHT: The geographical range of the viking explorations in the 300-plus year period, c. 800–1100 AD; **CENTER RIGHT:** A recreated viking longship in the Viking Museum, Oslo, Norway; **MAIN IMAGE:** Composite digital image of viking longship re-enactment.

VIKING CULTURE AND RITUALS

Viking culture was by turns progressive . . . and barbaric. Women had a far more equal standing than in Christian cultures, though conversely, the vikings did occasionally practice human sacrifice.

TOP: The Gjermundbu viking helmet, c. 900 AD, Viking Museum, Oslo, Norway; **ABOVE:** Viking spearheads, c. 900 AD, Melbourne Museum, Australia. The 2018 *Vikings Exhibition*.

The Norsemen had long-standing legal systems, class structures, and a rich oral tradition. Many Norse laws dealt with the concept of crime and punishment, particularly in cases revolving around issues of honor, feuds, and personal insults. In fairness, many of these conflicts were resolved through violence, but there was at least a system in place to guide the process to its bloody conclusion.

Norse society had a distinct class system that broke the population down into three classes: *jarls*, or chieftains, *karls*, or free men, and *thralls*, or slaves. There was some variation in terms of more minor positions and titles, of course, but this three-class system was a core concept of Norse culture. Most Norsemen were karls, and there was some potential for upward mobility in that class; it was possible to gain power and status through wealth and great exploits, and a karl could hope to someday become a jarl. Thralls had much more limited opportunities to rise above their station, but it was possible to for a thrall to be freed or buy their own freedom and become a *leysingi*, or "freedman." Freedmen were still below their former masters in social standing, but their grandchildren would be born as truly free karls.

Norse women had many more rights than women in other cultures of the time. Divorce was legal, for example, and could be initiated by a woman who felt that her husband was either not providing for her or treating her poorly. Women could inherit property, act as their own defense in legal matters, and own businesses;

many women were merchants, farmers, and brewers, for example. Women also held a certain amount of religious authority, as many aspects of Old Norse religion were assigned exclusively to women. As religious leaders, seers, medicine women, and runemasters, Women held sway in many cultural and spiritual aspects of Norse society. Most free Viking women were married, and the woman's standing in society was usually linked to that of her husband. Most marriages were decided by the family, however, and it was rare for a woman to choose her husband. Once Norse paganism gave way to Christianity, the then-unusual rights and freedoms of Norse women began to dwindle and eventually disappeared entirely.

One of the most important and well-documented practices of Old Norse religion was *blót*, or ritual sacrifice. Many texts, myths, and carvings depict animal sacrifices; this practice was most common during feast days, before battles, and during periods of hardship. Human sacrifice is also mentioned at length, the methods of which were numerous and varied; many sacrifices appear to have been made via hanging, and others via drowning in wells, lakes, and bogs. There were even some instances of willing self-sacrifice recorded, although many more sacrifices were carried out on slaves, prisoners of war, and criminals. Human sacrifices were less common than animal sacrifice, and were usually only carried out in particularly dire circumstances. More minor sacrifices of tools and weapons were also made frequently, usually by depositing them into a bog; most Vikings were also buried with their weapons and a good deal of their wealth. In some instances, swords appear to have been ritually "sacrificed" or "killed" before burial by being bent or broken into an unusable state; this may have been a way to commemorate a fallen Viking, or to protect the burial site from graverobbers by rendering valuable swords unusable.

Sports, contests, and tests of skill and strength were a popular pastime for Norsemen, particularly those that involved sparring and martial prowess. Many contests included spear throwing, wrestling, feats of strength and agility, and fist fighting. Skiing, ice skating, swimming, and diving were also popular both for recreation and as useful survival skills, depending on the climate.

TOP: Detail of the Stora Hammars I Stone, Gotland. A *valknut* rune sign, and ritual sacrifice, c. 600 AD; **ABOVE, CENTER:** Bracteate pendant c. 600; **ABOVE:** North Germanic bracteate pendant, c. 500–600 AD. Depicts Odin on horseback, surmounted by swastika symbol in *repousse*.

The northern lights at Alta, on the most northerly tip of Norway, in the Arctic Circle. Thousands of prehistoric rock carvings are at nearby Hjemmeluft Bay.

1

NORSE MYTHOLOGY

LEFT: A 17th century print edition of *Codex Regius*.

ABOVE, CENTER: Title page of a later, printed edition of the *Prose Edda*—the earliest written form of the Norse sagas, from the 13th century academic, Snorri Sturluson; **ABOVE:** Title page of Olive Bray's 1908 English translation of *Codex Regius*, also known as the *Poetic Edda*.

Norse mythology refers to the collection of myths, stories, and traditional beliefs of the early tribes of pre-Christian Scandinavia. It has roots in Proto-Germanic folklore, and some key concepts may trace as far back as the bronze age of Scandinavia. The height of Norse mythology was around the Viking Age, from the late 8th century AD to the early 12th century. Unfortunately, as much of Norse culture and storytelling was passed down as an oral tradition—at the time, great value was placed in the ability of *skalds*, or poets, to memorize poems and stories—almost no original record of Norse mythology survives today. The earliest reliable sources that we do have were mostly compiled years after the end of the Viking Age, primarily the *Prose Edda*, a Norse textbook composed in the 13th century by Snorri Sturluson, and the *Poetic Edda*, an untitled collection of poems also compiled in the 13th century. These two works are by far the most detailed and reliable sources of Norse Mythology available today; it is believed that these manuscripts contain faithful recordings of stories that were previously only passed down through oral history.

What we do know of Norse mythology is still a rich, colorful tapestry. The pantheon of the Norse canon is flush with gods, giants, and mortal heroes, all of which are given their own distinct personalities, strengths, and flaws. The gods of Norse mythology are humanized in their moments of weakness and bravery alike, while at the same time they are depicted as larger-than-life beings of unimaginable power. Although the gods did have individual domains and associations (Thor, for instance, is the god of thunder, while Loki is the god of fire and mischief), and Norse culture included many rituals that involved worshiping prime deities such as Odin in a public setting, many Norsemen chose to individually worship the god who they felt most personally in tune with.

In Norse Cosmology, the universe is broken up into nine realms, all of which are supported by or intersect with Yggdrasil, the world tree. Yggdrasil is the core axis of the entire universe, an impossibly large ash tree whose branches support whole worlds and whose roots stretch all the way down into the underworld.

The many gods can generally be divided into a few categories. The first—and arguably most important—faction is the Aesir gods of Asgard, including key figures such as Odin, Thor, Loki, Frigga, and Baldur. These gods are some of the most well-known in Norse mythology, and are generally the protagonists of the myths they feature in. Odin in particular stands out as the All-Father, king of the gods and partially responsible for the creation of the world.

Next is the smaller, lesser-known faction of the Vanir. These gods were originally introduced as outsiders to the Aesir, arriving from Vanaheim to wage war with the Aesir. The Vanir were associated with fertility, magic, and prophecy, and were perceived as the more warlike of the two factions. The Vanir include gods such as Freyja, Freyr, and Njord.

These two factions waged war upon first meeting, a conflict known as the Aesir-Vanir War, but eventually came to terms and formed a peace treaty that merged the Vanir with the Aesir.

Beyond the gods are the Jötnar, or giants, of Jotunheim, the eternal enemies of the Aesir. Dwarfs and Elves also commonly appear in Norse mythology as related but dissimilar races, as well as spirits such as the Norns and Valkyries.

CYCLICAL TIME

The concept of time as a cycle, rather than a linear progression with a beginning and end, is deeply rooted in Norse mythology and cosmology.

This recurring pattern—life, death, and rebirth—features in many myths, but most notably it is represented in the grand scheme of Norse cosmology. The pattern is as follows: the universe is created, life is born and history plays out, the world is destroyed in the fires of Ragnarök, and finally new life emerges from the ashes to rebuild the world, beginning the cycle all over again. The concept of Ragnarök, the inevitable twilight of the gods and end of the world as we know it, hints at a core aspect of the Norse worldview: death and entropy cannot be avoided, but life goes on. Líf and Lífþrasir, the two humans who survive Ragnarök and repopulate the earth, symbolize that continuation of life as the cycle resets; this is generally interpreted as a hopeful ending to the story, as it focuses more on the inception of new life than on the inevitable destruction to come with the arrival of the next Ragnarök.

Reincarnation in general was also a popular belief in Norse religion. This concept is at odds with the common belief that those who die in battle are sent to Valhalla to dine and fight alongside Odin until Ragnarök comes. Many Norse children were named after a deceased relative, and some stories make direct reference to the idea that the naming of a child may allow that dead relative to live again through them. Other myths also feature creatures that live in an eternal cycle of rebirth: Thor's twin goats, for instance, can be killed and eaten only to be revived the next day as long as their bones are intact, and the Asgardian boar Saehrímnir is slaughtered and cooked every night to feed the Aesir and *einherjar* (the spirits of Valhalla) only to be resurrected the next day.

TOP: A 19th century woodcut, depicts Ragnarök—the end of the world of the Aesir gods; **ABOVE:** The goats who pull Thor's chariot can be killed and eaten, but are renewed the next day.

TOP: A view of Mount Asgard, named for the home of the Aesir gods in Norse mythology, but majestically existing in space and time on Baffin Island, Canada; **ABOVE:** A page from the 17th century manuscript of *Skáldskaparmál*, the third section of the *Prose Edda*, originally documented from the Old Norse oral tradition in the 13th century.

It can be useful to draw a distinction between the concepts of myth and history when researching a culture with prehistoric roots.

Mythology, for instance, refers to the framework of traditional stories, myths, and folk tales of a given culture. Humans have relied on mythology and storytelling for thousands of years to try to explain the world around them; myths have long been a tool for understanding and exploring natural phenomena. Most mythologies also feature a *cosmogony*, a creation myth to explain the origin of the universe and human life, and an *eschatology*, a myth that predicts the end of the world. Myths tend to focus on the supernatural, usually revolving around gods, heroes, monsters, and the relationships and conflicts between them.

History, on the other hand, refers to the study and recording of actual events in humanity's timeline. Geography—location, *place*—is also integral to this real world timeline. Historical information should mark the passage of time, detailing interactions and conflicts between real, named groups and individuals; while mythology tends to be open to interpretation, history should refer to clear-cut facts.

Many cultures have interwoven mythology and history over the millennia, turning real historical figures into legends and treating ancient myths and folk tales as true retellings of history, and Norse culture was no different. Many of the kings, heroes, and conflicts of Norse mythology are based in some amount of fact, and the lack of true primary sources from the earlier centuries make it difficult to tell what is recorded history and what is a retelling of a long-standing myth. Both are valuable in their own way, and examining the two together can provide true insight into the culture and traditions of an era that might otherwise have been forgotten.

RUNES AND MAGIC

Before the year 100 AD, there was no formalized system of written language in ancient Scandinavia. The writing system that eventually developed was based on a runic alphabet; the earliest surviving artifacts displaying runic carvings are believed to have originated in around 150 AD.

The first of the runic alphabets was the Elder Futhark, which held out as the primary alphabet for the Norse folk until 800 AD, when it was replaced by the Younger Futhark—a simplified and streamlined evolution of the alphabet. From there, the runes branched out into several variations on the original theme, but the Elder and Younger Futhark are the most well-known today.

The runes each have their own individual sound as well as a specific meaning, which allowed for variation in how they were used; they could be written out to spell words phonetically, or the meaning of each individual rune could be relied upon instead. This may have had an impact on the prevailing idea of runes as a source of magic in Norse mythology; it was believed that those with mastery over and understanding of the runes could work them into spells, using them to predict the future or enact changes on the world around them. Runes could be formed into *sigils* (the pictorial identities of deities) and carved into blanks, armor, tools, and weapons, or written out in staves to form spell-like phrases.

The two other best-recorded forms of magic in Norse paganism were *Galdr* and *Seidr*. Galdr, literally meaning "spell" or "incantation" in Old Norse, is a form of magic that revolves around chanting poems and incantations in order to change the course of battles, control the weather, and speak with the dead. The chanting of an incantation also often involves specific ritual practices. The art of Galdr is associated directly with Odin, who—in his eternal quest for knowledge and magical secrets—is attributed with a deep understanding of the spells and charms that can be cast in this way. Galdr is generally a more practical, physical magic than seidr; its effects are intended to have concrete beneficial effects.

Seidr, comparatively, is a much more cerebral practice. Rather than invoking incantations to cause a specific effect, Seidr is primarily used for the purposes of prophecy and fortune-telling. Though Seidr is also associated with Odin, it was originally taught to the Aesir by Freyja, the Vanir goddess of love, war, and sorcery. Unlike Galdr and rune magic, Seidr was considered a feminine practice; men were able to practice Seidr, but doing so would break a cultural taboo and might result in persecution or exile. Odin, who was taught to use Seidr personally by Freyja, is the only male figure who seems to be permitted to practice this form of magic freely.

Though the practice of Norse magic declined after the Christianization of Scandinavia, there has been a relatively recent resurgence of these traditions in the 20th and 21st centuries. Now known more generally as Heathenism or Norse paganism, modern-day practitioners also place particular emphasis on runic divination.

TOP: A modern set of runes, based on carvings from c. 100–200 AD and the *Elder Futhark* and *Younger Futhark* systems of writing, c. 800–900 AD; **ABOVE:** Detail from *Freya*, 1890, by Irish painter James Doyle Penrose (1862–1932). Freyja is the Vanir goddess who teaches the Asgardians, and particularly Odin, the cerebral practice of *Seidr*—prophesising the shape of future events.

ORIGINS

Cosmogonic myths, or creation myths, are narrative attempts to explore and understand the origins of the cosmos, the earth, and human life. This concept is a core aspect of the mythological systems of cultures all over the world; almost every culture has its own variation on a creation myth.

ABOVE: A modern depiction of the frost giant Ymir; **MAIN IMAGE:** *Aurora Borealis*—the Northern Lights—over a frozen ocean, photographed in the Lofoten islands, Norway.

There have been some attempts to classify the similarities that can be found between the many creation myths of various cultures around the world; many, for instance, feature a creator deity constructing the world *ex nihilo*, or "from nothing," as seen in the Christian cosmogony. Others feature a cosmic egg or parent figure giving birth to the universe. The Norse creation myth can be categorized as both an "order from chaos" myth—that is, the formation of an ordered cosmos from a primordial, chaotic void—and a "world parent" myth, as Ymir's body is used to construct the nine realms.

In Norse mythology, the very first living beings to exist are instantly thrust into war with each other; once the fighting is over, the corpse of the first living being is dismembered by the victors

and used to build the world as we know it. As creation myths go, the Norse version is particularly bloody and full of conflict; given the harsh and dramatic environment that was the home of the Norsemen, it follows that the Norse creation myth should be just as violent. This myth is tinged with the core conflicts present in Norse culture; first, the fire of Muspelheim against the ice of Nilfheim and the warmth of Buri's heart against the frost giant Ymir are reminiscent of the warm, green summers and frigid, dark winters that were so characteristic of Norse life. Second, the immediate and violent conflict between the gods and the giants is a direct parallel to the warring, feuding tribes of Norse society. The feud between the giants and the gods is set in stone from the very beginning, never to end, a concept that echoes the long-running blood feuds that were characteristic of some aspects of Norse society. Both of these concepts—the beautiful, dangerous landscape, and the constant threat of violent conflict—were powerful influences on the Norse creation myth.

The following pages detail the events of the most commonly accepted version of the Norse creation myth. As with much of Norse mythology, many interpretations and translations of the source material over the years have resulted in quite a bit of variation in the characters, places, and events of the myth. For instance, in some versions, the giant Ymir is known instead as Orgelmir, or "seething clay;" In others, the trio of gods who give life to the first humans are Odin, Hoenir, and Loki, rather than Odin, Vili, and Ve. This version of the story is one of many, with some aspects of multiple versions borrowed for a more cohesive narrative.

ABOVE: As great glacial bergs of ice fall towards *Muspelheim*, the realm of fire, great clouds of primeval steam rise up, only to freeze again into hoarfrost. Eventually a giant figure is formed from the countless layers of ice . . . and the giant Ymir, first of the frost giants, comes to life. Illustration by Emil Doepler, from *Walhall, die Götterwelt der Germanen* (*Valhalla, the World of the German Gods*), 1905, by Martin Oldenbourg, Berlin (see pages 124–125).

The abyss had no end, no bottom, no bounds of any kind; it stretched on infinitely into the twilight that came before light or darkness had been formed.

North of Ginnungagap was Niflheim, the elemental realm of ice and mist. Niflheim was empty then, a world of cold, icy fog, at the center of which was a great river known as Hvergelmir, which fed into twelve magical springs called the Elivagar. The roaring waters of Hvergelmir poured from Niflheim and down into Ginnungagap, freezing and hardening into giant chunks of glacial ice as they fell, forming mountains of ice and filling the infinite void.

That ice fell then towards Muspelheim, the elemental realm of fire. The flames of Muspelheim rose to meet the falling ice, melting it as it crashed down. The melting ice and sparking fires met and produced great clouds of steam, which rose up to freeze again into hoarfrost. More steam billowed up and froze, over and over, until a giant figure was formed from the countless layers of ice. The giant Ymir, the first of the frost giants, came to life.

Alone in the darkness—although, born from frost, he did not feel the cold—Ymir searched for

CREATION OF THE COSMOS

At the dawn of time, before the earth or the gods or anything at all had been brought into existence, there was a great void called Ginnungagap.

some source of food in the vast mountains of ice. Eventually, he came across a giant cow, named Audhumla, who had been born from the ice just like Ymir. Ymir fed from the milk that flowed perpetually from the cow's udders; the cow, in turn, fed by licking the salt from a nearby block of ice. Over time, the cow's rough tongue wore away at the ice, and little by little, Ymir saw the outline of a man slowly being freed from the ice.

It took several days for the cow's licking to carve away the ice, and eventually Ymir fell asleep. As he slept, two giants—a son and a daughter—were born from the sweat of his armpits, and the six-headed giant Thrudgelmir was born from his feet. Thrudgelmir soon enough birthed his son, Bergelmir.

After three days, the man in the block of ice finally broke free. The man, whose name was Buri, was handsome, and he stood tall and strong; Ymir knew immediately and without doubt that Buri was not like him. Buri was a god, not a giant: his heart was warm, not frozen, and he was filled with all of the kindness and benevolence that Ymir lacked. Buri, ancestor to the gods, and Ymir, ancestor to the giants, were bitter enemies at first sight.

ABOVE: Two depictions of Audhumla, the giant cow whose udders sustain Ymir. Audhumla feeds by licking salt from a nearby block of ice, and, little by little, the outline of a man slowly being freed from the ice becomes evident. After three days the man breaks free. The tall, strong and handsome man is Buri, ancestor to the gods.

THE FIRST GODS

When the giants became aware of the existence of the god Buri, and of his son Borr (who had been born instantaneously from Buri after he was freed from the ice), they immediately went to war with the gods.

ABOVE: The giants going to war with the gods, from a 19th century woodcut; **OPPOSITE:** The giant Ymir is torn apart by Odin, Vili and Ve. His butchered body is used to form the world.

The gods represented all the things the giants hated: light, warmth, and goodness, while the giants were cold and cruel. The war went on for an unknowable time—eons, maybe, though time-markers such as the sun and seasons had not yet been created. Only when Borr married the giantess Bestla did the balance shift in the favor of the gods. Bestla gave birth to Odin, Vili, and Ve, and the three brothers joined Borr and Buri to finally slay Ymir. In death, Ymir's wounds poured enough blood to cause a great flood, drowning nearly all of the frost giants. The only survivors, Bergelmir and his wife, escaped by drifting in a rowboat on the sea of Ymir's blood to the end of the world, where they became the sole ancestors of all future frost giants.

The gods, who were collectively called the Aesir, celebrated their triumph. Then they began to look around, realizing that it was their responsibility to make the barren, frozen wasteland around them into a place that could support life. Eventually, the gods began to butcher the fallen body of Ymir; they rolled his great mass into the void and used his remains to craft the world.

Midgard, the earth, was made from Ymir's flesh; it rested in the very center of the void, and the gods planted a fence made of Ymir's eyebrows all around the realm to protect it from the giants. With Ymir's bones they made the hills, with his teeth the cliffs, and his hair became trees, bushes, and grass. The torrent of Ymir's spilled blood became the ocean, and his brains were used to form the clouds. Ymir's hollowed-out skull became the sky overhead, held aloft by four dwarfs standing strong at the four points of the compass.

All that was left, then, was to provide the world with light. So, taking sparks of flame from Muspelheim, the gods set them in the sky to create the first stars. They took swathes of bright, roaring fire and used them to create the sun and the moon, which they cradled in gleaming gold and silver chariots pulled by gold and silver horses.

The task of driving the chariots was given to Mani and Sol, the two most beautiful of the gods. Mani and Sol set out on their route, driving the sun and moon across the sky—not only giving light to the earth but marking out days and months to show the passage of time as well. The gloomy, dark daughter of the giants, Night, was sent out on her black horse to follow behind the moon. Behind her rode Day, the shining son of the Aesir, on his silver horse.

THE GIANTS

The giants (or *Jotnar* in Old Norse, meaning "devourers") descend from Bergelmir, the only frost giant to escape the flood of Ymir's blood that drowned the rest of his race.

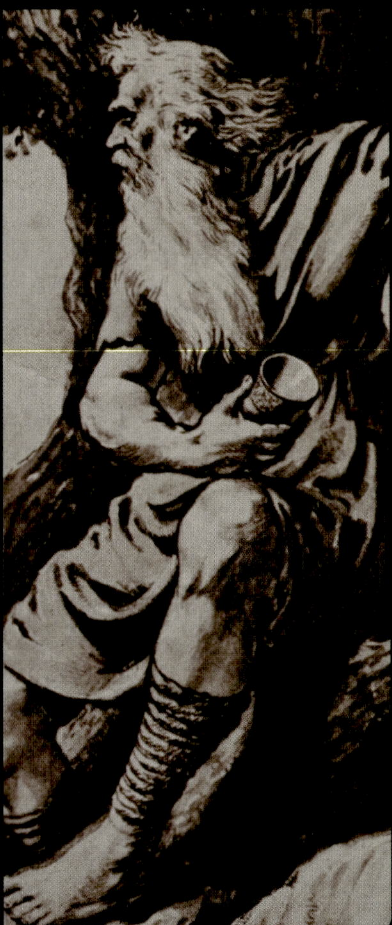

ABOVE: Mimir the giant. In Norse mythology he is the wisest living being.

Bergelmir traveled with his wife to the frozen wasteland at the very end of the world, where they established their new home: Jotunheim, the realm of the giants. Bergelmir fathered a new line of giants and raised them to uphold the hatred he held for the gods and all other living things. His descendants continued the blood feud with the Aesir, a war that would last until Ragnarök.

There were some, over the course of history, who proved to be exceptions to the usual nature of the giants. Mimir, for instance, the wisest living being, was also one of the kindest and gentlest despite his giant heritage. In fact, all of the Aesir have some amount of giant blood in them; Odin himself is half frost giant on his mother's side, as he was born of the union between Borr and Bestla. For the most part, however, the giants were cold-hearted, violent beings who hated anything that brought light or joy into the world. Although many of the giants possessed great wisdom, some holding secrets that were hidden even to the gods, that wisdom was rarely put to good use. The giants were not necessarily evil by nature, but they were the eternal enemies of the Aesir, and they rejected out of hand anything that the gods created or represented. They embodied the traits of cunning, selfishness, and cruelty, and they reveled in chaos in opposition to the order and peace of Asgard. Loki, the blood-brother of Odin and the personification of chaos, was born

to the giants before he joined the Aesir.

When the gods set the sun and the moon racing across the sky, casting gold and silver light down from their gleaming chariots, the giants were furious. They had been hidden away in Jotunheim, a barren land of ice and darkness, and they hated to see the rest of the world bathed in light and warmth. In retaliation, they sent the two giant wolves Skoll and Hati into the sky to chase down the sun and moon, swallow them whole, and return the world to perpetual darkness.

As fast as the wolves were, they could never quite catch up to the shining chariots long enough to devour them. Sometimes, however, they came so close that their great black shadows dimmed the brightness of the sun and blocked the light of the moon entirely, causing an eclipse. At the sight of this, the terrified people of Midgard would panic, scream, and raise such a commotion that the wolves would be startled into releasing their jaws and allowing the chariots to escape once again. The chase would only come to an end in the long, dark time of the Fimbulwinter, the precursor to Ragnarök, when the world would be ravaged with evil and smothered by ice and snow. Then, the newly-strengthened wolves would finally devour Sol and Mani, ridding the world of light and flooding Midgard in a sea of blood.

TOP: When the gods set the sun and moon racing across the sky, and bathe the world in warmth and light, the giants send the two giant wolves, Skoll and Hati to chase down the sun and moon and return the world to darkness; **ABOVE:** The hard times of the mythic Fimbulwinter is now believed to have actually happened—in 536 AD.

After the gods had finished their work, something was still missing from the realm of Midgard.

THE CREATION OF MEN

ABOVE: The first two humans—Ask and Embla, are magicked into life by Odin, Vili and Ve; **OPPOSITE:** After the apocalypse of Ragnarök, two new humans, Lif and Lifthrasir, emerge in the aftermath and repopulate the earth.

The gods felt the need for a race of beings that they could watch over, guide, and protect; this was the reason they created Midgard in the first place, but the world was still devoid of life.

One day, as Odin and his brothers Vili and Ve were walking along the shores of Midgard and looking out across the water, they came upon two trees, an ash and an elm. The trees had an unusual shape to them, and they looked almost like the gods. Odin, taking sudden inspiration, reached out and breathed on the trees, imbuing them with life. Their wooden forms gave way to flesh and bone, and they stood breathing and blinking in front of their creator. But, though the first human beings had been made, they were mindless, cold, and immobile, only able to stand and stare. Vili then reached out and touched their foreheads, granting them the gifts of wisdom, senses, and movement. Ve, in turn, gently stroked their faces, granting them speech, hearing, and warm lifeblood. At this, the two were truly alive, able to think for themselves, move freely, and speak to each other. The gods named the two humans Ask and Embla, after the trees they had been born from, and from those two followed the entire race of mankind.

As Ask and Embla began exploring the world that had been made for them, the Aesir retreated to Asgard to watch over them from afar. The gods had granted humans free will, after all, and although they often made efforts to guide and protect humans—especially Odin, known to wander the earth more than any other god—they had no interest in controlling their every movement. The descendants of Ask and Embla spread out across Midgard over the centuries, quickly establishing their own customs and laws, although they always remembered to give sacrifice and thanks to the gods who created them.

After Ragnarök, once Midgard has been consumed by fire, another pair of humans will emerge from the ashes. These two, named Lif and Lifthrasir, will go on to repopulate the earth, giving rise to a new age of mankind and renewing the cycle that began when Ask and Embla were first created.

Liv og Livthrasir

The realm the gods created was called Asgard, the home of the gods; it was a shining, beautiful city of golden palaces and great halls, a place where the gods could live happily and peacefully while keeping watch over the world of men. In a council of the gods that was held at the creation of Asgard, it was decided that no harm should ever come to anyone within the realm, and that it should remain a place of peace and harmony.

One day, however, the gods of Asgard learned that they were not the only gods in existence. They were visited by a goddess known as Gullveig, a traveler and sorceress hailing from a tribe of gods called the Vanir. She was a practitioner of *seidr*, a form of Vanir magic that dealt with the seeing and shaping of future events, and she had a great love for gold. The Aesir offered Gullveig hospitality at first, and she stayed for a time

THE AESIR VANIR WAR

After the creation of Midgard, the first humans, and the sun and the moon, the gods finally traveled to a plane high above the earth to create a home for themselves.

ABOVE AND OPPOSITE: The Aesir and Vanir gods wage war on each other. Both 19th century. Above: probable preparatory sketch for wood engraving. Opposite: *The war of the Aesir and Vanir gods*, wood engraving after drawing, by Karl Ehrenberg, 1887.

in Asgard. During her stay, she offered to help the Aesir with their difficulties through seidr and offered gold as gifts to those she spoke to. At first, her help was appreciated, and her magic made life easier for the Aesir—but before long, her presence in Asgard became less and less welcome. Her magic, though powerful, began to sway the minds of the Aesir towards selfishness, and her greed for gold was contagious, causing infighting and corruption among the gods of Asgard. Eventually the Aesir turned against Gullveig and attempted to execute her for the strife she had brought into Asgard; but although she was run through with a spear and burned, she was reborn. Gullveig was burned three times, each time returning to life, before she finally left Asgard and returned to Vanaheim.

It was not long before conflicts rose between the two clans of gods, especially after Gullveig's sowing of discord among the Aesir and—from the perspective of the Vanir—her barbaric treatment at the hands of her hosts. Early attempts at peacemaking fell through, and eventually there was full-scale war between the Aesir and the Vanir. The war was brutal and earth-shaking, as the gods tore entire mountains from the ground and icebergs from the sea to hurl back and forth. However, both sides of the war were evenly matched, and—seeing that there was no way either could win—it was eventually decided that a peace treaty must be signed. The Aesir and Vanir came together to hold a meeting, and came to the agreement that the only way to solve the conflict was to join the two clans as one. A large jug was brought out, and each of the Aesir and Vanir gods spat into the jar, mixing their spit together before shaking hands. Kvasir, a wise, kind man who became the greatest of all poets, was born from this mixture.

After this ritual was performed, the two clans exchanged hostages to ensure that they would be forever bound to each other. The Aesir send over Odin's own brother, Hoenir, who was a handsome and well-built man who would be perfectly suited to be a chief of the Vanir. Mimir, the wise and kind giant, was sent to serve as Hoenir's advisor. From the Vanir came the sea god Njord and his two children, Freyja and Freyr. The daughter, Freyja, was the most beautiful of all the gods, and her brother Freyr was equally handsome. From then on, Freyja, Freyr, and Njord lived among the Aesir in Asgard, and the two clans were united as allies.

THE WALLS OF ASGARD

In the early days of the gods, Asgard had no walls.

At first, it seemed as though the realm of Asgard would simply never need them, because the gods were so strong and wise and well-loved; surely no one would want to bring them harm, and no one who wanted to would dare. Then, of course, came the terrible war between the Aesir and the Vanir, which shook the gods' belief that no outsider could challenge their power. The giants, too, were growing in number, amassing their forces in the frozen realm of Jotunheim.

Since Asgard's creation, the city of the gods had been protected from the giants by Thor, the god of thunder. His fearsome strength and magical hammer, Mjölnir, were famous among the enemies of the gods, and that reputation alone was enough of a deterrent to keep Asgard safe for many years. However, Thor often left on long journeys, seeking out giants to fight and slay; before long, the gods realized that Thor would not always be there to protect them. One day, when Thor had been away for several weeks, the gods finally decided that Asgard needed walls strong enough to keep out the most fierce of the giants.

As the gods were debating how they would have the walls of Asgard built, the golden horn of Heimdall rang out through the city. All of the gods rushed to the gate of Asgard to see why he had called for them, and they saw that a strange man had come walking up the Bifröst, the bridge that connects Asgard to Midgard and the rest of the nine realms. The stranger wore a cloak, but even under his robes it was clear to see that he was massive and powerfully built—likely stronger even than many of the gods themselves. There was something about his appearance that Heimdall's sharp eyes did not trust.

"Why have you come here?" said Heimdall to the stranger, looking down at him from his high watchtower on the Bifröst. Although he was suspicious, Heimdall did not voice his concerns, as he was not one to make baseless judgements. The other gods stood back, waiting for the stranger's answer.

"I am a builder," said the man. "I have heard that the Asgardians are seeking fortifications built around their city, strong enough to keep out even the mightiest of giants. I am the only builder in the land capable of such a task, and I have come to offer my services."

The gods looked the stranger up and down and quickly agreed that he was the strongest and broadest man they had ever seen; surely, if anyone could build walls strong enough to defend against the giants, this man could. He was broad-shouldered and tall, and his muscles were like iron under his skin. To prove his strength, he reached down and hefted a massive boulder over his head with one hand, raising a stone heavier than any man or god could lift.

"How long will it take you to build the walls of Asgard? And what payment would you demand in return?" asked Odin after a long moment of consideration. "You should know first that we can only allow one stranger within our city at a time, and so you will have to complete this task without help."

"It will take me three and a half years," said the stranger. "As for my payment, I ask only for the hand of Freyja, the most beautiful of the gods, as my wife, and for the sun and the moon as our wedding gifts. This would be small payment for such a grand undertaking in so short a time."At this, the gods shook their heads with concern. Freyja was the most beautiful woman to ever live, and her presence in Asgard brought joy and light to the city of the gods. Without her there, life in Asgard would be bleak and cold. Similarly, the sun and moon brought joy and light to the world of men, and without them Midgard would be cast into darkness and misery. As badly as the gods needed walls around their city, they could not bear to part with any of these things.

Then the sly Loki spoke up, a cunning grin on his face as he leaned forward to whisper in Odin's ear. He had a plan to get the stranger to build their walls without ever having to make good on their promise of payment. Although Odin was wary of Loki's trickery and the gods were uncomfortable with his methods of guile and deceit, they allowed him to step forward and speak for them this time, as they knew that Asgard needed to be protected.

"Three and a half years is far too long to wait, my good man," said Loki to the stranger. "In that time, we would be as good as defenseless, and the walls would be of no use to us. If, however, you are able and willing to finish this project unaided within one winter, then you will be rewarded with Freyja as your wife, as well as the sun and moon. If, on the first day of summer, one single stone is missing from its place, or if you receive any help building the walls, then you will forfeit your reward." Loki spoke with grace and charm, making his case as though it were the most reasonable thing in the world, and the stranger took several minutes to consider the deal. Finally, he sighed, and nodded.

"Very well," said the stranger, "the walls of Asgard will be ready within one winter. However, you must allow me to use my horse, Svadilfare, to transport the stones. If I am to work alone and under such a short timeline, surely you will grant me at least this one small assistance."

The gods agreed to this, as it seemed a minor enough bit of help; they were sure that it would be impossible for the stranger to finish his task within a single season, with or without the help of his horse. The deal was made with a solemn oath sworn on both sides, and the stranger quickly got to work erecting a perimeter of heavy, dense stones all the way around the city of Asgard. They were as great as mountains and just as impenetrable, and the stranger worked

TOP: Freyja, most beautiful of all the gods; **ABOVE:** The builder of the walls of Asgard, with his horse Svadilfare; **OPPOSITE, TOP:** Heimdall, the god who keeps watch in his tower on Bifröst for invaders. He has a resounding horn, Himinbjörg, with which to raise the alarm; **OPPOSITE, BELOW:** "Thor, the protector of Asgard, often left on long journeys to fight with giants…"

"Later, Loki–still in the form of a mare–gave birth to the first of his children. His child was Sleipnir, an eight-legged horse who would prove to be unmatched..."

ABOVE: The plotting, scheming, shape-shifting trickster god Loki.

at a furious pace without rest, day and night. His horse worked just as hard as he did, if not harder, dragging enormous stones to and from the building grounds for hours on end.

With every passing day, the walls grew higher and stronger. The gods were delighted with the work the stranger was doing, but it quickly became apparent that he was going to finish his task well before the assigned deadline. Soon the gods began to panic, trying desperately to figure out some way that they could get out of paying the unreasonable fee the stranger had asked for, which they had already agreed to. It would be unthinkable for them to break their word. Especially within the Holy City of Asgard. But it would be just as unthinkable for them to give up Freyja, the sun, and the moon. Now finally, the gods realized who the stranger was. He was not a man or god, but a giant; this explained his size and his immense strength, and worst of all, it explained why he wanted this payment. Forever jealous of the gods, the giants wished to rid the world of light and warmth and joy, which is exactly what would happen if the sun, moon, and the beautiful Freyja were taken away to Jotunheim. Now the walls were all but completed, with only the gate left to build.

"This is all your fault, Loki," said the gods on the last night of winter, turning on him now that they realized that his plan was about to fail. As his plan was responsible for the mess they were in, it was agreed that he should be the one to fix it, and that he would be killed if he could not. Loki, desperate to save his life, once again turned all of his shrewd intelligence towards plotting and scheming. Finally, with a laugh of relief, he announced that he had yet another plan to cheat the giant out of his payment. Without any further explanation, he strode off into the darkness.

That night, the giant's horse was dragging the last of the enormous stone blocks up a great hill towards the gates of Asgard. These were the final stones that would be put in place to finish the wall and ensure the giant's payment. Svadilfare was distracted, however, by a beautiful mare that came charging out of the woods nearby.

"Follow me," said the disguised Loki to the giant's horse, "I know of a beautiful meadow where we can rest; I'll race you there." This temptation was more than enough to sway the horse, who had grown tired of dragging heavy boulders for weeks on end and wanted to gallop freely again. Loki turned and sped off, and the giant's horse charged after him, abandoning the heavy stones. The giant builder roared after them with rage, as even he was not strong enough to drag the massive stones such a great distance without his horse.

The next day, which was the first day of summer, there were still three stones missing from the high gates of the wall, which meant that the giant's payment was forfeit. He ranted and roared as he stomped up and down the streets of Asgard, his fury shaking the foundations of the city. He threatened to destroy the city himself if he did not receive his payment, and he might have done so if Thor had not finally returned home from his journey at that very moment. Just as the giant raised his fist to begin razing buildings to the ground, Thor leaped from his chariot, swung his hammer down, and shattered the giant's skull to pieces with a single mighty swing.

Later, Loki—still in the form of a mare—gave birth to the first of his children. His child was Sleipnir, an eight-legged horse who would prove to be unmatched in strength and speed by any other horse in all the nine realms. Sleipnir became the loyal steed of Odin, king of the gods, and carried him into battle and on his journeys in Midgard from that day until the final battle of Ragnarök.

"Sleipnir became the loyal steed of Odin, king of the gods, and carried him into battle and on his journeys in Midgard..."

TOP: Loki takes the form of a beautiful mare in order to lure the giant's horse Svadilfare away from the final completion of the walls of Asgard. Illustration by Dorothy Hardy; **ABOVE:** Thor returns to Asgard just in time to kill the enraged giant; **LEFT:** Odin rides Sleipnir, Loki's offspring with Svadilfare. Illustration by John Bauer.

2

YGGDRASIL AND THE NINE REALMS

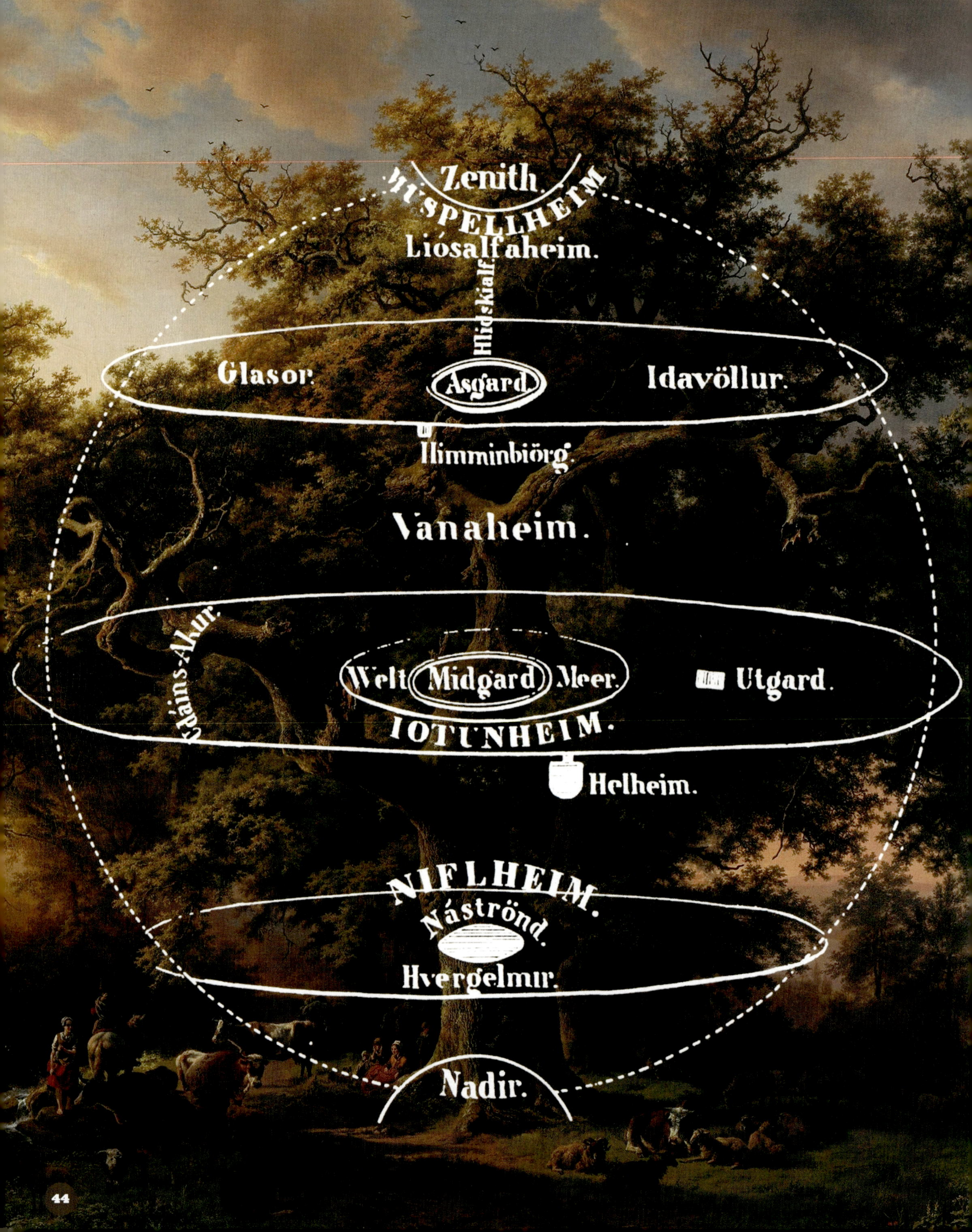
Zenith.
MUSPELLHEIM
Liósalfaheim.
Hlidskialf
Glasor.
Asgard.
Idavöllur.
Himminbiörg.
Vanaheim.
Odáins-Akur.
Welt
Midgard
Meer.
Utgard.
IOTUNHEIM.
Helheim.
NIFLHEIM.
Náströnd.
Hvergelmir.
Nadir.

The Norse mythological universe is composed of several worlds, each tending to correspond to a particular race of beings or element.

Aside from the usual variations that can be expected when attempting to collect or standardize the often fractured and conflicting stories of the Norse myths, it is generally accepted that there are nine major realms that make up the cosmos. These nine realms are—in rough order of prevalence—Asgard, Midgard, Jotunheim, Helheim, Niflheim, Muspelheim, Vanaheim, Alfheim, and Svartalfeheim. These nine realms can be found in and around the branches and roots of Yggdrasil, the world tree, which acts as a structural axis and centerpoint of the entire universe: everything that exists relies on the strength of the world tree's massive trunk and infinite limbs to do so.

Not all realms are equal, at least in terms of how often they appear in the surviving myths we have access to today. Asgard, for instance, is the home of the gods; dozens of stories are set in and around the shining city of the Aesir, as this is the home of the protagonists of most of the Norse myths. Midgard, similarly, is the home of man, and also features prominently in many stories. Realms such as Svartalfheim and Alfeim, however—the realms of the dark and light elves, respectively—are only mentioned a handful of times, and rarely if ever feature as core elements of any particular story. It may be

ABOVE: An 17th century interpretation of the World Tree, *Yggdrasil*, from a manuscript of the *Prose Edda*; **ABOVE, LEFT:** An early 20th century rendition of the bridge from Midgard to Asgard, and Valhalla; **OPPOSITE:** An early pen drawing diagram of the Norse universe, showing its various kingdoms, overlaid onto *Forest Scene*, 1841, by Dutch landscape painter Barend Cornelis Koekkoek (1803–1862). Although *Yggdrasil* is a "cosmically-large" Ash tree, great oaks were habitually called Wodan's Oaks (*Wodan* is a regional dialect form of *Odin*).

TOP AND ABOVE: The Norns, or Fates, are often depicted as three sisters sitting under the shelter of Yggdrasil. The Norns understand the destiny of every living thing, even of the Aesir themselves, and they alone know the truth of every aspect of creation. The main image at top is by Emil Doepler, from *Walhall, die Götterwelt der Germanen 1905, Berlin.*

that there were myths that focused on these other worlds more deeply which are now lost to time, or it may be that these other realms were intended for little more than world-building. Most of the mentions of the nine realms can be found in the *Poetic Edda* poems *Voluspá* and *Vafþrúðnismál* and the *Prose Edda* poem *Gylfaginning*, although they are never listed outright.

The original Norse myths depict the nine realms almost like separate countries on a map, although it is difficult to pin down such specific descriptions. Midgard, for instance, is often described as the earth itself—but it is also described as a specific region of the world, separated from Jotunheim only by the ocean and the great fence of Ymir's eyebrows. In modern media, they are often depicted as individual planets or alternate dimensions; this often functions as a more understandable narrative, especially when dealing with depictions of Asgard and Helheim.

Travel between the realms, especially between Asgard, Midgard, and Jotunheim, was possible, though only the gods did so with ease. Figures such as Thor, Loki, and Odin, regularly journeyed out from Asgard to go on adventures among the humans and the frost giants, but the giants and humans themselves rarely leave their home realms. Helheim, the realm of the dead, is an unusual case in this context, as many stories detail the exact path one must take to visit—but few ever entertain the possibility of a successful return to the world of the living.

Between and within the nine realms are a number of other, smaller locations, some of which are described as their own minor realms and others which are simply formless, briefly mentioned concepts. Ginnungagap, for example, is the primordial abyss that existed between Muspelheim and Niflheim at the dawn of time, although some myths imply that the void was filled with mountains of ice when the world came into existence. Asgard features some smaller realms, which function more like miniature kingdoms, that are the sole domain of certain individual gods.

YGGDRASIL

***Yggdrasil* is the cosmically large ash tree that stands at the epicenter of the Norse cosmological system.**

The tree, which was one of the first things to be created from chaos at the formation of the universe, is one of the most significant aspects of Norse Mythology. Known more poetically as the World Tree, Yggdrasil acts as the epicenter for the nine realms of the cosmos; it supports the worlds of Asgard, Midgard, and all the other realms with its near-infinite limbs, mighty trunk, and deep-reaching roots. The tree's roots extend into three mystical water sources for sustenance. The three sources--the wells Mimisbrunnr and Urðarbrunnr and the spring Hvergelmir--are deeply significant landmarks in their own right, but also provide the life force that sustains Yggdrasil and all nine realms by extension. Mimisbrunnr, the well of knowledge, is maintained by the wise giant Mimir and has particular significance in several myths: it contains all the knowledge and wisdom of the cosmos, something Odin sacrificed one of his eyes to obtain. Yggdrasil is sacred in Old Norse religion, and rituals and ceremonies in honor of the tree that was believed to hold up the universe were common.

The towering World Tree supports and unites the nine realms: Asgard, the realm of the Aesir gods; Midgard, the realm of humans; Alfheim, the realm of the bright elves; Vanaheim, the realm of the Vanir gods, Jotunheim, the realm of the giants; Hel, the realm of the dishonored dead; Muspelheim, the realm of fire; Niflheim, the realm of ice; and Svartalfheim, the realm of the dwarves. The trunk of the tree is the center-axis of Midgard, and no god or mortal knows where all of Yggdrasil's roots lead to. The highest leaves of Yggdrasil's canopy are layered with snow and buffeted ceaselessly with fierce winds.

The structural support that Yggdrasil lends to the cosmos is not the only value it holds, however. It acts as the meeting place where the gods gather for important councils and ceremonies, and the body of the tree itself is flush with life: its roots are surrounded and fed upon by giant snakes and the great dragon Nidhogg, while its leaves provide sustenance

ABOVE: Odin surprises Mimir, the wise giant, sitting by the trunk of Yggdrasil and watching over *Mimisbrunnr*, his well of knowledge. The well is one of the sustaining forces of the World Tree; **TOP LEFT:** A flowery 19th century lithograph depicting Yggdrasil, the World Tree.

"The World Tree's name also carries significance. The word *Yggdrasil* in Old Norse translates literally to "Odin's Horse," but the most common interpretation is "Odin's Gallows"..."

to the four stags (Dainn, Dvalinn, Duneyrr, and Durathror) that tirelessly race across its branches. An enormous eagle, the eternal enemy of Nidhogg, rests in the highest branches of the tree. The trickster squirrel Ratatoskr (also known as Drill-Tooth) travels up and down the length of Yggdrasil's trunk carrying insults and taunts between the eagle and the dragon, hoping to eventually provoke them into fighting. The tree itself is also sometimes treated as a sentient being; in the poem *Grímnismál*, Odin himself states that the World Tree is in perpetual agony as it is slowly devoured by both the animals it sustains and the erosion of time. In this interpretation, Yggdrasil's existence is depicted not just as a structural component of the cosmos, but as a sacrifice made in perpetuity by the oldest and largest living being in existence.

The exact organization of the nine realms around the World Tree has never been set in stone; some myths imply that all nine worlds are carried in the branches of the tree, while others place the "underworlds"—such as Hel and Niflheim—below the roots, Midgard and Jotunheim around the center of the trunk, and Asgard and Alfheim in the uppermost branches. Muspelheim, Svartalfheim, and Vanaheim are rarely given concrete locations around the tree.

The World Tree's name also carries significance. The word "Yggdrasil" in Old Norse translates literally to "Odin's Horse," but the most common interpretation of the name is "Odin's Gallows"—a name derived from the harrowing sacrifice Odin made by hanging himself from the branches of the tree in search of knowledge.

OPPOSITE: An early 20th century imagining of Yggdrasil for a sample card, advertising a newly-developed printing technique; **LEFT:** Odin hangs himself from Yggdrasil. A 19th century illustration.

BAXTERS Patent Oil Printing, 11, Northampton Square.

ASGARD

Asgard is the home of the gods. Of all the nine realms, Asgard is the most often depicted in myth; the shining city of the Aesir gods, the highest of all the realms, home to Odin and his subjects.

ABOVE: Asgard imagined in *The History of the Vikings* on Google; **MAIN IMAGE:** Marvel Studios' imagining of Asgard, in the motion picture *Thor: Ragnarok* (2017). Based on the Marvel Comics' character *The Mighty Thor*, the film is produced by Marvel Studios and distributed by Walt Disney Studios Motion Pictures.

The gods created Asgard only after they had finished constructing Midgard and Jotunheim and putting the sun, the moon, and the stars in the sky. Once the gods had created mankind and built a world to protect it, they then turned to create a home for themselves. Asgard was intended to be a perfect city, a monument to peace, happiness, and prosperity; an agreement was made that no harm should come to any guests dwelling within the walls of Asgard, and all those who lived there were eternally young, healthy, and happy. The food and drink of Asgard never ran out, and nobody fell sick or grew old, thanks in part to the magical apples of the goddess Idunn which ensured everlasting vitality.

Although a pact was made to avoid any violence within the walls of Asgard, the gods were not always able to maintain that ideal. Many myths—often the ones that involve Loki causing trouble and bringing it home to Asgard—feature an enemy of the Aesir charging the gates or infiltrating the city, only to be dashed to pieces by Thor's magical hammer. The lesser-known story of Gullveig, the gold-obsessed Vanir sorceress who the gods attempted to execute three times, ignores this concept entirely—possibly implying that the gods were pushed past the limit of their ideology, or simply displaying another example of the inconsistencies of Norse mythology.

The city itself is a shining marvel of palaces made entirely of gold, towers that soar into the clouds above, and impossibly grand great halls that can seat thousands at a time. Between the grand buildings of the city stand forests with shining gold leaves and rolling fields studded with flowers of otherworldly beauty.

Odin, the King of the gods, rules over Asgard from his high throne, a seat of power that no one but Odin himself would dare to claim. His wife, Frigga, occupies the second throne at his side. The thrones tower high above the rest of Asgard, a vantage point that allows Odin to look out across all nine realms.

TOP: Fallen warriors are brought to Valhalla by the Valkyries to feast with the gods; **ABOVE:** The gods crossing the bridge to Valhalla. A scene from Wagner's *Das Rheingold*, 1877. Lithograph.

VALHALLA

Valhalla, Old Norse for "Hall of the Slain," is one of the most iconic landmarks in the realm of Asgard, and the closest thing in the Old Norse religion to the concept of "heaven." The Norsemen believed that those who died gloriously in battle would have their souls brought to Valhalla, where they would feast and fight among the gods as equals until the coming of Ragnarök. Each time battle breaks out, Odin sends out the Valkyries, his loyal host of warrior maidens, to collect the souls of those who died with honor in battle. Half of the fallen warriors go with the Valkyries to Valhalla, where they become the Einherjar, an army of warrior spirits who will be called to aid Odin in the final battles of Ragnarök. The other half go to Freyja in her realm of Fólkvangr.

Valhalla stands in Glasir grove, a beautiful field surrounded by trees with red and gold leaves. The hall has five hundred and forty doors, wide enough for eight hundred warriors to pass through at once, and above the main gate stands a boar's head and a fierce eagle whose piercing gaze can see all the way to the farthest reaches of the world. The walls of this magnificent structure are made of gleaming spears that shine brightly enough to light the hall without a fire; the roof is made of golden shields, and the benches and long wooden tables are decorated with ornately crafted armor. When feasting, the Einherjar are attended by the Valkyries and eat the meat of the enchanted boar Saehrimnir. The meat of Saehrimnir never runs out no matter how many are present at the feast, and the boar is returned to life the next morning to provide the next night's feast. When not feasting, the warriors take up arms and head out into the field to fight; there they act out the heroic feats they accomplished in life. As all wounds are healed after each fight, the Einherjar fight recklessly with no fear of injury or death.

When Ragnarök comes, the Einherjar will be called upon to follow Odin into battle against the hordes of Jotunheim and the monstrous children of Loki. While Odin takes great pride in the numbers and combat prowess of his soldiers, he knows—due to the prophetic

"The Norsemen believed that those who died gloriously in battle would have their souls brought to Valhalla, where they would feast and fight among the gods as equals until the coming of Ragnarök."

knowledge granted by his great wisdom—that they will never be numerous or powerful enough to save him from the fate waiting for him at Ragnarök.

BIFRÖST

The Bifröst, also known as the rainbow bridge, connects Asgard to Midgard, the realm of mankind. Outside of flying or other magical means of travel, the Bifröst is the only way to travel to and from Asgard. It is watched over by Heimdall, the watchman and gatekeeper of the gods. Heimdall keeps a tower at the center-point of the rainbow bridge, where his magical eyes allow him to see for hundreds of miles in all directions. In Ragnarök, the sons of Muspelheim will ride across the Bifröst, shattering the delicate bridge under their thundering feet before Asgard itself is destroyed in turn.

FOLKVANGR

Folkvangr ("Field of the Host") is the realm that was granted to Freyja upon her arrival in Asgard. Not every god has their own distinct realm—that honor is reserved for the most beloved of the gods such as Thor and Baldur—but the Aesir were so immediately taken with Freyja that she was granted a realm and a hall of her own almost immediately. Her hall, Sessrumnir, is where the other half of the warriors who die in battle are sent if they are not taken to Valhalla. As Freyja's afterlife serves as a direct counterpart to Valhalla, there are conflicting theories of what the purpose of this separate hall might be. Some argue that Freyja's hall offers an afterlife to women who die with honor, or that Freyja's claim to half of the fallen soldiers for her own army is part of the peace treaty that was struck between the Aesir and Vanir after the war.

THRUDVANGR

Thrudvangr, or Thrudheim, is the realm of Asgard belonging to Thor and his wife Sif. Thrudvangr is the largest of the many sub-realms within Asgard, as Thor's role in protecting and providing for Asgard makes him one of the most significant figures in the pantheon. This is where Thor's home, Bilskirnir, can be found, an enormous hall that is said to be the largest building ever constructed. The hall has over 500 rooms, the grandest of which are reserved for Thor, Sif, and their children. When Ragnarok arrives, this domain will be partially destroyed when Surtr razes Asgard and destroys the Bifröst, although some versions depict Thrudvangr remaining whole enough to become a cornerstone in the new, revitalized Asgard that will be built after Ragnarök.

TOP: *The Ride of the Valkyries*, by the German painter William T. Maud, 1890; **ABOVE:** Bifröst, the bridge that connects Midgard (Earth) and Asgard. Watercolor by the English illustrator Stella Langdale, 1916.

MIDGARD

Old Norse *Miðgarðr*

MAIN IMAGE, AND ABOVE: Summer scenes in Midgard; **TOP:** Jörmungandr, the World Serpent, encircles Midgard. The serpent is depicted biting the end of its own tail. When the serpent releases its tail from its jaws, Ragnarök will begin.

Midgard is what we know as Earth; a realm constructed by the gods to defend humans from attacks by the giants of Jotunheim. The world of Midgard was built from the body of Ymir, the first living being and the progenitor of all other giants, after he was slain by the Aesir gods at the very beginning of time. His blood became oceans, his brain became clouds, his skull became the sky, and his eyebrows became the fence that encircles the human world and gives Midgard its name. In a similar fashion to Greek mythology's Atlas holding up the sky, Ymir's skuløøl is held aloft over the world by four dwarves: Nordri, Sudri, Austri, and Vestri, named for the four cardinal directions of a compass. The giant snake Jörmungandr, also known as the World Serpent, encircles the world of Midgard and acts as another boundary-marker between Midgard and Jotunheim. Jörmungandr—similar to the *ouroboros* of other world mythologies—is depicted biting the end of its own tail; when Jörmungandr finally releases its tail from its jaws, Ragnarök will begin. When this happens, Midgard—along with the rest of the nine realms—will be destroyed, and only two humans (Líf and Lífþrasir) will survive to repopulate the world.

Beyond its role as a homeland for humankind, Midgard also represents an important thematic element of Norse mythology and Norse culture in general: the fences, both physical and metaphorical, that distinguish civilization from the chaos of the wilderness. This concept, known as *innangard* and *utangard* (literally "within the fence" and "beyond the fence," respectively), was a core aspect of Norse society; fences were used to guard land, mark out property lines, and keep the outer world separate from distinct, law-abiding social groups. War and violence were constantly in the background of Norse society, and many disputes over honor, property, and individual feuds were traditionally solved with violence. A concrete legal system helped prescribe specific punishments and rules for conflict resolution through combat, which kept those disputes from spiraling out of hand.

This sense of boundary-marking was also deeply ingrained in the psychology of the time. Separating those within the society from those without allowed for firm adherence to law and custom, and the greatest punishment for breaking the law was outlawry. Literally referred to as *skóggangr*, meaning "going into the forest," this punishment stripped the outlaw of their rights and banished them from society, effectively forcing them beyond the "fence" of the civilized world. By extension, when the gods of Norse Mythology built a fence to protect the human world from those beyond—giants, monsters, and so on—this was a metaphor for the way those living in Norse society at the time placed great value on their tribal groups. In Norse mythology, the capital city of the Giants in Jotunheim is called "Utgard," after the same concept.

HELHEIM

Old Norse *Hel*

Hel is presided over by the similarly-named goddess Hel, or Hela, daughter of Loki and Angrboda. Depictions of the deity Hela herself are conflicting: in some recordings she is monstrous and inhuman, while in others she is—physically, at least—no different from the other Aesir and Vanir gods. As the daughter of the giant Angrboda and the (at least half-) giant Loki, Hela is technically closer to a giant than a goddess, although she is treated as a Goddess after she is given custody of the underworld.

Although Hel is most commonly referred to as simply "the underworld" in the context of Norse mythology, Hel is specifically the afterlife where dishonored or unworthy souls go to rest. Those who die noble deaths in battle are chosen to spend eternity in Valhalla, while those who die of old age, disease, or accident are sent to Hel.

There is an obvious comparison to be drawn between the "Hel" of Norse mythology and the "Hell" of many modern-day religions, but there are a number of important thematic differences between the two. Most notably, Hel is cold, not full of fire, and the souls condemned to eternity there are not punished in the way we often associate with the modern idea of Hell. In fact, while Hel is certainly dark, cold, and damp—to mimic the conditions of a grave, perhaps—there is little in the way of actual suffering recorded. In fact, many depictions of Hel imply that it simply mimics life on Earth, allowing the dead to eat, drink, sleep, and—for lack of a better word—live as they did when they were alive. There is also no notable connection between morality and the afterlife in Norse mythology; "good" and "bad" people are not automatically sorted into Valhalla or Helheim, and souls that travel to Hel do not do so as any kind of punishment. Several accounts depict Hela as almost a caretaker figure; she is cold and dark like the realm she governs, but she is also responsible for providing housing and protection to the souls in her domain. Hel is also known to be inescapable; the borders of the underworld are guarded by a Cerberus-like hound, Garm, and a shapeshifting giant, Hraesvelg, and the river Gjoll that wraps around Hel's border acts as an impassable moat. Even gods—who, on rare occasion, are also sent to Helheim after their deaths—are unable to escape. Baldur, for example, the most beloved of all the gods, is unable to be freed from Hel after his death at Loki's hands, despite the wishes of the rest of the Aesir to revive him.

Another notable characteristic of Helheim is that—in spite of the fact that escape from Hel is categorically impossible—there are many detailed iterations on ways for gods and mortals to travel to Hel from the other realms, either to attempt rescue a soul trapped there or to seek council from older and wiser spirits. Many myths feature gods and heroes journeying to Hel for one reason or another, but few are entirely successful.

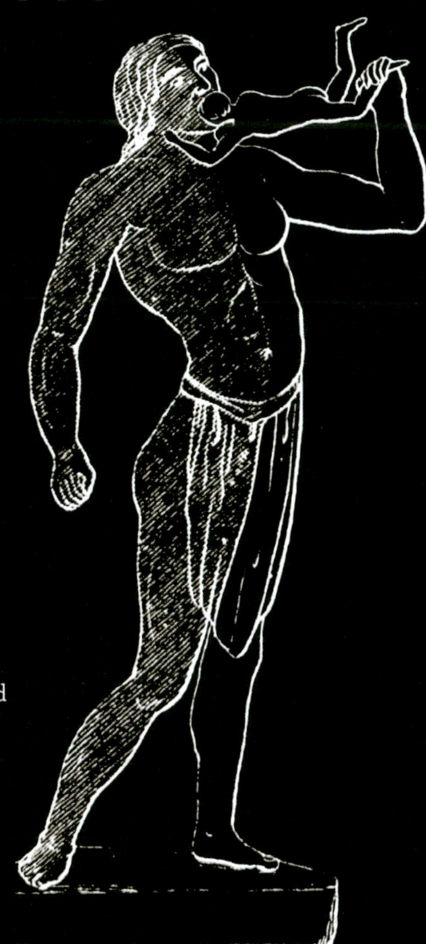

ABOVE AND RIGHT: Two differing depictions of the goddess Hela, daughter of Loki and Angrboda, and custodian of the Underworld.

JOTUNHEIM

Old Norse *Jötunheimr*

Jotunheim, literally "land of the giants" in Old Norse, is one of the most narratively significant of the nine realms.

ABOVE: Thrym, the King of the Frost Giants in Jotunheim.

Home to the Jotnar—meaning "giants," although the original translation would be closer to "devourers"—Jotunheim is a vast, chaotic expanse populated by monsters and magic. The world of Jotunheim is synonymous with the concept of wilderness, anarchy, and barbarism; it serves as a foil to the world of Midgard, where humans live peacefully in their law-abiding, civilized way. If Midgard and Asgard are examples of *innangard*, or "within the fence," then Jotunheim is *utangard*, "outside the fence." By natural extension of this concept, the capital city of the giants is named Utgard, which roughly translates to "outlands."

Because of its size and its wild, chaotic nature, the landscape of Jotunheim is varied and hostile. The realm of the giants features soaring, jagged mountain peaks, impenetrable forests, and vast stretches of ice and barren land. Jotunheim is a wasteland in almost all depictions, suitable only for the ravenous monsters roaming its borders and the bitter, exiled frost giants who forever resent being trapped there.

Jotunheim is ruled by Thrym, the king of the giants, while the city of Utgard is ruled by a giant named Utgard-Loki. Many of the most well-known Norse myths take place in or around Jotunheim; it was a common theme for the Aesir—Thor in particular—to journey to Jotunheim in an attempt to keep the giants in their place, quell any burgeoning plots to overthrow Asgard, and generally wage war with their eternal enemies. The theft and retrieval of Thor's hammer, the kidnapping of Idunn, and Thor and Loki's journey to Utgard, for instance, all involve perilous journeys to and from Jotunheim. As the Giants were so jealous of the light and warmth of Asgard and the rest of the nine realms, many of these myths feature giants kidnapping people from Asgard or from Midgard or stealing precious items and taking them back to Jotunheim to hoard. Many of the giants that can be reasoned with to some extent demand that goddesses such as Freya or Frigga be given to them as brides, and the idea of one of the Aesir being forced to live in Jotunheim is often presented as a worse fate than having to be wed to one of the giants.

Jotunheim is also home to Mimisbrunnr, or Mimir's well; this is the well to which Odin sacrificed his eye in exchange for a single sip of water, granting him almost unmatched wisdom. Mimir, the wisest and kindest of the giants, was stationed to guard the well before he entered into Odin's service.

NIFLHEIM

Old Norse *Niflheimr*

Niflheim is the region of ice and mist in Norse mythology.

Along with Muspelheim, the realm of fire, Niflheim was present at the very dawn of time on the northern side of Ginnungagap, the primordial abyss that existed before the world was formed. Niflheim is home to the frozen river Elivagar and the well Hvergelmir, which together are the source of all the rivers and streams of the world. The frozen waters from these two sources fell from Niflheim at the very dawn of time to meet with the fire rising from Muspelheim; the resulting steam and hoarfrost gave birth to Ymir, the first giant. In some tellings, the endless ice of Niflheim somehow managed to fill the endless void of Ginnungagap, creating mountains and plateaus of ice and snow. The well Hvergelmi feeds one of the three great roots of Yggdrasil.

It is also attested in the *Prose Edda* that Niflheim was created shortly after Muspelheim, making it the slightly younger of the two realms.

Niflheim is often conflated with the realm of Hel, the underworld where those who do not die in battle are sent to rest for eternity. Some versions of the Norse myths use the names interchangeably, while many others imply that Helheim is a smaller region within Niflheim. The realm of ice and mist is generally depicted as beneath the earth, similar to Helheim's place deep underground, or far above the earth in the void of space. In either case, there is no life in this realm; if Niflheim is an entirely separate plane from Helheim, then it is a barren expanse of ice and snow, devoid of all life and movement and warmth. If the two realms are linked, then Niflheim is a place of darkness and cold, where the only "living" beings are the drifting souls of the dead.

BELOW: A frozen sea amid the tundra of the Arctic Circle in Sweden.

MUSPELHEIM

Old Norse *Múspellsheimr*

Muspelheim, or Muspell, is the primordial realm of fire in Norse mythology.

ABOVE: Muspelheim, the primoridal realm of fire, is guarded by the fire giant Surtr, who brandishes a flaming sword.

The origin of the name is not known, but it may have its roots in a word meaning "end of the world" or "world-destroyers." Muspelheim was one of the two realms that were first present present, along with Niflheim, at the very dawn of time; the realm of fire stood on the other side of the great void of Ginnungagap from Niflheim, the primordial realm of ice and mist. The fires of Muspelheim met with the ice of Niflheim when the world was first created, leading to the birth of Ymir, the first giant. The sparks that fly from the fires of Muspelheim were used by the gods to put the stars in the sky, and the brightest of those sparks were used to create the sun and the moon.

Muspelheim is guarded by Surtr, the most powerful of the race of fire giants, who are rarely mentioned compared to the much more common frost giants that descended from Ymir. When Ragnarök arrives, Surtr and the sons of Muspelheim will ride out from their post to Asgard, where they will destroy the Bifröst, the city of the gods, and the rest of the world in an ocean of fire. As the name Muspelheim may mean "world-destroyers," and as there are some mentions of the "sons of Muspel" in Ragnarök myths, it may be the case that "Muspel" was originally the name of a giant, rather than simply being a realm of its own.

Little else is known of Muspelheim, partially because it serves primarily as a backdrop for the cosmological myth of Norse mythology, and partially because it is guarded by such a fearsome and impassable figure. There are few mentions of Muspelheim outside of the myths that detail the beginning and end of the world, and none in which any of the gods, giants, or men of Norse mythology dare to venture to the realm of fire.

VANAHEIM

Old Norse *Vanaheimr*

Another of the lesser-discussed realms of the Norse cosmos is Vanaheim, the homeland of the Vanir gods.

It is difficult to say where exactly Vanaheim would be situated in relation to the other realms; many depictions place Vanaheim on the same vertical plane as Asgard but far away, while others have Vanaheim included among the underworlds. Very little is said to describe Vanaheim in concrete terms; it is clear that the Vanir come from a far-off land, and that their customs and magical abilities are distinctly different from that of the Aesir, but there is little discussion of Vanaheim itself in the surviving source material.

However, it can be imagined that the realm of Vanaheim would echo the values of the Vanir gods. Asgard, for example, is a city of wealth, gold, opulence, and beauty, which mirrors the Aesir gods' love of wealth, treasure, and glorious exploits in battle. Many of the Vanir gods are deeply connected to nature; they are gods of the sea, the wind, fertility, and so on, and it would follow that Vanaheim would be a similarly natural environment.

After the Aesir-Vanir war, hostages were exchanged on both sides to bind the two tribes together permanently. Although this did end in Mimir being beheaded to send a message to the Aesir, it was generally a success, and the gods of both sides do not seem to have any trouble adjusting to their new realms.

One mention of Vanaheim in the *Poetic Edda* depicts the wise giant Vafthrudnir as he explains that the Vanir god Njord will return to his homeland after Ragnarök; this implies that Vanaheim as a whole may avoid the chaos of Ragnarök entirely, perhaps due to its distance from Asgard and the other realms.

ABOVE: Seated on Odin's throne Hliðskjálf, the Vanir god Freyr sits in contemplation of the panorama of earth and sky, in a 1908 woodcut by Frederic Lawrence.

ALFHEIM

Old Norse *Álfheimr*

Alfheim is the home of the light elves in Norse mythology.

The name literally literally translates to "elf land" or "land of the elves," but the realm of Alfheim is specifically reserved for the light elves—the kind, good-natured, and beautiful creatures who exist in stark comparison to the dark elves, or dwarfs. Alfheim is situated in the highest branches of Yggdrasil, the World Tree, usually depicted higher even than Asgard itself.

In some stories, Freyr—the twin brother of Freyja and the god of peace, good weather, and prosperity—is the ruler of Alfheim, which was given to him as a "teething gift," a gift that was traditionally given to infants to celebrate their first baby tooth (or perhaps the loss of their first tooth). This tradition happens to be one of the earliest depictions of what might have eventually developed into the modern idea of the "tooth fairy"; Norsemen believed that teeth held power, and would often pay children for their baby teeth, bury teeth that they had lost to keep them from being used by witches, and even wear necklaces of children's teeth into battle for good luck. Although the correlation is not exact, there are also some similarities between Alfheim and the "fairyland" concept present in the stories of many other cultures across the world, particularly in Scottish and Irish folklore. The inhabitants of Alfheim are less capricious than the morally-grey fairies of other cultures, but the idea of a higher natural world in which delicate, beautiful creatures live is a persistent one.

PICTURE: *Among the Sierra Nevada Mountains*, 1868, by the German-American painter Albert Bierstadt.

Old Norse *Svartálfaheimr*

SVARTALFHEIM

Svartalfheim is the home of the Svartalfar, or dark elves, also known as dwarfs.

ABOVE: An intricate bone carving, depicts the dark elves, or dwarves, of Svartalfheim, c. 10th century.

In direct contrast to the sunlit realm of Alfheim, the realm of the dark elves can be found deep, deep in the earth; the gods were offended by the dark elves' ugliness and cruel nature when they first emerged from the butchered corpse of Ymir, and so they were banished to live deep underground and never emerge during the light of day. The home of the dark elves is usually envisioned as a sprawling underground cavern system, labyrinthine and impossible to navigate for any but the creatures exiled to live out their days underground. The caverns are lit only by the fires of constantly-burning forges and smelteries used to refine ore, craft priceless artifacts, and forge weapons and armor.

This subterranean home may be why there is such a strong association between dwarfs and the trades of mining, smithing, and metalworking; due to their long proximity to the riches of the earth, the Svartalfar are deeply devoted to gold and jewels; they are renowned as master crafters despite the poor reputation their appearance and nature tends to bring them. The gods rarely visit Svartalfheim, but they often call upon its residents to create treasures, weapons, and magical artifacts for

them in times of need. Svartalfheim is also sometimes referred to as Niðavellir, meaning "dark fields."

The dark, hidden nature of Svartalfheim aids the metaphor that the light elf/dark elf distinction works towards. This clear-cut separation of these two races of what was originally the same species is the strongest instance of a pure black and white, good-versus-evil conflict—something that is rare in Norse mythology. Most of the creatures in Norse myths are complicated and characterized in shades of grey; for whatever reason, the light and dark elves stand out as polar opposites, one living high above the clouds and one banished deep beneath the earth. There is some possibility that Christian influence has impacted this depiction of the two realms, as the concept is fairly reminiscent of the angel/demon, heaven/hell dynamic of Christianity. Another possibility is that the two realms—and their two populations that originate from the same source—show us the possibility for both good and evil in each person, which may line up more closely with the complex nature of morality in Norse mythology.

ABOVE: The goddess Freyja, in Svartalfheim, watches the dwaves craft the necklace which they subsequently gift her.

3

THE AESIR GODS

THE AESIR GODS

TOP: From Wagner's *Ring* cycle: Wotan takes leave of Brünnhilde. Photograph by Konrad Dielitz, 1892; **ABOVE:** A modern wood construction of Odin, located on the shore of a Norwegian fjord; **RIGHT:** The Runic Stone, from Tjängvide, Götland, depicting Odin (riding his eight-legged steed, Sleipnir) and Frigga; and longship. c. 700 AD; **FAR RIGHT:** Modern, mass-produced statuette of Freyja; **OPPOSITE, MAIN IMAGE:** *Thor and the Dwarves*, Richard Doyle.

The Aesir gods are the primary deities depicted in the pantheon of Old Norse religion, and feature as the protagonists of the vast majority of stories from Norse mythology. The name "Aesir" refers specifically to the gods of Asgard, almost all of whom are descended from All-Father Odin, ruler of Asgard. These figures include gods such as Thor, Baldur, and Tyr, all children of Odin and his wife Frigga. A handful of the Aesir, however, were adopted into the clan later in life: Loki, the son of a giant, is one of the best-known examples of this. The Vanir—a distinct tribe of gods that once went to war against the Aesir—also allowed the gods Njord, Freyja, and Freyr to join the Aesir as part of a peace treaty.

Most of the gods are associated with one or more specific domains or attributes. Thor, for example, is the god of thunder, while Odin is the god of wisdom, victory in battle, the gallows, and poetry, among many other aspects. Unusually, the Norse gods were often believed to be the literal personification of their attributes; Thor was believed to be thunder itself, rather than simply controlling or creating it. Similarly, Loki is not a god "of" fire, mischief, or chaos, but instead is the personification of those concepts. This was more of a symbolic concept than a universal rule, of course; Thor was still often shown summoning and manipulating thunder, and the many gods of fertility and the harvest were believed to have direct agency over those aspects of mortal life.

Of the many characters of Norse mythology, the Aesir gods are the most thoroughly developed. Similar to the Olympians of Greek mythology, the Aesir gods were not believed to be perfect or infallible; they were very human in their behavior and personalities and often made mistakes. Although they were gods, they were just as liable to fits of jealousy, anger, and pride as any human. The Norsemen also believed that the gods—while ageless and extremely powerful—were not immortal. The gods could be killed, and those whose souls went to Hel after death (such as Baldur, the most beloved of the gods) could not return. The myth of Ragnarök, the prophesied end of the world and "twilight of the gods," promises that even the gods themselves cannot escape death forever. For all the extreme power and wisdom of the gods, they have no more control over fate than mortals.

ODIN

Odin is a complex god, one vitally important to the core structure of Norse mythology.

Odin has many names and titles; over 170 have been recorded in source material, a fact which features in several myths. Some of his best known titles are All-Father, High One, Grey Beard, Old One-Eye, and Lord of the Gallows. Odin was one of the first beings formed at the creation of the universe; he and his brothers Vili and Ve are the grandsons of Búri, the man who was licked out of a block of ice by the primordial cow Audhumla. Odin and his brothers slew Ymir, the father of all giants, and used his corpse to create the earth and the sky. This victory, along with Odin's leadership and wisdom, cemented his position as the ruler of gods—almost all of whom are descended from him—and mortals alike. He was also the catalyst that formed the first two humans, Ask and Embla, and built the realms of Asgard and Midgard by hand. He is known for his near-limitless wisdom, which he obtained by sacrificing one of his eyes to drink from Mimir's well, and his mastery over runes and magic. Even as the wisest being in the cosmos—except perhaps for Mimir himself—Odin's quest for knowledge is endless.

Generally, Odin is depicted as a sturdy older man, one-eyed and shrewd, with a long grey beard. Odin is often disguised or shrouded; many sources depict him wearing a dark grey or blue cloak, his face obscured by a deep hood or a wide-brimmed hat. As he was known to often wander the mortal realm to aid, observe, and converse with humans, his cloak and hat often helped hide his true identity so that he could pass unnoticed through Midgard. In other depictions—especially when riding into battle or making a display of strength—Odin dons a golden, eagle-winged helmet and wields Gungnir, his magic spear. He is almost always accompanied by his faithful Raven familiars, Hugin and Munin, who perch on his shoulders and act as his eyes and ears throughout the nine realms. His two wolves, Geri and Freki, are often seen around his feet; at feasts, Odin feeds the wolves by hand from his own plate. His eight-legged horse, Sleipnir, is the fastest and most noble horse in all of creation. Odin is the husband of Frigga, queen of the gods, and is the father or ancestor of almost all other gods—notably including his sons Baldr and Thor.

As Odin has been such an important figure for so long, he has come to represent many things over the centuries. He is primarily viewed as the patron god of wisdom, poetry, and victory in battle, although the full list of his associations would fill several pages. One particularly interesting association is that of Odin as the patron saint of hanged men and of the gallows, a belief stemming from Odin's self-sacrifice in hanging himself from the world tree in search of knowledge. He is also the patron god of the einherjar, the spirits of those who died nobly in battle, and feasts with them in the great hall of Valhalla. When Ragnarök comes, Odin will lead the einherjar into the final battle, where he will be slain while fighting the giant wolf Fenrir.

OPPOSITE: A deeply contemplative Odin sits on his throne, overlooking Asgard, accompanied by his two ravens, Hugin and Munin; **TOP:** Statue of Odin in Kronborg Castle, Helsingør, Denmark; **ABOVE:** Odin and his queen, Frigga. Illustration by Emil Doepler, from *Walhall, die Götterwelt der Germanen* (*Valhalla, the World of the German Gods*), 1905, by Martin Oldenbourg, Berlin (see pages 124–125).

LORD OF THE GALLOWS

Before Odin set out on his quest for knowledge, the runes–an ancient set of alphabets used in the earliest Germanic languages–were hidden from the world.

TOP: Odin Lord Of The Gallows, again by Emil Doepler, from *Walhall, die Götterwelt der Germanen* (*Valhalla, the World of the German Gods*), 1905, by Martin Oldenbourg, Berlin (see pages 124–125); **ABOVE:** Yggdrasil, the World Tree. Illustration by Friedrich Heine; **RIGHT:** Modern mass-produced runes; **OPPOSITE:** Odin the Wanderer.

The word "rune" literally means "secret" in Old Norse, and true mastery over the runes was believed to be the key to many forms of sorcery and spiritual ability.

Odin, eternally eager for knowledge and the gathering of secrets, knew that the runes were hidden at the bottom of the Well of Urd, one of the potent magical wells that feed the roots of Yggdrasil. The runes had a will of their own, however, and would not be revealed to the unworthy; an act of sacrifice and bravery was needed before they could be understood.

So, refusing assistance of any kind from the other gods, Odin hung himself by the neck from one of the highest branches of Yggdrasil and impaled himself with his magic spear, determined to endure until the runes revealed themselves to him. He stared down into the well for nine days and nine nights without food or water, bleeding and freezing in the brutal winds of Yggdrasil's high branches, half dead; on the ninth night, the runes finally revealed themselves to him. In moments, the shapes of the runes were burned into Odin's mind, and he understood all the secret knowledge they held within. Finally, with a scream, Odin cut himself down from the tree, armed now with a series of spells, charms, songs, and secrets that only he would ever know. Odin carved magic runes upon his spear Gungnir, into the teeth of his horse Sleipnir, and upon countless other creatures and objects, marking them with unique powers, protections, and abilities. From then on, he was known as a patron god of the gallows and of the dead, as some part of himself died that day in exchange for knowledge.

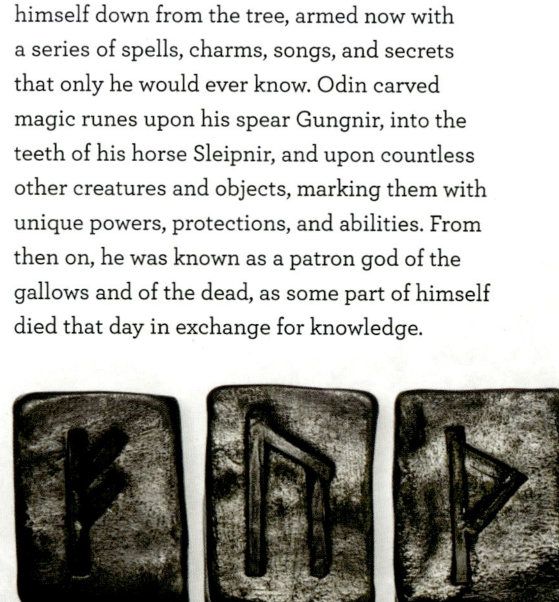

ODIN AND BILLING'S DAUGHTER

Billing, king of the Ruthenes, was wrought with fear when he heard the news that a great army was about to invade his kingdom.

The king was old, too old to fight, and his only child—a daughter named Rinda, of marriageable age—obstinately refused to choose a husband who could provide the additional soldiers the king so desperately needed. Things began to seem hopeless. Then, one day while Billing was sitting in his hall and contemplating his doom, a stranger suddenly entered his palace. Looking up, the king saw a middle-aged man wrapped in a deep blue traveling cloak, with a broad-brimmed hat drawn down over his forehead. The hat shrouded the man's face in shadow, but when the fire in the hearth illuminated his face for a moment, the king saw that he had only one eye. The stranger asked the king, kindly, what the cause of his depression was, and the king told him everything. There was something about the stranger that put Billing at ease and filled him with unexplainable confidence. When Billing was finished, Odin—the stranger's true identity, unknown to the king—offered to lead the Ruthenes' forces against the invading army.

ABOVE: *Odin as the Wanderer*, by the English artist Arthur Rackham, 1910; **BELOW:** Modern plastic models of Odin and two of his cohorts.

He succeeded, of course, as an army led by the king of the gods would be hard-pressed to fail, and when he returned, he asked Billing for his daughter's hand in marriage. The king agreed to Odin's request at once, but his daughter Rinda refused outright.

Undeterred, Odin returned the next week in a new disguise, this time taking the appearance of a master smith. He gave the king and princess gifts of fine gold and silver trinkets, and once again asked for Rinda's hand; once again, the king agreed, and once again, the princess rejected him with scorn.

When he returned a third time to ask the princess to be his bride, she rejected him once more, this time shoving Odin away hard enough to make him lose his balance and drop to one knee. Furious at this added insult, Odin pointed at the princess and cursed her, casting a spell that rendered her limp and lifeless as a corpse. Odin was gone from the castle by the time she awoke, and the King and his attendants found with dismay that she had been stricken with a deep and incurable depression by the god's curse. When the king had begun to lose all hope of reviving his daughter, an old woman presented herself to the court and claimed that she could undo the curse. The old woman claimed that the princess must be given over into her care for the cure to work, and the king agreed without question. Then, Odin—who had been disguised as the old woman in question—revealed himself. As the king had given the princess to him, Odin now had the power to compel Rinda to marry him, and so he released her from the curse only after she promised to be his bride.

THE MEAD OF POETRY

After the great war between the Aesir and Vanir, when peace had been agreed upon, the signing of a peace treaty was to be marked by a particular ritual.

A large vase was brought into the meeting place, and every god from both tribes approached the vase and spat into it. From the mixed saliva of the gods, the being Kvasir was born: he was quickly renowned for his wisdom and goodness, and soon went about the world of gods and men answering all questions asked him, teaching and educating as many as possible.

Everyone loved the wise, kindhearted Kvasir—everyone, that is, except for the two cruelest of the dwarfs, who had become jealous of Kvasir's glowing reputation and undeniable talents. So, one day when the poet was walking on the seashore, the two dwarfs named Fialar and Galar came up to him and begged him to visit their cave deep in the cliffs near the sea. Kvasir, pure of heart as he was, never suspected

ABOVE: *Odin and Gunlod*, illustration by Emil Doepler, from *Walhall, die Götterwelt der Germanen* (*Valhalla, the World of the German Gods*), 1905, by Martin Oldenbourg, Berlin (see pages 124–125).

anyone of wrongdoing, so he willingly followed the dwarfs into their dark cavern miles underground. The two dwarf brothers killed him, then, and drained his blood into three jars in which they had already placed some honey. From that mixture of sweet honey and the great teacher and poet's blood, Fialar and Galar brewed the Magic Mead, which would grant anyone who drank it the same gifts of poetry and kindness as Kvasir.

When the dwarfs had mixed the mead, they took great care to hide it in a secret cave. And then, proud of their success, they set off in search of some new adventure. Soon they encountered the giant Gilling asleep on the seashore; they pinched and kicked him awake, then asked him to row them a little way out to sea in his boat. The giant, who was both good-natured and naïve, took the dwarfs aboard and began rowing out into the water. Then Galar suddenly pulled the boat sharply to one side so that it struck on a rock and capsized. The kind giant, who could not swim, quickly drowned, left behind by the two cruel brothers as they floated back to shore on the shattered remains of the boat.

Still not content with the day's cruelties, they went straightway to the giant's house and called to his wife to come quickly, for Gilling was drowning. The giantess rushed out of the house to save her husband, and as she came through the doorway, Fialar suddenly dropped a millstone from the roof down onto her head, killing her instantly.

As the dwarfs were celebrating their success, the giant's son—whose name was Suttung—came home. When he saw his mother lying dead upon the ground, and the little men jumping and cackling with glee, he knew what they had done. He seized Galar and Fialar, one in each hand, and carried them far out into the sea, where he set them on a tiny crag of rock which would be quickly submerged when the tide rose. As he turned to leave, the dwarfs screamed with fear and begged him to save them. In their terror, they promised to give him anything he asked for.

Suttung had heard rumors of the Magic Mead in the days since Kvasir's death, and he longed to taste it and gain the gift of poetry, so he made the dwarfs promise to give him the three jars in exchange for their lives. Although Galar and Fialar were furious at his request, they had no choice but to agree if they wanted to live. As soon as they were on land again, they delivered the precious mead into his hands. As Suttung could not be at home all day to guard his treasure, he hid the jars in a deep recess in the rocks, and asked his daughter Gunlod watch over them night and day. The mouth of the cavern was sealed up with an enormous stone so that no one could enter except by a passageway known only to Gunlod, and Suttung felt that his treasure was safe from both gods and men.

OPPOSITE: Sittung the giant confronts the dwarves; **BELOW:** Odin, taken from the early print edition of the *Prose Edda*, published in the 17th century.

Baugi
Rati.

Meanwhile, the news of Kvasir's death had been brought to Odin by his ravens Hugin and Munin, and he—in his eternal quest for knowledge and arcane secrets—was equally determined to claim for himself the mead that had been brewed from the poet's blood. So he disguised himself as a traveler, pulled his big gray hat low over his face, and set out for the country where the Magic Mead was hidden. As he neared the giant's home, he saw a field in which nine sturdy thralls were mowing hay, servants of Sutting's brother Baugi. He went quickly up to the thralls and said: "Your scythes seem very dull; imagine how much faster you could work if they were sharper. Shall I sharpen them for you?" The men were surprised at this unexpected offer of help; but they accepted the stranger's assistance gladly. When they found how sharp he had made their scythes, they begged him to sell or give them the whetstone. To this Odin replied, "Whoever can catch it may have it as a gift," and with these words he threw the stone among them. Immediately greed overwhelmed the nine men, and they slashed at each other so savagely with their scythes that by evening every one of them lay dead in the field.

Meanwhile, Odin sought out Baugi's house and begged for a meal and a night's shelter. The giant received him hospitably, and as they sat eating, word was brought to Baugi that his nine servants were dead. Odin listened as Baugi mourned his bad luck and despaired over all the wealth he would lose with no one to care for his fields. Eventually, he offered his services to Baugi, promising to do as much work as the nine thralls. The giant was very doubtful, but he accepted the offer all the same, and next morning Odin got to work in the fields.

Before long, all the hay on Baugi's land was carefully stored away in the barns, and Odin came to the giant to demand his payment. "What payment shall I make you?" asked Baugi, fearing that the stranger would charge a huge amount of money for such efficient work. He was surprised, then, when Odin answered, "All I ask is a draught of the Magic Mead which your brother Suttung keeps hidden in a cavern."

"That is not an easy thing to get," replied the giant, "for though I would be glad to fetch you some of the mead, my brother has never let me enter the cave. However, I will ask him to bring you a single draught." So Baugi went in search of his brother and told him of the service that Odin had rendered. Then he asked for one drink of the Magic Mead for his guest. This infuriated Sutting, and he shouted: "Do you think I would give any of the mead to a stranger who can do the work of nine thralls? No man could have such power; that can only be a god that you have been calling your servant, and the gods have been our enemies since the beginning of time."

Baugi feared and hated the gods as much as his brother, but he had given his word to Odin to help him get the Magic Mead, and he did not dare to break his promise. So when he returned to his guest and told of his failure to retrieve the mead, Odin answered: "Then we must try some other way. Take me to the cavern where the mead is hidden; but see that your brother does not see us there."

Reluctantly, Baugi agreed to show Odin the secret cave; as they walked, he tried to think of a plan to get rid of his troublesome guest. When they finally reached the cave, Odin drew a hand-drill from his pocket and began to bore a hole in the great stone that stood at the cave's mouth. As soon as he grew tired, he made Baugi take his turn at the drill; and, owing to the giant's great strength, a hole was soon bored through the rock. Then Odin quickly turned himself into a snake and crept into the opening while Baugi, seeing the god no longer beside him and realizing what the sudden transformation meant, made a stab at the snake with the drill, hoping to kill it. But Odin had slid safely through the hole and was already inside the cave.

OPPOSITE: The giant Baugi drills into the mountain to allow Odin to retrieve Sutting's Magic Mead hidden in there. From the 17th century print edition of the *Prose Edda*; **ABOVE:** *Odin's Hunt*, by August Malmström, 19th century.

ABOVE: *Odin drinks of the magic mead.* Illustration by Katharine Pyle, 1930; **BELOW:** Bragi, by Carl Emil Doepler (see pages 124–125).

Taking his rightful form, Odin now began to look eagerly about him, and when his eyes grew accustomed to the dimness of the cavern, he saw the daughter of Suttung seated in the furthest corner beside the three jars that contained the Magic Mead. He came softly to Gunlod's side, and spoke to her gently so as not to frighten her at the sudden appearance of a stranger. He smiled at her kindly, and she asked, "Who are you, and why are you here?"

"I am a traveller, tired and thirsty after my long journey," answered Odin. "Will you not give me something to drink?"

Gunlod shook her head. "I have nothing here save the Magic Mead, and that I dare not give you," she said sadly. Odin begged for just a single sip, but the giant's daughter firmly refused to let him touch the jars.

At last, after hours of debate, Gunlod allowed her visitor to take one sip of the mead; but as soon as Odin got the jars in his hands, he drained each one dry before the astonished woman could stop him. Then he changed himself quickly into a snake, and glided out through the opening in the rock, before turning then into an eagle and taking flight back to Asgard. He knew well that there was no time to lose, for Baugi had already gone to his brother with the news of what had happened at the cave's mouth.

When Suttung heard Baugi's story and realized that his precious mead was being stolen by one of the gods, he rushed straight to the cavern. Just as he reached it, he saw an eagle soar up into the air, and he knew this was some god in disguise bearing away the Magic Mead to Asgard. So he quickly changed himself into an eagle and took off in pursuit. Odin could not fly very fast, for the mead made him heavy, and he was understandably distressed to see that the giant was easily gaining on him. As they both neared the gates of Asgard, some of the gods were looking out and happened to see the two birds approaching. It was not until the eagles neared the outer walls that the watchers realized that it was Odin fleeing from an enemy, straining his weary wings to reach Asgard.

In a hurry, the gods of Asgard laid a great pile of wood on the inner walls, setting it alight the moment that the first eagle had passed safely overhead. The flames shot up violently as Suttung approached; the fire scorched his great wings, and the smoke blinded his eyes so that he fluttered helplessly down to the earth and burned to death on the way down. Meanwhile the Magic Mead was safe in Asgard, and there it was put in care of Bragi, the white-haired son of Odin. The the mead remained with the gods from then on, but sometimes a favored mortal is given a single drop of the mead on the day of their birth, fating them to grow into a renowned poet later in life.

ODIN'S EYE

ABOVE: Statue of Odin, with his ravens and wolves; **MAIN IMAGE:** "Heimdall an der Himmelsbrücke" ("Heimdall and the Sky Bridge"), Emil Doepler, from *Walhall, die Götterwelt der Germanen* (*Valhalla, the World of the German Gods*), 1905, by Martin Oldenbourg, Berlin (see pages 124–125).

One night, when all was quiet in Asgard and the Aesir had gone to rest, Odin sat awake on his high throne, his thoughts racing. At his feet crouched his two faithful wolves, and upon his shoulders perched his twin ravens who served as his messengers and spies in the realms beyond Asgard's walls.

As the ruler of all things, the All-Father was burdened with heavy responsibility, and he felt that he needed greater wisdom than he—or anyone, for that matter—possessed in order to succeed at his task. After thinking a long time on the matters which needed his care, he suddenly started up, and went forth with long strides from his palace of Gladsheim into the night. He soon returned, leading his beautiful, eight-footed steed, Sleipnir, and it was plain that Odin was going on a journey. He quickly mounted Sleipnir, and rode swiftly away toward Bifröst, the rainbow bridge. When Sleipnir stepped upon the bridge, it trembled and seemed hardly strong enough to bear the horse and his rider, but they had no fear of its giving way, and Sleipnir galloped swiftly onward.

BELOW: Norse carved stone relic c. 300–600 AD: Heimdall blowing the Gjallarhorn. Heimdall, watchman of Bifröst, the whitest of all the gods, with gold teeth and acute vision and hearing; **BOTTOM:** Odin rides Sleipnir.

Soon Odin saw Heimdall, the watchman of the bridge, riding toward him on a fine horse, with a golden mane that reflected light upon the noble face of his rider.

"You must be out on some important errand, Father Odin, to be riding from Asgard so late at night," said Heimdall.

"It is indeed a most important errand, and I must hurry," replied Odin. "It is well for us that we have such a faithful guardian of the rainbow bridge; if it were not for you, Heimdall, our enemies might long ago have taken Asgard by storm. You are so watchful, you can hear the grass grow in the fields, and the wool gather on the backs of the sheep, and you need less sleep than a bird. I myself stand in great need of wisdom, in order to take care of such faithful servants, and to drive back such wicked enemies!"

They hurried over the bridge until they came to Heimdall's castle. This was a lofty tower which was placed so as to guard the bridge, and it shone forth such a wonderful, clear light, that Heimdall could see, even in the darkest night, anyone who came toward the bridge from miles away. Here Odin stopped a few moments to drink the mead which the good Heimdall offered him.

Then said Odin, "As I am journeying into the land of our enemies, I shall leave my good horse with you; there are not many with whom I would trust him, but I know that you, my faithful Heimdall, will take good care of him. I can best hide myself from the giants by going on as a wanderer."

With these words the All-Father left Heimdall's castle, and started off toward the north, through the land of the fierce giants. During all the first day there was nothing to be seen but ice and snow; several times Odin was nearly crushed as the frost giants hurled huge blocks of ice after him. The second day he came to mountains and broad rivers. Often when he had just crossed over a stream, the mountain giants would come after him to the other bank, and when they found that Odin had escaped them, they would howl so fiercely that the echoes sounded from hill to hill.

At the end of the third day, Odin came to a land where trees were green and flowers blooming. Here was one of the three fountains which watered the world tree, Yggdrasil, and nearby sat the wise giant, Mimir, guarding the waters of this wonderful fountain, for whoever drank of it would have the gift of great wisdom. Mimir was a giant in size, but he was not one of the fierce giant enemies of the gods, for he was kind, and wiser than any other being living or dead. Mimir's well of wisdom was in the midst of a wonderful valley, filled with rare plants and bright flowers, and among the groves of beautiful trees were strange creatures, sleeping

dragons, serpents, and lizards, while birds with bright plumage flew and sang among the branches. Over all this quiet valley shone a soft light, different from sunlight, and in the center grew one of the roots of the great world tree. Here the wise giant Mimir sat gazing down into his well.

Odin greeted the kindly old giant, and said, "Oh, Mimir, I have come from Asgard to ask a great boon!"

"Gladly will I help you if it is in my power," said Mimir.

"You know," replied Odin, "that as father of gods and men I need great wisdom, and I have come to beg for one drink of your precious water of knowledge. Trouble threatens us, even from one of the Aesir, for Loki, the fire-god, has lately been visiting the giants, and I fear he has been learning evil ways from them. The frost giants and the storm giants are always at work, trying to overthrow both gods and men; great is my need for wisdom, and even though no one ever before has dared ask so great a gift, I hope that since you know how deep is my trouble, you will grant my request."

Mimir sat silently, thinking for several moments, and then said, "You ask a great thing, indeed, Father Odin; are you ready to pay the price which I must demand?"

"Yes," said Odin, eagerly, "I will give you all the gold and silver of Asgard, and all the jeweled shields and swords of the Aesir. More than all, I will give up my eight-footed horse Sleipnir, if that is needed to win the reward."

"And do you suppose that these things will buy wisdom?" said Mimir. "That can be gained only by showing bravery, and through personal sacrifice. Are you willing to give me a part of yourself? Will you give up one of your own eyes?"

At this Odin despaired at first; but after a few moments of deep thought, he looked up with a bright smile, and answered, "Yes, I will even give you one of my eyes, and I will suffer whatever else is asked, in order to gain the wisdom that I need!"

And so, in exchange for one of his eyes—which was plucked from his head that very evening—Odin was granted a single drink from Mimir's well of knowledge, granting him all the wisdom of the nine realms. From that day on, Odin was the wisest being alive, second only to Mimir himself. And despite the pain and injury of his sacrifice, never once was the All-Father sorry for what he had given up or for the suffering he had borne for the sake of the gods and mortals under his protection.

TOP: "Odin Mimir Befragend" ("Odin questioning Mimir") by Emil Doepler, from *Walhall, die Götterwelt der Germanen* (*Valhalla, the World of the German Gods*), 1905, by Martin Oldenbourg, Berlin (see pages 124–125); **ABOVE:** Copenhagen University 400th anniversary medal; Odin consults with Mimir, the guardian of the well of wisdom.

THOR

Thor is the son of Odin, the All-Father, and Jörd, the Earth, though some myths state that his mother was Frigga, queen of the gods.

He is usually represented and described as a man in his prime, tall and fit, with muscular limbs and bristling red or blonde hair and beard. In moments of anger, sparks often fly from his eyes and hair. His wife is Sif, the golden-haired goddess of grain and fertility.

Thor is the proud owner of a magic hammer called Miölnir, which always returns to his hand after being thrown at an enemy. As this huge hammer, the mythologized origin of thunder, was generally red-hot, some depictions show Thor wearing an iron gauntlet which enabled him to grasp it safely. He could hurl Miölnir a great distance, and his strength, which was always remarkable, was doubled when he wore his belt of might.

As a child, he was remarkable for his great size and strength, and soon after his birth he amazed the assembled gods by playfully carrying out feats of strength that would have been impossible for a grown man. Although generally good-tempered, Thor would occasionally fly into a terrible rage, and as he was very dangerous at these times, he was once sent away from home and entrusted him to the care of Vingnir and Hlora. These foster-parents, who are considered the personification of sheet-lightning, taught Thor patience and self-control, and raised him to be the hero and defender of the gods that he is now known to be. Thor himself, recognizing all he owed them, later assumed the names of Vingthor and Hlorridi, by which he is also occasionally known.

Thor holds pride of place in the halls of Asgard; he is known to be the strongest and bravest of the Aesir gods, and occupies one of the twelve seats in the great hall of Valhalla. He also rules his own realm of Thrudheim, where he built a palace called Bilskirnir, the most spacious in all Asgard. It contains five hundred and forty halls for the accommodation of his many servants, who after death were welcomed to his home, where they received equal treatment with their masters in Valhalla. Thor is also the patron god of the peasants and lower classes.

OPPOSITE: *Thor's Fight with the Giants*, Mårten Eskil Winge; **BELOW:** The Valley Of Thor, Iceland.

As a personification of fire and lightning as well as of mischief, Loki is often seen paired with Thor, as both friend and foe. Although they are often depicted as good friends, the two are constantly at odds in many myths, and their personalities are direct opposites: Thor is brave, selfless, and kind, while Loki is cowardly, selfish, and often cruel, making him a narrative foil to Thor. In many tellings, Thor is not allowed to pass over the Bifröst (the rainbow bridge connecting Asgard to the other realms) for fear that his size and the heat he radiates would destroy it. In these myths, Thor is forced to travel on foot or in his chariot, usually pulled by two goats.

When Ragnarök comes, Thor's fate is to die in battle alongside his father, Odin, along with many of the other Aesir gods. At the final battle, Thor will fight and slay Jörmungandr, the Midgard serpent, before drowning in the flood of blood and venom that pours from Jörmungandr's fallen corpse.

TOP: Thor in his Chariot, by Carl Emil Doepler (see pages 124–125); **THIS IMAGE:** An early 20th century rendition of the bridge from Midgard to Asgard, and Valhalla.

Ugliest and wickedest of all the giants was Geirrod, who lived in a great gloomy castle away in a dark corner of Jotunheim, with his two giant daughters, Gialp and Greip.

THOR AND GEIRROD

Gialp and Greip were hideous, with misshapen figures and lopsided features. One had red eyes and the other had perfectly black teeth. When Geirrod heard of the death of Thrym, his brother, he was filled with wrath, and swore an oath that he would never rest till he had taken revenge on Thor. Loudly, he described all the terrible things he would do to Thor if only he could catch him without his hammer, his belt of power, and his gloves of might; as he ranted, his daughters wailed and gnashed their teeth, and both clamored to have whatever might be left of the god of thunder when their father had finished with him.

Meanwhile, Thor was not even aware of the existence of these particular giants, and it did not seem at all likely that he would ever encounter them under his own power. About the time that Geirrod was screaming his threats against Thor to the world, Loki was growing restless within the walls of Asgard, and, recalling the fun he had had when he visited Jotunheim in the guise of a bird, he went to Freyja once more with intent to borrow her falcon dress. But Freya would not lend it to him again, as she had no particular fondness for Loki. So the mischievous god simply waited for a moment when she was distracted and stole the dress while she wasn't looking. Taking to the air, Loki directed his flight towards Jotunheim, until he found himself hovering above the towers of Geirrod's castle.

The giant and his family were sitting at their great table as Loki arrived upon the scene. Peering through the open window, he could see the ugly trio snatching chunks of charred meat from smoking dishes, half choking themselves in their efforts each to eat faster than the rest. Perching on the windowsill, Loki could not resist a croaking chuckle of amusement, and at the same time his great wings shut out much of the light. This attracted Geirrod's attention, and he quickly looked up.

TOP: Jotunheim; **ABOVE:** *Freia, the Fair One*. By the English artist Arthur Rackham, from *The Rhinegold and the Valkyrie*, 1910; **LEFT:** Loki's flight to Jotunheim.

ABOVE: Peregrine Falcon, *Falco peregrinus*. The fastest animals in the world; **MAIN IMAGE:** Thor, Loki and Gialp. Illustration by Emil Doepler, from *Walhall, die Götterwelt der Germanen* (*Valhalla, the World of the German Gods*), 1905, by Martin Oldenbourg, Berlin (see pages 124–125); **OPPOSITE:** Mjölnir, Thor's Hammer.

"Catch me that bird!" he cried to one of his servants, for there was something about the appearance of the falcon that revealed the truth to Geirrod at a single glance. The servant leapt for Loki, but the ledge was too high for him, and Loki chuckled at his vain attempts, keeping all but within reach in order to watch the servant struggle.

But suddenly the servant, jumping just a little higher, managed to get a grip of the sill, and as Loki spread his wings in flight he found his feet firmly caught in a tangle of ivy. As he struggled to get free, the servant held him fast and carried him off in triumph to Geirrod.

"Who are you?" asked the giant, but Loki only blinked and made no reply.

"What are you doing here?" he demanded again; but still he got only a blink for an answer.

"Who sent you to spy upon us?" roared Geirrod; Loki gave only another blink.

Then the giant stood up in a fit of rage, and, declaring that hunger and thirst were the best things in the world to teach a bird to talk, he locked the unfortunate Asgardian in a strong cage, with neither food nor drink.

For three whole months Loki languished in the cage, and then at last, at the point of death, he croaked out feebly that he was in fact Loki, and promised anything in his power if Geirrod would only set him free.

This was the chance the giant had been waiting for.

"Bring to me," he said, "Thor, the god of thunder, and be sure that he comes without his hammer or his belt of strength or his gloves of might."

Loki promised to do exactly that. As soon as he was able, Loki flew back to Asgard, composing a story as he flew. He told Thor that during his three months' absence he had been a welcome guest at the hall of a friendly giant named Geirrod, and that, when he had reluctantly torn himself away, the giant had begged him to come and visit again, and to bring the great Thor the Thunderer along with him next time. Flattered, Thor agreed to accompany Loki to Geirrod's hall. He even left behind his hammer, girdle, and gloves, when Loki pointed out that bringing weapons would be rude to their friendly host.

On their way, they passed the house of Grid, a kindly old giantess, who had long been a friend of Thor's. Sitting in her doorway, she saw them pass by, and beckoned to Thor to come to her, while Loki, unsuspecting, went on his way.

"Where are you going, Thor?" asked the old giantess.

"To Geirrod's hall," he cheerfully replied. "Do you know him?"

"Know him!" said Grid, with a hoarse chuckle. "Is there anyone who does not know Geirrod? But why, my son, do you go unarmed to the hall of the strongest and wickedest of all the giants?"

Hearing this, Thor ground his teeth, exclaiming: "This is another trick of that rascal Loki! And now, what can I do? If I return to fetch Miölnir, my girdle of strength, and my gloves of might, they will say that Thor is afraid."

Luckily, it just so happened that Grid possessed of a girdle of strength, a staff of power, and gloves of might of her own, and these she produced and gave to Thor, bidding him to say not a word about them.

Before long, Thor and Loki came to the brink of the largest river in the world, where the waves rose far above their heads. Then Thor buckled on the belt of strength and, taking the staff firmly in his grasp, he stepped boldly into the water, while Loki clung to his belt, for he was afraid. Higher and higher rose the waves, and if Thor had not kept a firm grip on the staff of power he would have been washed away. But Loki, overcome with fear, let go of the belt and was carried by the waves back the way he came; and from there he hurried back to Asgard as fast as he could run.

ABOVE: Thor. Woodcut 1834, London; **BELOW:** Thor's journey to Geirrod's hall: "So, stooping quickly, he pulled an enormous rock from the water and threw it at her..."; **OPPOSITE:** Thor and Loki set out for Utgard.

When Thor had reached midstream he saw Gialp, the red-eyed daughter of the giant, stirring up the water at its source in an attempt to drown him. So, stooping quickly, he pulled an enormous rock from the water and threw it at her. He was not one to miss his mark, and the giantess fled, howling. At once the waters lowered, and Thor, seeing a mountain ash over-hanging the river, grabbed at a branch and pulled himself safely ashore.

Weary, Thor gladly turned towards Geirrod's hall, which loomed out of the darkness nearby. He was received with grace by the giant's servants, though Geirrod himself had not yet returned home. A banquet had been prepared within the hall, but somewhat to his surprise, Thor could see only one chair. This, however, was large and roomy, draped round the legs and comfortably cushioned, so the Asgardian was glad to throw himself into it and rest.

Scarcely had he done so, however, when the chair began to rise beneath him, and it ascended towards the rafters with such force and speed that in another moment Thor would have been crushed to death had he not still been holding the staff of power. He pushed the staff against the rafters, and at the same time he pressed down on the seat with such force that he plummeted to the floor again with a loud crash, a sound also mixed with shrieks and screams. Gialp and Greip, the giant's daughters, had hidden themselves under the chair, intending to kill Thor, and had now met the very same fate. After this, Thor happily ate the meal laid out in front of him, and scarcely had he finished when the giant Geirrod finally came striding into the hall. Geirrod gnashed his teeth horribly when he saw Thor sitting quite at home at his table, but he pretended that he was pleased at his visit, and at once invited him into another hall, where a number of large fires were burning. Here he proceeded to challenge Thor to a contest of skill. Thor agreed to the challenge, but Geirrod, thinking to catch Thor off his guard, snatched up a red-hot wedge of iron from the fire and flung it at him while Thor was still speaking. Quick as lightning, Thor caught the wedge in his glove of might and threw it back so hard that it passed straight through the giant, through the pillar in front of which he stood, through the wall of his castle, and at last buried itself miles deep in the rocky ground outside. At the touch of the red-hot iron, Geirrod was turned into stone. Thor took the grotesque statue and set it on top of a high mountain in Jotunheim, and it was a long time before any of the folk of that realm dared test Thor's strength again.

THOR AND UTGARD-LOKI

One morning, Thor asked Loki if he would like to go forth with him to Utgard, the stronghold of the giants, where he was going to try to conquer the fiercest enemies of Asgard.

Loki was happy to go with him, and the two gods set out in Thor's chariot, drawn by two goats. Toward evening the travelers stopped at a peasant's hut, and Thor, stepping down from his chariot, went to the door of the house to ask shelter for the night.

"I will gladly give you a room, but I have no food in the house," said the man who opened the door.

"Oh, never mind that," said Thor, "I will provide the food." So Thor and Loki stopped for the night at the peasant's hut. They found the family within, the man, his wife, and two children, a boy and a girl. All looked on in great surprise to see Thor kill his two goats and cook them for the evening meal. "Eat all you wish of the meat," said Thor, "but be careful not to break any of the bones. Throw them all into the two skins which I have spread upon the floor."

ABOVE: Thor, Loki, and young Thialfe and his sister Röskva, left the goats and chariot and set off on foot. Children's book illustration, mid-20th century; **BELOW:** Thor, Loki and Thialfe journey to Utgard. British newspaper illustration, mid-20th century; **OPPOSITE:** *Thor's Journey to the Land of Giants*, by the English artist Arthur Rackham, early 20th century.

The boy, whose name was Thialfe, wondered why Thor should say this, and as he happened to have a piece of the leg bone, he thought there could be no harm in breaking it open to eat the marrow inside. The next morning, however, the boy learned a lesson that he never forgot. When Thor was ready to start off again the next day, he held his magic hammer over the skins in which lay the bones. All at once the goats became whole again, and stood there just the same as before, except that one of them limped with his hind leg.

Then the young Thialfe knew why Thor had told them not to break the bones. At first, when he saw Thor's angry face, and how he grasped his hammer, the boy was frightened, and wanted to run away; but soon he remembered it would be cowardly to do that, so he went to Thor and asked his forgiveness. Thor, though often quick to anger, was always just and kind; after scolding the boy as he deserved, he freely forgave him, and said that he and his sister should come along with Loki and himself on their journey. The four set off, after saying goodbye to the peasant and his wife, leaving in their charge the chariot and goats, for it seemed best to finish the journey on foot. At nightfall they entered a thick forest, through which they wandered on for miles, when all at once they came upon a strange-looking house. The wide front door opened into a big room; at the left was a small room, and just opposite the front door were four long, narrow rooms.

The travelers were glad to have shelter for the night, and all lay down for a good rest. Soon after midnight they were awakened by groans and strange sounds, and the earth began to tremble. Thor sent his companions into the farthest room, grasped his hammer, and stood guard by the door. At daybreak he set out to find out what had caused the noise. He had not gone far when he came upon a huge giant, lying on the ground asleep, and Thor realized that he was making the earth tremble with his snoring, which must have been the sound they had heard in the night.

While Thor was looking at the giant, he awoke, and spoke to the god. "Hello there! I think you, little fellow, must be Thor. Really, I did not think you were quite so small! Now the sun is up, and I must be off. But where is my other glove? Oh, here it is, on the ground!" And the giant stooped and picked up his glove, which was the very house in which our four travelers had spent the night.

"If you are going my way, you may come along with me," said the giant. So they journeyed together for one day, but even mighty Thor could hardly keep up with the giant's long strides. When night came, the giant stopped under a large oak tree, and said, "I am going to sleep. You may eat your supper, if you wish;

here is a bag full of food." Saying this, he fell asleep, and was soon snoring. But when Thor tried to open the bag of food, he could not untie the cord. This made him angry, for the giant had tied up their food with his own. He looked at the huge figure lying before him asleep and, growing angrier still, Thor seized his magic hammer and threw it at him.

"Did a leaf fall on me?" said the giant, sleepily. "Haven't you eaten your supper yet? Well, I am going to sleep again." And soon he was snoring louder than before. Thor grasped his hammer tighter than ever, and threw it with such strength that it seemed as though it must surely have killed the giant; but again he rubbed his eyes, and said, "Did an acorn fall on my head?" He had hardly spoken when he was asleep again.

Then a third time Thor hurled his hammer with all his strength, and it seemed to hit his enemy in the forehead, and was buried out of sight, but the giant only said: "I think there must be birds overhead in this tree; I believe a feather dropped down on me. Are you awake, Thor? I think we'd better be going on with our journey, but I advise you to go home instead; you will find bigger fellows than I in Utgard!"

But Thor had made up his mind to go on, and nothing could make him change. At noon the four friends left their giant guide, whose path led another way. They had not traveled far when Thor spied a large city looming up before them, and soon they came to Utgard, the home of the giants. Although it was surrounded by high walls, Thor and his friends were able to creep through the bars of the great gate. When they came to the palace and found its door open, they went in, and there sat all the giants with their king, Utgard-Loki—of no relation to Loki the fire god—at their head.

Upon seeing the four strangers, the king of the giants said: "Why, this must be the god Thor. I really did not suppose that you were such a little fellow, Thor! Hopefully you are stronger than you look. Now, before you sit down at our table, you must each show some proof of your strength!"

Then Loki, who was very hungry, said he was sure he could eat more than anyone else; so the king called one of the giants to come forth, saying to Loki, "If you can indeed eat more than one of my men, you will perform a great feat."

A huge trough full of meat was brought in, and Loki began eating at one end, while the giant began at the other. They reached the center together; but Loki had eaten only the meat, while the giant had devoured meat, bones, trough, and all.

Thialfe, the peasant boy, took his turn next, and boasted that he was the fastest runner of them all. "Oh," said the king, "it will be a most wonderful feat if you can win a race against one of my men!" The first time Thialfe ran the course he kept ahead until near the end and was beaten by only a few yards. The second time he came off worse, and the third time he was only halfway around when the giant had reached the goal.

Thor, however, was not at all worried by the failure of the others, and he proposed a drinking contest. So the king brought forth a long drinking horn, saying, "My men usually empty this in one draught, if they are very thirsty, though sometimes they have to take it in two swallows, or even three."

Then Thor put his lips to the drinking horn, and took one long, deep pull, thinking he had surely emptied it, but to his surprise, the water had lowered only a few inches. Again he lifted the horn, feeling sure he should empty it this time, yet he did no better than before. The king said, "You have left a great deal for your last drink!"

This made Thor try his very best; but it was of no use, he could not empty the horn.

"So you are not as strong as you seemed, after all! Do you care to try anything else?" said the king of the giants in a mocking tone.

"Oh, certainly, anything you like!" replied Thor.

"Well," said the king, "I will give you something easy this time, since I see you are not as strong as I expected. You may try to lift this cat from the floor; it would be mere child's play for one of my men."

Thor put out his hand to lift the cat, but he could raise only one paw, though he used all his strength.

"Well, it is no more than I expected!" said the king; "you boast of your strength, but you do not show it to us."

By this time Thor was getting very angry, and he spoke fiercely, "I will challenge any one of you to fight with me!"

The king looked about the hall to find some one small enough to wrestle with Thor. Then he said, "All my men are too large, I shall have to send for one of the women!" Soon a bent old woman came hobbling in, and Thor thought it would be nothing to beat her; but the longer they wrestled, the stronger the old woman became, and at last, when it was plain that she was going to win, and Thor had been thrown to the floor, the king called to them to stop.

Thor and his friends were then invited to sit down at the feast, and the next morning, after a good breakfast, they started on their journey homeward. Utgard-Loki went with them to the city gate, and when he was about to leave them, said, "Did you find it as easy as you expected to overthrow the giants?"

"No," said Thor, who was too honest to hide his shame, "I am vexed that I have done so little, and I know that after this failure, you will all laugh at my weakness."

"No," replied the king, shaking his head. "Since you are now well outside our stronghold I will tell you the truth about what you saw there, and I will take good care not to let you get in again. You have greatly surprised us all with your strength, and I have had to use magic to hold out against you.

"When you met the first giant in the forest you would have killed him with your hammer if he had not put a mountain between himself and you. Loki was a wonderful eater, but we matched him against fire, and who can devour more than fire? The boy was a swift runner, and I had to make him race against thought, in order to beat him; what can be swifter than thought? The horn, from which you drank, was the ocean, and you took such a mighty draught that the people in Midgard saw the tide ebb. It was really not a cat you tried to lift, but the Midgard Serpent, and you pulled him so far that we feared he would let go his hold on his tail. Then you wrestled with Old Age, and who is there that can overcome Old Age?"

With these words the giant king vanished, and Thor, upon looking around, saw the city of Utgard was also gone. Then, silently, Thor and Loki, with the boy and the girl in tow, made their way back to Asgard.

OPPOSITE, TOP LEFT: "Thor bei Skrymir," Emil Doepler, from *Walhall, die Götterwelt der Germanen* (*Valhalla, the World of the German Gods*), 1905, by Martin Oldenbourg, Berlin (see pages 124–125); **OPPOSITE, BOTTOM LEFT:** Thor attempts to lift Miðgarðsormr the cat. British newspaper illustration, mid-20th century; **ABOVE:** Thor and the giant Skrymir, by Louis Huard. From *The Heroes of Asgard: Tales from Scandinavian Mythology* by A & E Keary, 1900. MacMillan & Co, London.

In the meadows of Asgard, the gods raised noble horses that were more beautiful and more swift than any known in the mortal world.

THOR AND HRUNG

There was Hrîmfaxi, the black, sleek horse who drew the chariot of night across the sky and scattered the dew from his foaming bit. There was Glad, behind whose flying heels sped the swift chariot of day. His mane was yellow with gold, and from it beamed light which made the whole world bright. Then there were the two shining horses of the sun, Arvakur the watchful, and Alsvith the rapid; and the nine fierce battle-chargers of the nine Valkyries. Each of the gods had their own glorious steed, with such pretty names as Gold-mane and Silver-top, Light-foot and Precious-stone; they galloped with their masters over clouds and through the air, blowing flame from their nostrils and glinting sparks from their eyes.

THIS IMAGE: *Valkyries Riding into Battle*, by the Swedish painter Johan Gustaf Sandberg.

But best of all the horses of heaven was Sleipnir, the eight-legged steed of Odin, who could gallop faster over land and sea than any horse which ever lived. Sleipnir was snow-white and beautiful, and Odin was very fond and proud of him. One day Odin galloped off from Asgard on Sleipnir straight towards Jotunheim, for it was a long time since the All-Father had been to the cold country, and he wished to see how its mountains and frozen rivers looked. As he galloped along a wild road, he met a huge giant standing beside his own giant steed.

"Who goes there?" cried the giant gruffly, blocking the way so that Odin could not pass. "You with the golden helmet, who are you? For I have been watching you from this mountain-top. Truly, that is a fine horse you ride."

"There is no finer horse in all the world," boasted Odin. "Have you not heard of Sleipnir, the pride of Asgard? I will match him against any of your big, clumsy giant horses."

"Ha!" roared the giant angrily, "an excellent horse he is, your little Sleipnir. But I warrant he is no match for my Gullfaxi here. Come, let us race, and then I shall repay you for your insult to the horses of Jotunheim."

So saying, the giant, whose name was Hrungnir, sprang upon his horse and spurred straight at Odin in the narrow road. Odin turned and galloped back towards Asgard with all his might; for not only did he need to prove his horse's speed, but he had to save himself and Sleipnir from the anger of the giant, who was one of the fiercest and wickedest of all his fierce and wicked race. Like a flash of lightning Sleipnir darted across the sky, and the giant horse rumbled and thumped along close behind like the thunder following the flash.

Already the rainbow bridge was in sight, with Heimdal the watchman prepared to let them in. His sharp eyes had recognized the flash of Sleipnir's white body and of Odin's golden helmet from miles away. Soon the twelve hoofs were upon the bridge, the giant horse close behind the other. At last Hrungnir knew where he was, and into what danger he was rushing. He pulled at the reins and tried to stop his great beast, but Gullfaxi was tearing along far too fast to stop. Heimdal threw open the gates of Asgard, and in galloped Sleipnir with his precious burden, safe. Close upon them bolted in Gullfaxi, bearing his giant master, puffing and purple in the face from hard riding and anger. Heimdal shut and barred the gates behind them, and now the giant was trapped within the walls of Asgard.

OPPOSITE: Odin wood carving, part of a twelve-panel frieze; **ABOVE:** *Natten* (*Night*). Hrîmfaxi, the black, sleek horse who drew the chariot of night across the sky, by Norwegian painter Peter Nicolai Arbo (1831–1892); **BELOW:** "Walhall" ("Valhalla"), Emil Doepler, from *Walhall, die Götterwelt der Germanen* (*Valhalla, the World of the German Gods*), 1905, by Martin Oldenbourg, Berlin (see pages 124–125).

BELOW: Sif, by English artist and illustrator John Charles Dollman (1851–1934); **OPPOSITE:** An 1887 engraving of Thor.

The Aesir were courteous folk, unlike the giants, and they were not the type to slaughter a single enemy thrown at their mercy. They invited him to enter Valhalla with them, to rest and eat before the long return journey ahead of him. Thor was not present, so they filled Thor's great cups for the giant, as they were nearest to the giant size. But, while Thor was famous for his power to drink deeply, Hrungnir's head was not so steady; Thor's draught was too much for him. He raged like a madman, and threatened to pick up Valhalla like a toy house and carry it home with him to Jotunheim. He said he would pull Asgard to pieces and slay all the gods except Freya the fair and Sif, the golden-haired wife of Thor, whom he would carry off like little dolls for his toy house.

The Aesir weren't sure what to do, for Thor and his hammer were not there to protect them, and Asgard seemed in danger with this enemy within its very walls. Hrungnir called for more and more mead, which Freya alone dared to bring and set before him. Finally, they asked Heimdal to blow his horn and summon Thor.

In only moments, Thor dashed into the hall, hammer in hand, and stared in amazement at the scene.

"A giant feasting in Asgard?" he roared. "This is a sight which I never saw before. Who gave the insolent fellow leave to sit in my seat? And why does fair Freya wait upon him as if he were some noble guest at a feast of the high gods? I will slay him at once!" and he raised the hammer to keep his word.

Thor's coming had sobered the giant somewhat, for he knew that this was no enemy to be trifled with. He looked at Thor sulkily and said: "I am Odin's guest. He invited me to this banquet, and therefore I am under his protection."

"You shall be sorry that you accepted the invitation," growled Thor, lowering his hammer and looking very fierce; for Sif had sobbed in his ear how the giant had threatened to carry her away.

Hrungnir now rose to his feet and faced Thor boldly, for the sound of Thor's threatening voice had restored his scattered wits. "I am here alone and without weapons," he said. "You would do ill to slay me now. It would be little like the noble Thor, of whom we hear tales, to do such a thing. The world will count you braver if you let me go and meet me later in single combat, when we shall both be fairly armed."

Thor dropped the hammer to his side. "Your words are true," he said, for he was a just and honorable god.

"I was foolish to leave my shield and stone club at home," went on the giant. "If I had my arms with me, we would fight at this moment. But I name you a coward if you slay me now, an unarmed enemy."

ABOVE: Title page of the 17th century print edition of the *Prose Edda*; **BELOW:** *Thor und Hrungnir*. Thor throws his hammer and slays Hrungnir. Pen drawing by German painter, feature writer, and critic Ludwig Pietsch (1824–1911).

"Your words are just," said Thor again. "I have never before been challenged by any foe. I will meet you, Hrungnir, at Utgard, midway between heaven and earth. And there we will fight a duel to see which of us is the better fellow."

Hrungnir departed for Jotunheim, and great was the excitement of the other giants when they heard that one of their number was to fight with Thor, the deadliest enemy of their race.

"We must be sure that Hrungnir wins!" they cried. "We will make a second hero to aid Hrungnir."

All the giants set to work at once. They brought great buckets of moist clay, and heaping them up into a huge mound, molded the mass with their giant hands until they had made a man of clay nine miles high and three miles wide. "Now we must make him live; we must put a heart into him!" they cried. But they could find no heart big enough until they thought of taking one from a mare, and that fitted nicely. A mare's heart is the most cowardly one that beats.

Hrungnir's heart was a three-cornered piece of hard stone. His head also was of stone, and likewise the great shield which he held before him when he stood outside of Utgard waiting for Thor to come to the duel. Over his shoulder he carried his club, and that also was of stone. By his side stood the huge clay man, Möckuralfi.

But at the very first sight of Thor, who came thundering to the place with his servant Thialfi the swift at his side, the timid mare's heart in the man of clay throbbed with fear; he trembled so much that his knees knocked together, and his nine miles of height rocked unsteadily.

Thialfi ran up to Hrungnir and began to mock him, saying, "You are careless, giant. I fear you do not know what a mighty enemy has come to fight you. You hold your shield in front of you; but that will serve you nothing. Thor has seen this. He has only to go down into the earth and he can attack you conveniently from beneath your very feet."

At this terrifying news Hrungnir hastened to throw his shield upon the ground and to stand upon it, so that he might be safe from Thor's attacks from below. He grasped his heavy club with both hands and waited. He had not long to wait. There came a blinding flash of lightning and a peal of crashing thunder. Thor had cast his hammer into space. Hrungnir raised his club with both hands and hurled it against the hammer which he saw flying towards him. The stone club was like glass against the power of Mjölnir; it was dashed into pieces instantly. Some fragments fell upon the earth; and these, they say, are the rocks from which whetstones are made unto this day. One splinter of the hard stone struck Thor himself in the forehead, with so fierce a blow that he fell forward upon the ground, and Thialfe feared that he was killed. But Mjölnir, not even stopped in its course by meeting the giant's club, sped straight to Hrungnir and crushed his stony skull, so that he fell forward over Thor and his foot lay on the fallen hero's neck.

Meanwhile Thialfe the swift had fought with the man of clay and had found little trouble in toppling him to earth. For the mare's cowardly heart in his great body gave him little strength to meet Thor's faithful servant, and the trembling limbs of Möckuralfi soon yielded to Thialfe's blows. He fell like an unsteady tower of blocks, and his brittle bulk shattered into a thousand fragments.

Thialfe ran to his master and tried to help him up. The giant's great foot still rested upon his neck, and all Thialfi's strength could not move it away. Swift as the wind he ran for the other Aesir, and they came rushing to the spot with fear and concern. Together they all attempted to raise Hrungnir's foot from Thor's neck, hoping to see whether their hero lived or not, but all their efforts were in vain.

Then arrived Magni, the son of Thor himself. Magni was but three days old, yet already in his infancy he was almost as big as a giant and had nearly the strength of his father. Thor's son came running to the place where his father lay surrounded by a group of sad-faced and despairing gods. When Magni saw what the matter was, he seized Hrungnir's enormous foot in both his hands, heaved his broad young shoulders, and in a moment Thor's neck was free of the weight which was crushing it.

Finally, the gods saw that Thor was not dead, only stunned by the blow of the giant's club and by his fall. He stirred, sat up painfully, and looked around him at the group of eager friends. "Who lifted the weight from my neck?" he asked.

"It was I, father," answered Magni modestly. Thor clasped him in his arms and hugged him tight, beaming with pride and gratitude.

"Truly, you are a fine child!" he cried; "Now as a reward for your first great deed you shall have a gift from me. The swift horse of Hrungnir shall be yours—that same Gullfaxi who was the beginning of all this trouble. You shall ride Gullfaxi, as only a giant steed is strong enough to bear the weight of such a young prodigy as you, my Magni."

This did not please Odin, for he thought that a horse so excellent ought to belong to him. He took Thor aside and argued that without him there would have been no duel, no horse to win. Thor answered simply, "True, Father Odin, you began this trouble. But I have fought your battle, destroyed your enemy, and suffered great pain for you. Surely, I have won the horse fairly and may give it to whom I choose. My son, who has saved me, deserves a horse as good as any. Yet, as you have proved, even Gullfaxi is scarce a match for your Sleipnir. You should be content only with the best."

Satisfied, Odin said no more.

Over time, Thor was healed of all his hurts except that which the splinter of stone had made in his forehead. For the stone was imbedded so deep that it could not be taken out, and it caused Thor great pain. Sif, his golden-haired wife, was in despair. At last she thought her of the wise woman, Groa, who had skill in all manner of herbs and magical charms. Sif sent for Groa, who lived all alone because her husband Örvandil had disappeared and no one could find him. Groa came to Thor and, standing beside his bed while he slept, sang strange songs and gently waved her hands over him. Immediately the stone in his forehead began to loosen, and Thor opened his eyes.

"The stone is loosening, the stone is coming out!" he cried. "How can I reward you, gentle woman? What is your name?"

"My name is Groa," answered the woman, sadly, "wife of Örvandil who is lost."

"Now, then, I can reward you, kind Groa!" cried Thor, "for I can bring you news of your husband. I met him in Jotunheim, where I sometimes visit for a bit of good hunting. It was by Elivâgar's icy river that I met Örvandil, and there was no way for him to cross. So I put him in an iron basket and myself bore him over the flood. His feet stuck out through the meshes of the basket, and when we reached the other side one of his toes was frozen stiff. So I broke it off and tossed it up into the sky, where it became a star. There is a new star shining over us at this very moment; from this day it shall be known as Örvandil's Toe. I promise that your husband shall soon return to you, safe and sound, but for the small loss of his toe."

At this wonderful news, Groa was so overcome that she fainted. Unfortunately, that put an end to the charm she was weaving to loosen the stone from Thor's forehead. The stone was not yet wholly free, and from that day on it could never be removed; Thor would always carry the splinter of stone in his forehead.

ABOVE: Gullfaxi the horse, from *The Crimson Fairy Book*, 1903.

THOR GOES FISHING

The sea giant Aegir was the ruler of the ocean, and his home was deep down below the waves, where the water is calm and still. His palace hidden in the coral caves was beautiful; its walls were hung with brightly-colored seaweed, and the floor was made of white, sparkling coral sand.

One day the gods in Asgard held a feast, and Aegir was invited. He could not often leave home to visit Asgard, for he was always very busy with the ocean winds and tides and storms; but calling his daughters, the waves, he asked them to keep the ocean quiet while he was away and to look after the ships at sea.

Then Aegir went over Bifröst, the rainbow bridge, to Asgard, where the feast was so wonderful and lasted so long that he was sad when the time finally came to go home. At last he said goodbye to Odin and the rest of the Aesir. He thanked them all for the joy and hospitality they had given him, saying, "If only I had a kettle that held enough mead for us all to drink, I would invite you to visit me."

Thor, who was always eager to be involved in anything relating to eating and drinking, said, "I know of a kettle a mile wide and a mile deep; I will fetch it for you!"

Aegir was pleased, and set a day for them all to come to his own great feast.

So Thor took his brother, the brave Tyr, who knew how to find the kettle, and together they set out. The two rode in Thor's chariot, drawn by goats, and headed to Jotunheim, the home of the giants.

When they reached the realm of the giants, they soon found the house of Hymir, the giant who owned "Mile-deep," as the giant kettle was called. The gods were happy to find that the giant was not at home, and his wife, who was

MAIN IMAGE: "Thor bei Hymir," by Emil Doepler, from *Walhall, die Götterwelt der Germanen*; **OPPOSITE, BELOW:** "Aegir," Emil Doepler, also from *Walhall, die Götterwelt der Germanen*.

TOP, INSET: Runic Stone, Götland, depicting Odin, Sleipnir (his horse), viking longship and other symbolic carvings. c. 700 AD; **ABOVE:** Tyr, one of the Aesir gods, shown doing battle; **OPPOSITE:** Thor with Hymir, fishing for the Midgard serpent Jörmungandr, using the head of Hymir's best ox as bait. Painting c. 1790.

far more gentle than most of her people, asked them to come in and rest. She cautioned them, however, to be ready to run when they heard her husband coming, and to hide behind a row of kettles which hung from a beam at the back end of the hall. "For," she said, "my husband will be very angry when he finds strangers here, and a single glance from him is fierce enough to kill."

It was not long before they heard the heavy steps of Hymir returning home, and Thor and Tyr were lucky that the giantess had told them to hide: when the giant heard that two of the Aesir gods were in his home, a flash of light shot from his eyes and broke the beam from which the kettles hung. All of the kettles, except Mile-deep, fell to the floor and shattered.

After a while the giant grew quiet, and at last even began to be polite to his guests. He had been unlucky at his fishing that day, so he had to kill three of his oxen for supper. Thor being hungry, as usual, made Hymir quite angry by eating two whole oxen. When they rose from the table, the giant said, "If you keep on eating as much at every meal as you have tonight, Thor, you will have to find your own food."

"Very well," said Thor; "I will go fishing with you in the morning!"

Next morning Thor set forth with the giant, and as they walked over the fields toward the sea, Thor cut off the head of one of the giant's finest oxen, for bait. Hymir was not pleased at this, but Thor said he would need the very best kind of bait, for he was hoping to catch the Midgard serpent itself, the enormous sea monster who lived at the bottom of the ocean, coiled around the world with his tail in his mouth.

When they came to the shore where the boat was ready, each one took an oar, and they rowed out to deep water. Hymir grew tired first, and called to Thor to stop. "We are far enough out!" he cried. "This is my usual fishing place, where I find the best whales. If we go farther the sea will be rougher, and we may run into the Midgard serpent."

As this was just what Thor wanted, he rowed all the harder, and did not stop until they were far out on the ocean; then he baited his hook with the ox's head and threw it overboard. Soon there came a fierce jerk on the line; it grew heavier and heavier, but Thor pulled with all his might. He tugged so hard that he broke through the bottom of the boat, and had to stand on the slippery rocks beneath.

All this time the giant was looking on in wonder, but when he saw the hideous head of the Midgard serpent rising above the waves, he was so frightened that he cut the line; and Thor, dismayed, saw him fall back again under the water. Even Miölnir, the magic hammer, was not fast enough to strike the serpent dead before it retreated into the water. Defeated, the two fishermen had to turn back and wade to the shore, carrying the broken boat and oars with them.

The giant was proud to have bested Thor, and after they reached the house he said to the thunder god: "Since you think you are so strong, let me see you break this goblet; if you succeed, I will give you the mile-wide kettle."

This was just what Thor wanted, so he tightened his belt of strength and threw the goblet with all his might against the wall; but instead of shattering, the goblet broke the wall instead.

He tried again, but did no better. Then the giant's wife whispered to Thor, "Throw it at his head!" And she sang in a low voice from her place at her spinning wheel:

"Hard the pillar, hard the stone, Harder yet the giant's bone! Stones shall break and pillars fall, Hymir's forehead breaks them all!"

Thor threw the goblet one more time, now against the giant's head, and it finally shattered to pieces.

Then Tyr tried to lift the Mile-deep kettle, for he was in a hurry to leave the land of ice and snow; but he could carry it alone, and Thor had to help him before they could get it out of the giant's house.

When Hymir saw the gods he hated carrying off his kettle, he summoned all his giant friends, and they set out to chase the two gods down. But when Thor heard them coming, he turned, raised Miölnir above his head, and hurled it into the horde of giants, turning them all instantly to stone.

WAGNER'S VIKINGS

Der Ring des Niebelungen. Notes on Richard Wagner's *Ring* cycle.

TOP: Richard Wagner, photographed in Paris in 1861; **CENTER:** A 19th century illustration of Wagner's *Götterdämmerung*, Siegfried hiding the ring, with the Rhinemaidens; **ABOVE:** The Norwegian operatic soprano Kirsten Flagstad, in the role of Brünnhilde.

Richard Wagner (1813–1883) was a German Romantic composer who revolutionized opera through his artistic vision of "Gesamtkunstwerk"—"the total work of art." His mammoth 15-hour four-opera cycle *Der Ring des Nibelungen* (*The Ring of the Nibelung*), is more well-known in English as the *Ring* cycle, and it embodies his concept of fusing the musical, poetic, and dramatic arts into a complete auditory and visual experience. He greatly influenced classical music in the 19th century, and his opera *Tristan und Isolde* is considered one of the harbingers of modern 20th century music. The young philosopher Friedrich Nietzsche was, for some time, a Wagner disciple, but the two were estranged after Nietzsche rejected Wagner's perceived pro-Christian and anti-Semitic views.

Wagner felt passionately that the Germanic and Scandinavian folk stories told profound truths about the human condition, and he hungrily incorporated them into his vision. His direct inspiration for the *Ring* cycle was five-fold: the *Prose Edda*, and the *Poetic Edda* (the two 13th century Icelandic epics discussed elsewhere in the book); the *Völsunga* saga, the Germanic heroic legend whose themes and characters overlap with the Old Norse oral tradition; the Old Norse saga of *Þiðrekr (Didrek) of Bern*; and finally, the *Niebelungenlied*, a 13th century epic poem based on the oral tradition of Germanic heroic legend.

Wagner immersed himself in these great sagas of Norse and Germanic mythology and freely took and adapted aspects of all the stories, but fundamental parallels with the Norse myths remain. His characters are split into gods, mortals, valkyries, Rhinemaidens, giants, and Niebelungs: the character *Wotan* is Odin, the one-eyed All-Father, king of the gods; *Fricka* is based on Odin's queen, the goddess Frigga; *Fricka*'s brother is *Donner*, who is modeled on Thor (the German expression "donner und blitzen" translates into English as "thunder and lightning"); *Fricka*'s sister is *Freia*, who is based, of course, on Freyja, the most beautiful of all the gods. And the character *Loge* is Loki, the half-god, half-giant, trickster whose loyalties are forever wavering. A significant aspect of the *Ring* cycle is Wagner's use of the *leitmotif*—whereby a character, emotion or subject is denoted and expressed by his, or her, or its, own passage of

ABOVE: Brünnhilde, foremost of the Valkyries, daughter of Wotan and Erda, bearing a wounded warrior to Valhalla. Illustration for the opera *Die Walküre*, thematically, the second work of the *Ring* cycle; **LEFT:** Lithograph illustration of a set design for *Die Walküre*, from the 1890s; **BELOW:** Wagner's *Ride of the Valkyries* is famously, or notoriously, used in the "Death from above!" helicopter attack scene in Francis Ford Coppola's 1979 Vietnam War movie, *Apocalypse Now*. Robert Duvall's character, Lt-Col. Bill Kilgore, has an enormous sound system strapped to his lead helicopter and the music is relayed to the VC army and civilians on the ground, both to announce their arrival—and as the helicopters decimate the village.

music, or melody, or similar. Wagner called them his "guides-to-feeling."

The *Ring* cycle comprises four discrete parts, or works, and each has been performed separately on many, many occasions, but they are, in thematic order: 1) *Das Rheingold* (*The Rhinegold*) a continuous, two and a half hour-long Prelude; Then, the Trilogy proper: 2) *Die Walküre* (*The Valkyrie*), subtitled *First Day*; 3) *Siegfried*, subtitled *Second Day*; 4) *Götterdämmerung* (*Twilight of the Gods*), subtitled *Third Day*.

The first complete performance of the *Ring* cycle took place in the specially-constructed festival hall at Bayreuth on the 13th to the 17th of August 1876—some 26 years since Wagner began writing it. Anthony Freund, the Stage Director responsible for organizing the operas described the Bayreuth premiere as "the high-water mark of our artform, and the most massive challenge any opera company can undertake."

With regard to our modern conception of the appearance of Viking warriors, there is an significant aside to this event. The Costume Designer was the German painter and illustrator Carl Emil Doepler, and he devised helmets that were adorned with eagle wings and bull horns—something which had never existed in real Viking history, but which is now subsumed into our concept of the appearance of a Viking warrior. The *Ring* cycle, too, is now so utterly entrenched in European culture that even some of the characters' names have become interchangeable with the names of the original gods they were based upon.

LOKI

Loki is a complex figure whose moral alignment and depiction in Norse mythology has had a tendency to shift over the years.

Although he was originally described solely as the god of fire—his full name was often written as Loki the Red, after his fiery red beard and hair—he has since come to be known as the god of mischief, trickery, and chaos. His role in Norse mythology is often as both an antagonist and an ally to the gods of Asgard; he regularly instigates conflict and causes problems through his trickery and selfishness, only to be forced to fix those problems himself once the consequences of his actions come back to bite him. His actions range from petty mischief to outright malevolence, but he is rarely depicted as entirely evil. For the most part, Loki is described as selfish, capricious, and irreverent, but he almost always takes the side of the Asgardians. It isn't until Loki is finally banished from Asgard that he turns his back on the Aesir for good, eventually leading the Jotunn into battle against his former family during the events of Ragnarök.

Loki's status as a perpetual outsider in Asgard is not only due to his behavior. Although Loki is treated as a member of the Aesir, he is not an original member of the clan. Loki's father, Farbauti, is a Jotunn, making Loki at least half frost giant; although his mother's heritage is never directly stated, she is often believed to be either a giant as well or a minor forest deity. Because of this, Loki has much more giant blood in his veins (even if he is not a full-blooded giant) than the average Asgardian. This may explain why he alone among the gods has the ability to shapeshift, an ability that many giants have been shown to possess. Alternatively, Loki's ability to shapeshift and his use of magic may just be a factor of his nature as a trickster god, as many of the other gods have unique abilities that reflect their character and domains.

Although Loki is often at odds with the gods of Asgard due to his unpredictable and often outright antisocial nature, he is frequently shown to be particularly close to the gods Thor and Odin. Loki is Thor's uncle and Odin's adoptive "blood brother"; it is hinted in some of the earlier myths that Thor and Odin once performed a ritual to mix their blood and bind themselves to each other for life. This may be why Odin tolerates Loki's behavior for so long, despite the many crimes he commits. Despite his behavior towards Thor on some occasions, Loki has also been shown to be a readily helpful ally to the god of thunder, often accompanying him on quests and aiding him in battle. Similarly, although Thor is often quick to assume that Loki is at fault whenever something goes wrong—which is often accurate—Loki is also the first person he turns to when he needs to solve a problem. For instance, when Thor's hammer goes missing, Loki is the first and only person he tells. Loki is also depicted as the god of lightning in some sources, making him a counterpart to Thor's thunder.

Although Loki was not explicitly evil, many later interpretations of myths featuring Loki tend to depict him in much more black and white terms. It is likely that Christian influence is to blame for this, as many Christians who were introduced to Norse mythology related Loki to Satan, making him a similarly archetypal antagonistic figure. In truth, Loki is closer to true neutral than purely good or evil; he is driven by his own impulsive desires, regardless of the consequences.

ABOVE: "Iduna Giving Loki the Apple," From Asgard Stories: *Tales from Norse Mythology*, Mary H. Foster, 1901. Silver, Burdett and Company; **OPPOSITE:** *The Punishment of Loki*, 1912, by the English painter James Doyle Penrose (1862–1932); **BELOW:** Loki theTrickster. By the English artist and illustrator Arthur Rackham, c. 1900s.

LOKI'S CHILDREN

Loki, the most wicked of the Aesir, had done something that even he was deeply ashamed of.

TOP: "Lokis Gezücht" ("Loki's Breed/ Brood"), Emil Doepler, from *Walhall, die Götterwelt der Germanen*; **ABOVE:** Loki's Children, c. early 20th century.

He had married Angrboda, the ugliest, fiercest, most dreadful giantess that ever lived; of course, he didn't want anyone to know what he had done, because he knew Father Odin would be furious with him for marrying one of the Aesir's enemies, and none of his brothers would be grateful to him for giving them such a hideous sister-in-law.

But, at long last, All-Father discovered Loki's long-hidden secret. Worse, he discovered that Loki and the giantess had three ugly children hidden away in the dark recesses of the earth, three children Loki was even more embarrassed of than of their mother, despite the fact that he loved them as well in his way. Hela, his daughter, was the least hideous of the three, yet she was far from lovely. Half of her body was black and the other half white, which gave her a strange, unearthly appearance; she was easily recognizable from afar. She was fearsome and grim to behold, and the mere sight of her terrified and sometimes even struck dead those who stared at her.

The other two of Loki's brood were the most dreadful beasts the world had ever seen. One was a gigantic wolf with long, sharp teeth and piercing red eyes. And the other was a scaly, slimy, hideous serpent, bigger than any ever seen and a hundred times more vicious. It should have been impossible for Loki to find anything to like about them at all, but Loki's heart secretly loved evil, and it was the wickedness in his three children that made them so ugly.

When Odin realized that three such monsters had been living in the world without his knowledge, he was both angry and worried, for he knew that these children of the wicked Loki and his monstrous giantess-wife were a threat to Asgard's safety. He went to the Norns, the three wise maidens who resided beside the Urdar-well and could see into the future to predict what would happen in the coming years, and they warned him to be wary of Loki's children. The Norns said that the three monsters would bring tremendous misery to

ABOVE: Loki's Children, c. 19th century pen drawing; **BELOW:** Statue of the three Norns in Düsseldorf, Nordrhein-Westfalen, Germany.

Asgard, for the giantess their mother would teach them all her hatred of Odin's kind, while they would have their father's crafty wisdom to aid them in all kinds of mischief. So Odin understood that his fears were not misplaced; something had to be done to keep the threats to Asgard at bay.

Father Odin summoned all the gods and commanded them to go forth into the world, seek out Loki's offspring in the secret places where they were hidden, and bring them to him. The Aesir then mounted their horses and went off on their mission. They searched Asgard, Midgard, and Jotunheim, the home of the giants. Finally, they discovered the three dreadful monsters hiding in their mother's cave. They dragged them out of the cave and carried them up to Asgard, where they were presented to Odin as he sat on his throne.

The All-Father had been debating what to do with the three creatures, and when they arrived, he had made up his mind. Hela, the daughter, was less terrible than the other two, but her face was dark and dismal, and her stare killed anybody who gazed at her. She had to be imprisoned somewhere out of sight, where her sad eyes couldn't bring misery to men's lives and death to their souls. So he cast her down into the dark, frozen realm of Niflheim, which lay beneath one of the great tree Yggdrasil's roots. There she would stay forever, but because she wasn't entirely wicked, Odin made her queen of that land, and she was to have all the folk who died on Earth as her subjects, except the heroes who died in battle, whom the Valkyries transported straight to Valhalla in Asgard. All who died of sickness or old age, all who died as a result of accident or murder, were sent to Queen Hela, who housed them in her dreary palace. Her realm was vast, as large as all the nine realms combined, and it was enclosed by a high wall, so that no one who had gone there could ever return. And Loki's daughter reigned among the shadows from then on, herself half dark and half light, half good and half bad.

Jörmungandr, the serpent, on the other hand, was a more terrible beast than Death herself. Odin frowned as he saw the monstrosity writhing before his throne. He snatched the scaly length in his powerful arms and threw it over Asgard's wall; down went the enormous serpent, twisting and spinning as he plummeted, turning the sky dark with smoke from his nostrils and shaking the world at the sound of his hissing. He plummeted with a tremendous splash into the vast ocean that encompassed the earth. He lay there writhing and twitching, getting larger and larger until he was so massive that he extended like a ring around the entire earth, biting the end of his tail in his mouth, his cruel eyes looking up through the sea at Asgard and the gods he despised. Sometimes he pushed himself up, great body and all, in an attempt to flee the ocean that had become his prison. This caused tremendous waves in the sea and snow, harsh winds, and rain on the earth, and everyone was terrified that Jörmungandr would escape and destroy the world, although he never quite managed to break free.

The third and most terrifying of the three monsters was the wolf, Fenrir. He was so dreadful that Father Odin decided not to let him out of his sight at first, and he was permitted to live in Asgard, among the Aesir. Day by day, he grew bigger and bigger, fiercer and fiercer, until all of the Aesir lived in fear of the wolf roaming their halls and only Tyr the Brave had the fortitude to feed him. When All-Father saw how massive he had become, and how he was now strong enough to bring ruin upon all Asgard if he were free to roam and rage as he pleased, even he grew afraid of the monstrous wolf; something, he decided, must be done. (See The Binding of Fenrir, page 188)

SIF'S GOLDEN HAIR

Sif was the thunder-god Thor's wife, and she was very proud of her lovely golden hair, which she meticulously combed and braided each day.

When she awoke one morning, however, she was filled with grief and dismay to discover that her beautiful hair had been cut off in the middle of the night while she slept. Her husband was away that day, but when he returned home late at night, Sif was careful to avoid his gaze as she was ashamed of her now shaved head.

Thor, however, eventually called Sif to his side, and quickly became enraged when he saw what had been done to her. Thor had a fiery temper, and everyone feared his outbursts of rage. "Who could have committed such a heinous crime?" he wondered. "Only one of the Aesir would even consider doing such a thing!"

Thor wasted no time in apprehending Loki, who was quickly forced to admit that he was indeed the guilty party, but he begged Thor to give him just a few days, and he promised to

MAIN IMAGE: *Sif was Queen of the Fields*; **BELOW:** Loki and Sif. Near a wood, the goddess Sif rests her head on a stump while the half-deity Loki lurks behind, blade in hand. Loki holds the blade to cut Sif's hair, from the myth recounted in the *Prose Edda* book *Skáldskaparmál*. From *Legends of Norseland*, Mara Louise Pratt-Chadwick. Educational Publication Company.

find a gift for Sif that would make her look more beautiful than ever. So Thor decided to give him a chance and instructed him to return Sif's golden hair to her.

Now Loki knew a place where some unmatched craftspeople lived, so he flew as fast as he could to Svartalfheim, the home of the dwarfs beneath the earth, and asked one of them to make some golden hair for Sif as soon as possible. In addition, he requested two gifts to be delivered to the gods Odin and Frey in order to sway them to support him if Thor brought his charges before the Aesir.

Loki didn't have to wait long for the dwarf to bring him a large amount of beautiful hair spun from the finest golden thread. When it came into contact with anyone's head, it had the amazing ability to grow just like real hair. Next was a spear forged for Odin, enchanted so that it never missed its target no matter how far it was thrown, and a ship for Frey that could sail through the air as well as the sea. Although the ship was large enough to hold all of the gods and their horses, it could be folded to fit in a pocket.

Loki was overjoyed with the gifts and declared that this dwarf must be the most skilled craftsman of them all. Another dwarf, Brock, overheard him say this and told Loki that he and his brother could create even more wonderful things than these. Loki didn't think it was possible, but he told Brock to try his skill; the Aesir would judge them, and the one who failed the trial would lose his head. Brock then summoned his brother, Sindri, and they immediately got to work. Sindri started a large fire and threw a lump of gold into it; then he told Brock to blow the bellows while he went out, and not to stop until he returned.

Brock thought this would be a simple task, but his brother hadn't been gone long before a huge fly began buzzing around his face, bothering him so much that he couldn't keep on blowing; still, he finished his work, and when Sindri returned, they took out of the fire an enormous wild boar, which glowed with light and could travel through the air with incredible speed.

Sindri threw another piece of gold into the fire on the second day, once again leaving his brother to blow the bellows. The buzzing, stinging fly returned, and this time it was even more bothersome than before; but Brock tried hard to be patient, and was able to tolerate it without stopping his work until Sindri returned. Then they took a magical gold ring from the fire, from which eight new rings fell each week.

On the third day, a lump of iron was thrown into the fire, and Sindri left Brock alone once more. The cruel fly swooped in again; by now, Brock was certain that the fly was actually Loki in another form, trying to cheat. The fly bit the poor little dwarf so hard on the forehead that blood ran down into his eyes, blinding him so he couldn't do his job.

Brock had to come to a halt just before Sindri arrived home, but not before the hammer they were working on in the fire was nearly finished, albeit with a rather short handle. The hammer was given the name Mjölnir. It had the ability to hit its target every time when thrown, and would always return to the hand that threw it.

When Loki finally appeared before the assembled Aesir with the two dwarf brothers and their gifts, it was declared that they had made the finest things, as the hammer—which was given to Thor—would undoubtedly be very useful in keeping the giants of Jotunheim out of Asgard.

When Loki discovered that the verdict was against him, he attempted to flee, but Thor quickly forced him to stay still by threatening to throw his new hammer at him.

Panicking, Loki searched for some way to avoid losing his head. He was silent for a long time, thinking over the terms of the bargain. At last, he told Brock and Sindri that they could have his head, according to the agreement. However, the bargain had made no mention of any harm coming to Loki's neck, and so the dwarfs were forced to spare him.

TOP: Loki, the god of wickedness, cuts off the hair of Sif, Thor's wife. To help make good this wicked deed, Dwalin the dwarf brings Loki a large amount of hair—spun from the finest golden thread; **ABOVE:** The gold hair that Loki presents to the Aesir.

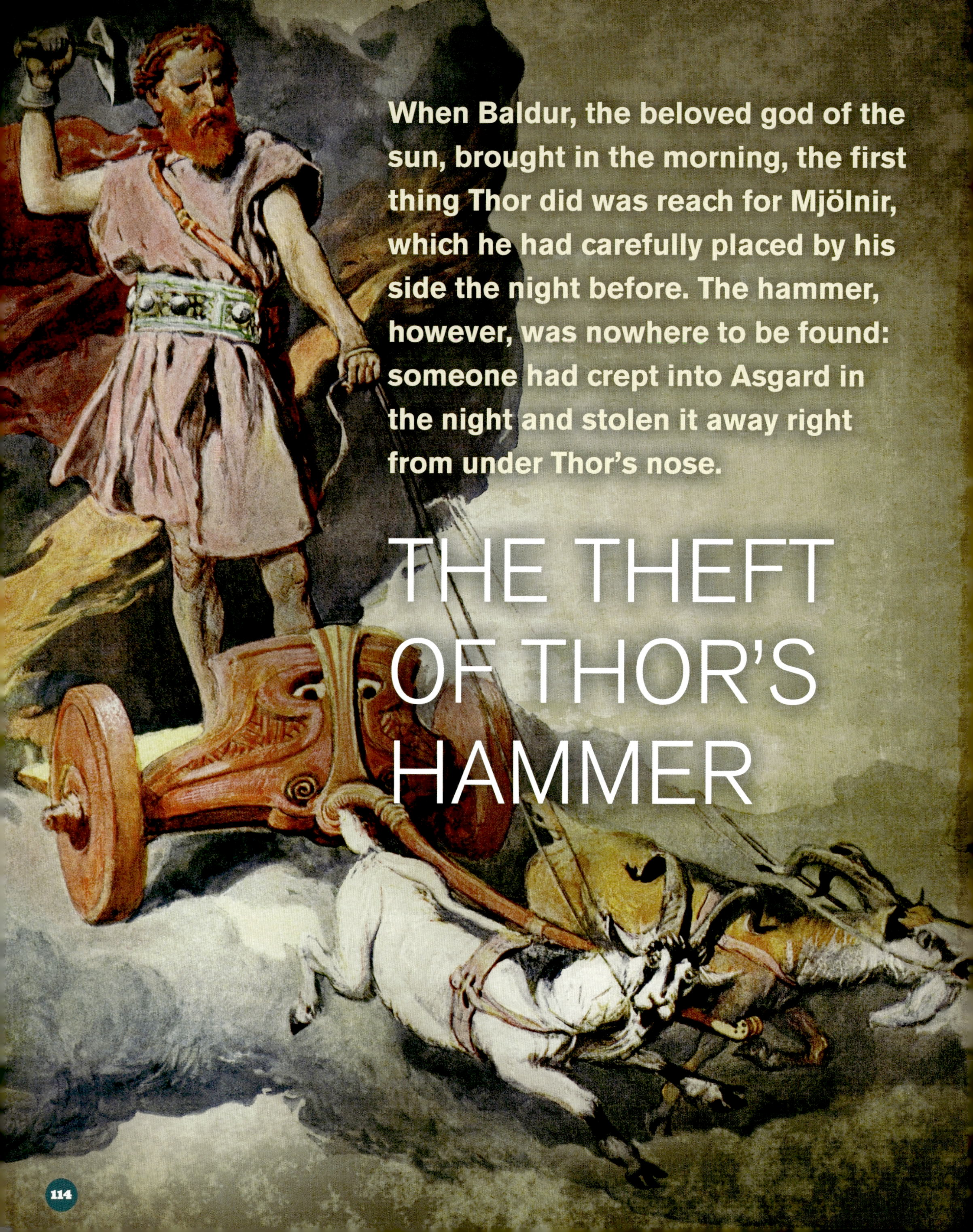

When Baldur, the beloved god of the sun, brought in the morning, the first thing Thor did was reach for Mjölnir, which he had carefully placed by his side the night before. The hammer, however, was nowhere to be found: someone had crept into Asgard in the night and stolen it away right from under Thor's nose.

THE THEFT OF THOR'S HAMMER

"My hammer! My hammer!" thundered Thor, his rage carrying the shout far enough that all the gods of Asgard awoke with a start. Thor went first to Loki, the god of mischief, only to find that—for once—Loki was innocent.

"If not you, Loki," he said, "Then those evil frost giants must have taken it from me while I slept. How will we defend Asgard without my hammer? They will surely destroy our beautiful home!"

"We must go quickly and find it!" exclaimed Loki. "Let us ask Freyja to lend us her falcon cloak."

Freyja, the goddess of love, war, and gold, had a wonderful garment made of falcon feathers, and whoever wore it could transform into the shape of a bird at will. So Thor and Loki raced to Freyja's palace, where they found her sitting among her maidens. "Asgard is in great danger!" exclaimed Thor, "and we have come to you, fair goddess, to ask if you will lend us your falcon cloak, for my hammer has been stolen, and we must go in search of it."

"Certainly," Freyja replied, "I would lend you my falcon cloak, even if it were made of gold and silver!"

Then Loki—lighter and more nimble than Thor—quickly dressed himself in Freyja's robe and flew away to the land of the frost giants. There, Loki found Thrym, the king of the giants, making gold collars for his dogs and combing his horses. As Loki approached, Thrym looked up and said, "Ah, Loki, how fare the mighty gods in Asgard?"

"The Aesir are in great peril," Loki replied, "and I have been dispatched to retrieve Thor's hammer."

"And do you think I'm going to be foolish enough to give it back to you after all the trouble I've gone to get it into my power?" asked the king. "I've buried it deep, deep, deep in the earth, and there's only one way to get it back." You must bring the goddess Freyja to be my wife!"

Loki was at a loss for words, because he knew Freyja would never agree to leave Asgard to live among the fierce giants; but, seeing no chance of obtaining the hammer, he flew back to Asgard to see what could be done.

OPPOSITE: Thor, swinging Mjölnir, his hammer, and being pulled in his chariot by his two goats. Emil Doepler, from *Walhall, die Götterwelt der Germanen*; **ABOVE:** Thrym, the king of the Frost-Giants; **LEFT**: Loki in flight by Lorenz Frølich, 1898. From *Den ældre Eddas Gudesange* by Karl Gjellerup.

RIGHT: Freyja shows Thor and Loki her feather cloak. Lorenz Frølich, 1898. From *Den ældre Eddas Gudesange* by Karl Gjellerup; **BELOW:** Freyja disguises Thor in her clothes; **OPPOSITE:** "Thor bei dem riesen Thrym als braut verkleide," Thor is dressed in disguise as a bride for the giant Thrym, in order to retrieve Mjölnir from him. Emil Doepler, from *Walhall, die Götterwelt der Germanen*.

Thor was on the lookout for him. "What news do you bring, Loki?" he cried. "Have you brought me my hammer yet?"

"Alas, no!" Loki exclaimed. "I bring only a message from the giant king. He will not relinquish your hammer until you persuade Freyja to marry him!"

Then Thor and Loki went together to Freyja's palace, and the fair goddess greeted them kindly, but when she heard their news and discovered they wished her to marry the cruel giant, she became very angry, and said to Thor, "You should not have been so careless as to lose your hammer; it is all your fault that it is gone, and I will never marry a giant to help you get it back."

Thor then went to tell Odin, who convened a meeting of all the Aesir to discuss the matter. If the king of the giants only knew the power of the mighty hammer, he could storm Asgard and take the fair Freyja as his bride. So the Aesir gathered in their great judgment hall, Gladsheim, and talked long and anxiously about their peril, trying to devise some plan to save Asgard from their enemies. Finally, Heimdall, the stalwart guardian of the rainbow bridge, proposed a solution.

"Let us dress Thor in Freyja's robes, braid his hair, and let him wear Freyja's wonderful necklace and a bridal veil!" he said.

"No!" cried Thor angrily, "you would all laugh at me in a woman's dress; I will not do such a thing!"

"We must find another way." But, when no other solution could be found, Thor was eventually persuaded to try Heimdall's plan, and the Aesir set to work dressing the mighty thunder-god like a bride. He was the tallest of them all, and, of course, he looked very strange to them in his woman's clothes, but he'd be small enough next to a giant. Then they disguised Loki—who was so delighted at Thor's predicament that he demanded to go along with him and watch—as the bride's waiting maid, and the two set off for Utgard, the giants' stronghold.

When the giant king saw them approaching, he ordered his servants to prepare the wedding feast and invited all of his giant subjects to come and celebrate his marriage to the lovely goddess Freyja.

So the wedding party sat down to the feast, and Thor, who was always a good eater, ate one ox and eight salmon and drank three casks of mead. The king stood there, surprised to see a woman eat so much, and exclaimed, "Where hast thou seen such a hungry bride?"

But Loki, the bride's waiting-maid, who stood nearby, whispered in the king's ear, "Eight nights has Freyja fasted and refused to take food, so anxious was she to be your bride!"

This pleased the giant, and he approached Thor, saying he had to kiss his fair bride. When he lifted the bridal veil, a gleam of light shot from Thor's eyes, and the king froze, wondering why Freyja's eyes were so sharp.

"For eight nights the fair Freyja has not slept, so greatly did she long to arrive here!" Loki replied again, only barely hiding his laughter. This pleased the king once more, and he said, "Now let the hammer be brought and given to the bride, for the hour has come for our marriage!"

Thor had been so eager to get his treasure back that he couldn't sit still, and if it hadn't been for what the cunning Loki said, he might have been discovered too soon. But, eventually, the precious hammer was brought and handed to the bride, as was customary at weddings; as soon as Thor grasped it in his hand, he threw off his woman's robes and stood out in front of the astonished giants.

He swung the hammer once, and before the eye could follow its movement, it had crashed through Thrym's skull and knocked over a dozen of his guests. It swung in his hand yet again, and this time it left no giant standing in the hall. A third time it was swung, and this time the roof and walls of the palace collapsed on all sides, leaving only Thor and Loki alive among the ruins.

"Ha!" laughed Loki, "that was nicely done, fair Freya."

Thor, who was now busy ripping off the clinging robes and veil, turned to stare threateningly at his companion. "No more of that, Loki," he said, "the thing had to be done, 'tis true, but don't speak to me of this woman's work again. We will only remember that I am the Thunderer, and that my misplaced hammer has been found."

Then, with Loki still laughing to himself, they flew peacefully home to Asgard.

ABOVE: Statue of Aegir, the sea god in Kungstradgarden, Stockholm, Sweden. Fountain by J.P. Molin, opened in 1866; **TOP:** "Loki bei Aegirs gastmahl" Loki, insulting the gods at Aegir's banquet. Emil Doepler, from *Walhall, die Götterwelt der Germanen*.

LOKI'S FLYTING

The gods had never forgiven Loki for killing Baldur, and they yearned to drive him out of their beautiful city, which had never harbored anything evil before Loki. But Loki was Odin's brother, and they dared not punish him until the All-Wise One gave his approval.

(SEE: BALDUR'S DEATH, PAGE 130)
Odin, like them, knew that the murderer of Baldur was unfit to live among the gods, but he waited for Loki to commit one more cruel act before driving the offender out of Asgard. This moment arrived sooner than Odin had anticipated.

One day, all the gods were invited to a feast in the halls of Aegir, the sea-king, and a plentiful supply of ale was brewed in the great mile-wide kettle brought from Hymer's castle by Thor. Thor was not present at the feast because he was on a long journey, but Loki was, looking sullen and angry. No one spoke to him, and he sat silent and alone, trying to appear unconcerned about the hostile stares directed at him.

The sea-god's palace was stunning, with walls and ceiling made of mother-of-pearl so delicately laid that light filtered softly through them. The finest golden sand was strewn across the floor, and all the food was served in opal-tinted seashells. The only thing that detracted from the scene's beauty was Loki's sullen, wicked face.

The gods almost forgot about Loki's presence as the meal progressed and they grew merry over their cups; but Loki brooded in angry silence, waiting for some opportunity to wreak his ill-will on the entire company.

"Your servants have been well instructed," one of the gods said to Aegir as he stopped beside him to refill his horn with the foaming ale. "They treat Loki with the utmost respect, as if he were a distinguished guest."

When Loki heard these words, he flew into a rage and, seizing a knife from the table, he killed the innocent servant.

The gods sat speechless in the face of such heinous cruelty; but Odin rose, looming dark and terrible in his wrath, and with a resolute voice he banished Loki to exile. "Never tread our sacred halls again, nor pollute Asgard's pure air with your presence," he commanded. Odin looked so dreadful that Loki skulked out of the hall without a word, and the gods resumed their feasting. Soon after, a loud noise was heard outside the hall, and all the servants ran in, terrified. Behind them came Loki, who boldly approached the table and dared Odin to send him out before he said the words he had returned to say.

Then he began to speak to each of the gods in turn, telling them of all the foolish, mean, or wicked things they had ever done, mocking their mistakes and exposing all their flaws in such a dishonest way that each minor offense appeared to be an act of monstrous wickedness. Not content with attempting to humiliate Asgard's heroes, Loki began to speak disparagingly of the goddesses, attributing to them all the heinous things that his malicious imagination could conjure up. He was just beginning to say something particularly vile about Sif when he heard the rumble of chariot wheels outside, and Thor rushed into the hall brandishing his hammer. He had heard Loki's final words about his wife and charged straight at the slanderer, intending to crush him with a single blow of Mjölnir. Loki, however, quickly transformed himself into a sea-serpent and slid out of the room before Thor's vengeful hammer could strike him down. Loki was well aware, now, that he had finally lost all hope of forgiveness.

ABOVE: The Daughters of Aegir and Rán; **BELOW:** "Loki began to speak disparagingly of the goddesses...He was just beginning to say something particularly vile about Sif when he heard the rumble of chariot wheels outside, and Thor rushed into the hall brandishing his hammer..."

LOKI'S PUNISHMENT

When the mighty Thor drove Loki out of Aegir's palace-hall, Loki knew he would never be allowed back among the gods in Asgard.

This mischievous fire god had brought the Aesir much trouble and sorrow in the past, but now he had done the cruelest deed of all: he had slain Baldur the Good and driven all light and joy from Asgard.

Far away into the mountains he fled, hoping no one would find him; he eventually stopped to rest near a lovely mountain stream, and there he built for himself a hut with four doors looking north, east, south, and west. This way if Odin, watching from his high throne in Asgard, should see him and send messengers to punish him, Loki could see them coming and escape through the opposite door.

He spent most of his days and nights trying to figure out how to get away from the Aesir. "I wonder if they could catch me if I ran to the stream and turned myself into a fish," he thought. "I could avoid a hook, but there are nets; Aegir's wife has a wonderful thing like a net for catching fish, and that would be far worse than a hook!"

When Loki thought about the net, he wondered how it was made, and the more he thought about it, the more he wished he could make one to see how a fish could avoid getting caught in it. He sat by the fire in his small hut, took a piece of cord, and began to weave a fish net. He was almost finished when he noticed three Aesir approaching his hut from the distance through the open door. Loki was well aware that they were on their way to capture him, so—throwing his net into the fire—he dashed to the stream, transformed himself into a beautiful spotted salmon, and leapt into the water.

The three gods entered the hut a moment later, and one of them noticed the fish-net burning in the fire. "Look!" he exclaimed, "Loki must have made this net to catch fish; he's always been a good fisherman, and now this is exactly what we need to catch him!"

OPPOSITE: *The Punishment of Loki*, by Louis Huard; **ABOVE:** Loki with fishing net, from the 17th century print edition of the *Prose Edda*; **LEFT:** Loki (center), with his offspring: Hela, Fenrir, and Jörmungandr.

TOP: *The Punishment of Loki.* The statue of Loki with snakes, in the gardens of Stockholm City Hall, Sweden; **ABOVE:** Eruption of Strokkur, the most famous geyser in Iceland; **RIGHT:** Loki shapeshifts to a salmon; **OPPOSITE:** Loki, chained to a cliff, is helped to survive by his wife, Sigyn.

So they snatched the last bit of the net from the fire and learned how to make another by looking at it, which they took with them to the stream's bank.

The first time the net was dropped into the water, Loki hid between two rocks, and the net was so light that it floated past him; however, the next time it had a heavy stone weight, which caused it to sink, until Loki realized he couldn't get away unless he leapt over the net. When Thor saw him, he waded out into the stream and threw the net again, forcing Loki to jump a second time or else go on out into the deep sea.

Thor stooped and caught him in his hand as he leaped, but the fish was so slippery that Thor could hardly hold it. The salmon's tail was pinched so tightly by the thunder-strong god's fingers during the struggle that it was drawn out to a point, and the old stories say that is why salmon tails have always been pointed.

Loki was thus caught in his own trap, and his punishment was dreadful. The Aesir chained him to a high rock and hung a large, poisonous serpent from the cliff above his head.

Loki would have quickly died from the poison that fell from the snake's mouth if it hadn't been for Sigyn, his loving and faithful wife. She knelt next to her husband, raising a cup above him to catch the dripping poison. Only when she had to turn aside to empty the cup did the drops fall upon Loki, causing him such terrible pain that he shook the earth with his struggles, and the people of Midgard fled from the terrible earthquakes. When he screamed, great geysers of hot water burst through the earth in Iceland, and burning ashes and lava poured down the mountainsides in the south.

The cruel, mischievous Loki was to lie there, chained to the cliff, until the Twilight of the Gods; on the dark day of Ragnarök, when all the evil things of the nine realms would be freed, Loki would lead his monstrous family in a final terrible battle against the gods of Asgard.

Pictures of the viking culture have continually evolved down the centuries, and say much about the artists and their times.

SHAPESHIFTERS

William Blake's illustrations for Thomas Gray's 1761 work *The Descent of Odin*, painted c. 1792; **TOP:** "Him the Dog of Darkness Spied"; **ABOVE:** "The Serpent and the Wolvish Dog. Two Terrors in the Northern Mythology."

WILLIAM BLAKE (1757–1827)

English Painter and Poet

A visionary outsider, the Londoner William Blake was a committed Christian who despised organized religion, and many of his Soho neighbours considered him, at the very least, eccentric. He had studied at the Royal Academy, but thought his tutor, Sir Joshua Reynolds, was an artist with suspect taste, and a hypocrite. Blake had a deep psychic reaction to the early industrializing that had begun in England—the increasing mechanization, its new methods of commerce—with its factories and its rapidly-expanding urban population. For Blake, this alien new world was immoral and deeply unethical. It was against nature. As such, he is one of the harbingers of the coming Romantic Age in European art. The Old Norse deities and culture was a good fit for Blake, and several of the Romantics. He was one of the earliest English artists to portray the Norse universe, when he took a commission to illustrate *The Descent of Odin*, Thomas Gray's poetry edition of the Northmen. Blake's extensive poetry embodied his attitude of rebellion against the abuse of class power. He sold very little of either his paintings or his poetry during his lifetime, though today he is considered a giant—and still stubbornly difficult to classify. He is buried in the dissenters' graveyard at Bunhill Fields on the City Road, London.

CARL EMIL DOEPLER (1824–1905)

German Painter

In 1876, after twenty-six long years in gestation, Wagner's great 15 hour-long opera project, the *Ring* cycle, was realized at Bayreuth in southern Germany. It literally brought the concept of the Norse sagas to front center stage of European art. As we have seen (pages 106–107) Wagner chose the painter Carl Emil Doepler as his Head of Costume, and his ideas for the visual appearance of the characters have changed our modern conception of the vikings—his use of eagle wings adorning the helmets of the Valkyries was a 'gamechanger.'

EMIL DOEPLER (1855–1922)

German Painter and Illustrator

The son of Carl Emil Doepler (above). Doepler the Younger was taught as a child by his father, and went on to study at the Arts and Crafts Museum in Berlin. After his studies, he became a freelance illustrator and teacher at the Museum, later becoming Professor. He designed the coat of arms of the German publishing industry (motto: "Books Have Their Destiny"), and later, the coat of arms of Weimar Germany (the new constitution formed after the collapse of the German Empire in 1918, at the end of World War One). Doepler was a significant re-imaginer of the Norse deities, and illustrated *Walhall, die Götterwelt der Germanen* (*Valhalla, The World of the German Gods*), a popular book of 1905 by Martin Oldenbourg. Many of the illustrations in *Walhall* enrich this book you are reading now. Pictures of the entire panoply of the Norse universe became part and parcel of the culture in Germany, to such an extent that Doepler was commissioned to design a memorable set of trading cards on Norse cosmogony, that were issued by the Stollwercks Chocolade company.

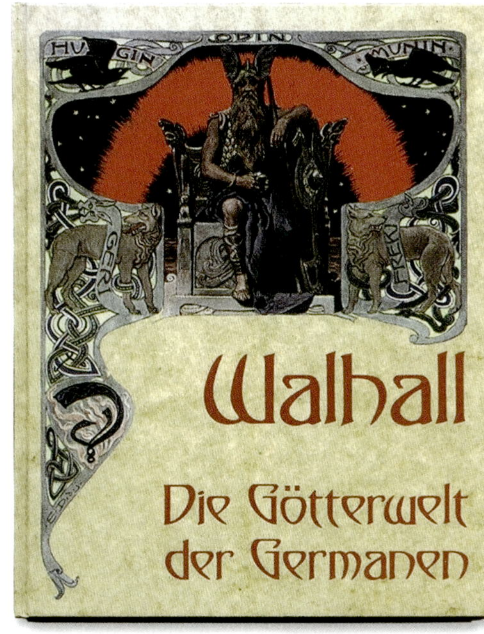

JOHN BAUER (1882–1918)

Swedish Painter and Illustrator

Bauer studied at the Royal Swedish Academy of Arts. He then traveled through Germany and Lapland—in the Arctic Circle in the north of Sweden. His work was deeply influenced by the spectacular landscapes of northern Europe and his primary inspiration was landscape, and the mythology of the North. He came to prominence in Sweden after illustrating the popular publication *Bland tomtar och troll* (*Among Gnomes and Trolls*). His paintings, using a muted palette, broadened the context in Sweden of early Northern folklore. Tragically, he and his wife and child were drowned in 1918, during their trip on the ill-fated Steamship Per Brahe, which sank on Lake Vättern, southern Sweden.

TOP, LEFT: John Bauer photographed in his studio, c. 1908; **TOP, RIGHT:** *Walhall, die Götterwelt der Germanen* (*Valhalla, the World of the German Gods*), 1905, by Martin Oldenbourg, with illustrations by Emil Doepler; **ABOVE:** *Freja* (*Freyja*), oil sketch on canvas, 1905, by John Bauer.

Baldur, the god of light and love, is the son of Odin and Frigga, husband of Nanna, and father of Forsetti. He is described as one of the most beautiful of the gods, with skin and hair so fair that he literally glows—hence his reputation as a god of light.

BALDUR

Beyond his physical beauty, Baldur is also the kindest, most gracious, and most good-natured of the gods; he is beloved by all, and he brings happiness and joy to everyone around him. His home is Breidablik, a towering palace with a polished silver roof supported by golden pillars; the palace is so pure and clean that nothing unclean can ever pass through the door.

Baldur has some knowledge of rune magic, although he is likely not as adept as Odin. His tongue is adorned with several runes, and his glowing eyes grant him sight that few other gods possess. On occasion, Baldur is even able to see into the future, although his visions are unclear. Whatever future he sees, it is not enough to warn him of his fate at the hands of his brother, Hodur, who is manipulated by Loki into killing him.

Despite his kind and benevolent nature, Baldur is central in the events that lead to Ragnarök. This is through no fault of his own, of course, but instead occurs as a result of his death; Baldur's light and positivity represent the hope, joy, and warmth that can be found in the world, and his death means that all of those things are stripped away. Without Baldur's light, the rest of the gods fall into hopeless grief: their powers weaken, their morale falls, and the world itself becomes a darker, colder place. This is the first stage of the beginning of Ragnarök, as the giants of Jotunheim are able to take advantage of the gods' weakness and the world's descent into darkness to stage their uprising.

After Ragnarök, when the dust has settled and all the fighting is done, Baldur and his brother will finally emerge from the darkness of Hel and return to the world of the living; Baldur is instrumental in the rebuilding of the world and the protection of the last remnants of the human race.

Baldur and his brother are often interpreted as two sides of the same coin; the shining, beloved Baldur, god of light, and the sullen, blind outsider Hodur, god of darkness. Baldur's death at the hands of Hodur and Loki foreshadows the eventual chaos of Ragnarök, when the world will be plunged into darkness just as Asgard was after Baldur's death. Another interpretation casts Baldur and Hodur as summer and winter; here, their conflict represents a season of light and warmth giving way to one of cold and darkness.

ABOVE: Hodur, Baldur's blind brother, and the god of darkness, is tricked by Loki (left) into shooting an arrow of mistletoe at Baldur. Sculpture by the Swedish artist Carl Gustav Qvarnstrom (1810–1867); **OPPOSITE:** *Balder the Good*, by Jacques Reich; **BELOW:** Baldur dies after Hodur shoots him with mistletoe. Emil Doepler, from *Walhall, die Götterwelt der Germanen*.

LEFT: Baldur, as depicted by Emil Doepler, from *Walhall, die Götterwelt der Germanen*; **OPPOSITE, TOP:** Baldur tells his mother, Frigga, of his dark and terrifying dreams. British newspaper illustration, mid-20th century; **OPPOSITE, CENTER:** *Odin, disguised as a traveler*, photograph by Emilie Kip Baker, from *Stories from Northern Myths*, 1914, New York: The Macmillan Company; **OPPOSITE, BELOW:** Odin and his horse Sleipnir meet with an unnamed *völva* in Hel, as described in *Baldrs draumar*. Sleipnir and the Helhound Garm stare at one another. Published in *Den ældre Eddas Gudesange*, by Karl Gjellerup, 1895.

BALDUR'S DREAMS

Baldur, the most beloved of all the Aesir, was only ever seen to be smiling and happy. He was always in good spirits, and nothing ever seemed to trouble him; so, when the other gods saw that a cloud had fallen over his face, it became cause for great concern.

It was getting worse, day by day: the gleaming light in his blue eyes started to go out, and he looked more and more tired and walked with slower, heavier steps.

Odin and Frigga, who saw their son's obvious misery, begged him to tell them what was making him so sad. He resisted at first, but eventually relented and agreed to tell them what was wrong. Baldur explained that he had never suffered from nightmares before, but now he was assailed by dark, terrifying dreams every single night. Every morning he woke with a feeling of overwhelming terror and doom, but he could never remember a single moment of the dream itself.

Odin and Frigga were concerned when they learned of this, but they vowed that nothing in the world would be permitted—or willing—to harm their universally adored son. When the worried parents discussed the situation further, they admitted that they, too, were plagued by a similar sense of dread, and they eventually came to believe that Baldur's life was in danger. So, rather than wait anxiously for the worst, Baldur's parents set out to do whatever they could to protect him.

First, Odin mounted his eight-legged horse and rode off at once, making the long journey down to the underworld. A grand feast was already set, and the floor was scattered with gold and jewels, but Odin knew that the extravagant welcome was not prepared in his honor. Odin, disguised as a traveler by the name of Vegtam the Wanderer, Odin dragged up the spirit of a long-dead seeress and demanded that she read Baldur's future. The seer, relenting, prophesized that Baldur would certainly die soon and be welcomed to Hel with open arms. Miserable, Odin returned to Asgard and told his wife what he had learned.

Frigga, desperate for any chance of saving her son, demanded that every last thing in creation, living or not, swear an oath to never harm Baldur. Frigga dispatched her servants in all directions, commanding them to travel the world and dispense her orders, and they set out at once with grim determination. The task proved to be easier than expected; there was not a single creature, object, or plant that did not love Baldur, and every single thing quickly swore to never cause him harm. So the servants returned to Frigga, telling her that every last thing had sworn the oath—except for a small mistletoe plant that grew at the base of a large tree outside the gates of Valhalla, which was certainly too small and too harmless to bother worrying about. Frigga, Odin, and the rest of the Aesir rejoiced, confident that the god they loved most would be protected from all harm.

When the gods realized that no weapon could harm Baldur, it wasn't long before they invented a game around his new invulnerability.

BALDUR'S DEATH

The gods lined up and threw all manner of stones and spears at the god of light, knowing that no matter how precisely they hit their mark, the objects would simply glance aside or fall harmlessly to the ground. Baldur was happy to stand around as the gods entertained each other, laughing when he remained uninjured after each volley. Once again Baldur was a beacon of light and happiness in Asgard, all worries forgotten.

However, there was still one god who held no love for Baldur. Loki, jealous of all the attention and praise Baldur was getting, stood back and watched the game play out in sullen silence. He refused to join in, but he couldn't bring himself to simply walk away. Eventually, however, Loki heard Frigga laughing nearby as she spoke to another god.

"It's only natural," Frigga said, "that no one would want to hurt Baldur. He is so beloved that every single being in the world has sworn an oath not to cause him harm. Well—every being except for the young mistletoe near Valhalla's gate, that is, as it would be impossible for such a small thing to do any harm."

Elated, Loki headed out immediately in search of the mistletoe. When he found it, he knelt down and whispered words of magic that nurtured the plant unnaturally quickly, causing it to grow several feet at once and develop sturdy, sharp branches. Loki cut one of these branches, whittled it down into a slender javelin with a razor-sharp point, and returned to the game.

Quietly, Loki approached blind Hodur, who was standing away from the crowd looking dejected. After some needling from Loki, Hodur admitted that he was ashamed that he could not join the other gods in honoring Baldur's newfound strength; he had no weapon to throw, and he could not aim without the use of his sight.

With feigned kindness, Loki placed the mistletoe shaft in Hodur's hand, offering to guide his throw so that he might participate in the game. He led Hodur forward, turned him to face his brother, and Hodur hurled the javelin with as much confidence as any of the gods.

This time, however, no laughter rose up from the crowd. A shocked gasp of horror rang out instead as the mistletoe sunk straight into Baldur's chest, piercing his heart. Baldur collapsed to the ground, dead. There was a moment of silence, and then the gods began to howl with anger and grief. Loki slunk away then, leaving Hodur behind—but all the Aesir had seen him guide the blind god's hand, and they knew what he had done.

Baldur's light was already beginning to fade, and the world began to grow dark and cold in his absence. In desperation, Frigga demanded that one of the gods travel again to Hel to beg the goddess of death to let Baldur go free. Hermod, Odin's son, volunteered, and within moments he was on his way to the underworld astride Odin's own horse. He explained to Hela that everything in the world loved Baldur, and that his death would open the way for the coming of Ragnarök. In response, Hela decreed that if every single being would weep for Baldur, he would be allowed to return.

At first, the gods had hope; every stone, plant, and animal readily wept over Baldur's death, and it seemed that he would soon be returned to Asgard. Then, however, the Aesir came across an old giant woman sitting alone in a cave. In a voice that the gods recognized as Loki himself in disguise, the old woman bitterly refused to weep for Baldur, sealing his fate and trapping him in Hel forever.

TOP: *Baldr Dead* by Danish painter Christoffer Wilhelm Eckersberg (1783–1853). Baldur is lying dead in the foreground. Hodur, his blind brother, is standing on the left, stretching his arms out. To his left, Loki tries to conceal his smile. Odin and Thor sit in the middle of the Aesir. Yggdrasil and the three Norns can be seen in the background; **ABOVE:** Hermod presents his case to Hela to return Baldur back to the upperworld. Hela agrees, but only if all things dead and alive weep for him; **OPPOSITE, MAIN IMAGE:** Baldur lies dead, from *A Book of Myths*, by Helen Stratton, 1915. New York: G.P. Putnam's sons; London, T.C. & E.C. Jack; **OPPOSITE, TOP LEFT INSET:** *Each arrow overshot his head* by Elmer Boyd Smith.

HODUR

Hodur, sometimes referred to as Hodur the Blind, is the son of Odin and Frigga, and the brother of Baldur.

Although Hodur does have his own aspect—he is depicted generally as a god of darkness—he seems to exist only in the context of Baldur, specifically Baldur's death. Hodur has the unfortunate fate of being his brother's unwitting killer; he was tricked by Loki into impaling Baldur with a javelin made of mistletoe, the only substance that could hurt him, a guilt Hodur never recovered from. (Many visual depictions show Hodur killing Baldur using a bow and arrow.) After Hodur killed Baldur, Odin sired a young god named Vali to avenge Baldur's death, as Odin could not harm Hodur by his own hand. Vali then slew Hodur, allowing the god of darkness to be with his brother again in Hel. Though it was clear to the gods that Hodur's part in Baldur's death was an accident, and that Loki was the one truly at fault, it was still his hand that threw the javelin, and by custom, vengeance had to be exacted against him. During their time in the underworld, Hodur and Baldur reconcile and learn to live peacefully together. After Ragnarök, the two brothers rise from Hel to rejoin the living and help rebuild Midgard.

Despite the lack of narrative myth featuring Hodur, his existence is thematically interesting at the very least. He is the foil to Baldur, the other side of the same coin; this is a concept that recurs frequently in Norse mythology. While Baldur is bright and shining, literally glowing with goodness and joy, Hodur is described as somber, blind, and solitary. If Baldur is the light of day, Hodur—his killer—is the night. Hodur is a perpetual outsider, his sullen nature eclipsed by Baldur's perfection.

In another telling of Baldur's death, Hodur is cast as a warrior rather than the innocent we see in the *Eddas*. In this version (from the *Gesta Danorum*, a 12th century collection of Danish history and poetry), Hodur and Baldur are rival warlords fighting over the hand of Nanna, Baldur's wife in most sources. Hodur, inferior to Baldur in strength and skill, journeys to the underworld to find a magical weapon that will be able to slave Baldur. After Hodur succeeds in defeating Baldur, he is once again killed to avenge Baldur's death. The events of the two stories are similar—Hodur strikes Baldur down with a magical weapon, only to be killed in revenge himself—but the depiction of Hodur himself is starkly different.

MAIN IMAGE: Hodur, the blind brother of Baldur, with Loki, the instigator of the crime (left) shoots the mistletoe at Baldur. Illustration by Emil Doepler, from *Walhall, die Götterwelt der Germanen*; **TOP, INSET:** Hodur, from the manuscript of *Prose Edda*, 17th century; **ABOVE:** "There broke forth a wailing and a lamentation at the killing of Baldur." Woodcut, 1901.

Heimdall is the watchman of the gods and the guardian of Bifröst. He is occasionally known as Rig or Vindler.

HEIMDALL

ABOVE: Staue of Heimdall by Rolf Adlersparre in Djurgardsbron, Stockholm, Sweden; **BELOW:** *Heimdallr and Gulltoppr*, by Dorothy Hardy, 1908; **OPPOSITE:** Heimdall, with his acute hearing, listens for any sounds of approaching danger which may disturb the tranquility of Asgard, c. 1890s.

Heimdall is often described in unusual but distinct terms; his teeth are of shining gold, and his eyesight allows him to see for miles in every direction with fantastic accuracy. He can see in the dark as easily as in the day, and needs less sleep than a bird. His hearing is as acute as his eyesight; he can hear the sound of grass growing as well as the wool growing on a sheep's back. Some sources imply that Heimdall sacrificed one of his ears to Mimir's well for his perfect hearing, similar to Odin's sacrifice of an eye for great wisdom. Heimdall is also described as being born of nine mothers, although the exact implications of this are unclear. As an infant, Heimdall was nourished by the earth, the sea, and the sun, the same elements (earth, water, and fire) that make up the Bifröst he is sworn to protect.

As the watchman of Asgard, Heimdall spends most of his time in his watchtower Himinbjörg, where he drinks fine mead and watches for invaders approaching from the rainbow bridge. Heimdall's watchtower stands either between Asgard and the Bifröst or directly at the Bifröst's center. His supernaturally strong eyesight allows him to see potential threats coming from several miles away and so he is able to alert the Aesir well in advance. When Ragnarök comes, Heimdall will use his horn Gjallarhorn to sound the call that marks the end of the world and summons the gods to their final battle. For reasons that are not made explicitly clear—beyond Loki's general behavior, that is—Heimdall and Loki have a bitter rivalry, and the two are fated to kill each other during the events of Ragnarök. There are a few reasons that might explain the animosity between Heimdall and Loki. For one, Heimdall takes the role of the rational, reasoned problem-solver in many Norse myths, which often puts him at odds with Loki and the trickster god's scheming. Heimdall is also shown to be a suspicious and shrewd observer of those around him, a trait suitable for a watchman; he was the only one to be suspicious of the giant who built the walls of Asgard, for instance, though he said nothing at the time to avoid making baseless accusations. Given his keen senses and suspicious nature, his hatred of Loki may imply that he sees something malevolent in the god of mischief that the rest of the Aesir do not.

BIFRÖST

The Bifröst, also called the rainbow bridge, is the magical bridge that connects Asgard to Midgard and the rest of the nine realms.

ABOVE: Heimdall, by J.T. Lundbye, 1907; **BELOW:** *Rainbow Bridge* by Hermann Hendrich; **OPPOSITE:** Bifröst, the bridge that connects Midgard (Earth) and Asgard. Watercolor by the English illustrator Stella Langdale, 1916.

As the name might suggest, the most common visual depiction of the Bifröst is a rainbow that stretches from the ground high into the clouds. In some original texts, however, the bridge is described as a perpetually burning path of several intermingled primordial elements (the *Aurora Borealis*?). The Bifröst was created from water, fire, and earth when Asgard itself was first created by the gods; it was created so that the Aesir would have a way to get in and out of their city when they needed to travel or on the rare occasion that guests were welcomed in Asgard. The Valkyries who bring the spirits of the honored dead—the *einherjar*—from the battlefields of Midgard to the hall of Valhalla must cross the Bifröst on their way into Asgard. The elements that make up the bridge are responsible for its multi-colored appearance, as each element is represented visually: red for fire, blue for water, and so on.

The bridge is guarded by Heimdall, the watchman of the gods, who spends most of his time in his high tower Himinbjorg at the highest point of the Bifröst. From there, Heimdall's magically-enhanced eyesight allows him to see for miles in every direction so that he can warn the other gods of potential invaders from Jotunheim. Heimdall was said to have been nurtured by the same elements as a child that make up the substance of the Bifröst, which may partially explain his role as the bridge's guardian.

Several myths mention the Bifröst, although this is usually in passing; we see figures such as Odin setting out across the bridge to wander the world of men, and we often see Loki sprinting or flying back across the bridge towards Asgard, pursued by another newly-made enemy. Full-force invasion attempts across the Bifröst are rare, likely due to the fact that the bridge is often depicted as narrow and delicate; some sources refer to it as the "shaking" or "swaying" path, for instance, and it is occasionally mentioned that Thor's thundering steps are too heavy to safely cross the bridge. During Ragnarök, Surtr the fire giant and the forces of Muspelheim are prophesied to ride across the Bifröst, shattering it to pieces on their way to burn Asgard. In other versions of the story, the gods shatter the Bifröst in their wake as they march across it towards the final battle.

FRIGGA

Married to Odin, Frigga is the Queen of Asgard and the highest of the goddesses. As the mother of Thor, Baldur, Tyr, and Hodur, she is the goddess of motherhood, and marriage, but is also associated with other aspects, such as prophecy, and the weather.

She is depicted as a beautiful and statuesque woman, usually wearing dark robes or snow-white clothes. Mirroring the relatively progressive Norse culture of the time (compared to other civilizations of the era) Frigga held a huge amount of power over the Asgardians rather, than simply being Odin's wife. She was often placed in direct competition with Odin, in fact, as the two were both extremely competitive and valued victory and shrewdness highly. Many myths featuring Frigga revolve around contests or wagers between her and Odin, with one or both sides often cheating or bending the rules in an attempt to guarantee victory. The poem *Grímnismál*, for instance, features the king and queen of Asgard choosing sides between the two young princes of a human kingdom; when Frigga wants to prove that Odin's favored prince has grown into a cruel, tyrannical king, she sends word ahead of Odin that the king should be wary of a sorcerer coming to bewitch him. This results in Odin being captured and tortured when he pays the king a visit, proving Frigga right. In another myth, Frigga and Odin disagree on which of two armies should have victory over the other. Odin declares that whichever army he sees first, upon rising at dawn the next day, will be the winner, knowing that he will be able to see his favored army from his bedroom window. To ensure her victory, Frigga advises the women of her favored tribe to tie their hair in front of their faces like beards. She then turns Odin's bed to face the opposite window while he sleeps; when he wakes the next morning and exclaims at the bearded soldiers he sees through his window, he is forced to declare Frigga's favored army the victors.

Some interpretations of Norse myths combine Frigga and Freyja—for a number of confusing reasons. One of which is that their names are phonetically similar, and some of the multiple spellings and iterations of their names crossover between the two. Both gods are also associated with sorcery and prophecy, and are attested to have taught the practice of *seidr* (the form of magic related to both the telling, and the shaping of, the future) to the Asgardians. In some tellings of the story it was Frigga who taught Odin the art of seidr, while in others Freyja brought the practice to Asgard when she arrived from Vanaheim.

Frigga is shown to be very protective of her children and of the other Asgardians in general, for instance. When Baldur tells her of the dark, prophetic dreams he has been having, she takes it upon herself to demand that every single living and non-living thing in all of creation swear an oath to never harm her son. After Baldur's death, Frigga demands that one of the gods set out from Asgard at once to bring her son back from the underworld, something that had never been attempted successfully before. There is some implication that this goes against the custom and tradition of The Aesir, but Frigga's grief is so immense that nobody would dare question this decision.

OPPOSITE, MAIN IMAGE: *Frigga Spinning the Clouds*, by John Charles Dollman (1851–1934); **ABOVE:** *Odin and Frigga*, by Harry George Theaker, 1920; **BELOW:** Frigga and her servants. The one on the right is possibly Gná, whom Frigga sends on errands. Behind her is presumably her horse, Hófvarpnir. The one sitting beside Frigga is Fulla, who protects Frigga's *eski* (box); **BOTTOM:** Women look up to Odin and Frigga, with their long hair tied to appear as beards. From *Walhall, die Götterwelt der Germanen* (*Valhalla, the World of the German Gods*), 1905, by Martin Oldenbourg, with illustrations by Emil Doepler.

TYR

Tyr, the son of Odin and Frigga (or, in some versions, the son of Hymir the frost giant and a personification of the raging sea) was known as the bravest of the Asgardians.

Tyr was particularly renowned for his fearlessness in battle, even more so than gods like Thor and Odin. Notably, Tyr was the only god unafraid enough to feed Fenrir the great wolf, after it had become large enough to easily swallow a grown man whole. Later, when the time came for the Aesir to bind Fenrir the wolf before he could destroy Asgard, Tyr was the only god to volunteer to put his hand between the wolf's teeth; Tyr made this sacrifice knowing that Fenrir would bite off his hand when he failed to escape the gods' magical bindings. Given the prevalence of this myth, Tyr is usually depicted with one hand. Some sources mention that, after losing his right hand, Tyr used his right arm to hold his shield and became just as adept with a sword in his left hand as he had been with his right. The loss of Tyr's hand is another instance of the recurring theme of physical sacrifice for the greater good in Norse mythology—such as Odin's sacrifice of his eye for the wisdom required to lead the Aesir. It's also a reminder of the mortality of their gods. As the events of Ragnarök draw closer and we see the gods' vulnerabilities—Baldur's death, Tyr's hand—we are reminded each time they suffer an injury like this that the gods can be killed. When Ragnarök comes, they will have to face that mortality themselves. In the final battle, Tyr is fated to die while slaying the hellhound Garmr.

Although there are not as many myths that feature Tyr as the main focus, he was clearly a significant figure in Old Norse religion. There is some evidence, given the etymology of Tyr's name, that he was once held in as high regard as Odin himself, if not higher. Tyr's name comes from a word that literally means "god" or "the god," which implies that he was once viewed as a king among the gods, similar to Odin. The Tiwaz rune and the word "Tuesday" both come from Tyr's name. Some sources also attest that Tyr had some command over the forces of the Valkyries, and that it was his responsibility to determine which battlefields to send the Valkyries to in search of honorable fallen warriors. This elevated view of Tyr's station may have been a holdover from an earlier sect of Old Norse religion, before the canon of Norse mythology we know today was popularized. Over time, Tyr's popularity diminished, and he shifted somewhat to the sidelines of the pantheon of Norse gods.

ABOVE: The Tiwaz rune (and the word "Tuesday"), both come from Tyr's name; **BELOW:** Thor and Tyr in their goat-drawn chariot; **OPPOSITE:** 17th century Icelandic manuscript depicting the story of Tyr (the Norse god of single combat, victory and heroic glory) losing his hand to the monstrous wolf Fenrir.

IDUN

Idun is a goddess of fertility and health. She is best known as the caretaker of the apples of youth, a specially-nurtured crop of magical apples that are responsible for providing the Aesir gods with their eternal youth, vigor, and perfect health.

In some sources, Idun is the keeper of a magical apple orchard and picks apples each day to give to the rest of the Aesir gods. More commonly, however, Idun is said to carry a basket, or bag of apples with her wherever she goes. In both cases, the apples never run out—the basket is bottomless and the trees always bear fruit—and only Idun is allowed or able to retrieve the apples.

Idun's name translates to "ever-young" or "rejuvenator," correlating with her role as the provider of the gods' eternal youth. Idun is the wife of Bragi, the god of poetry. Idun and Bragi met as Bragi was strolling through a forest, playing his harp and causing the trees and flowers around him to bloom into life. Idun came across him there and was impressed by his ability to bring life to the natural world around him, and the two were quickly married. In the *Lokasenna*, the poem containing the story of Loki's series of taunts against the gods, Loki claims that Idun is sleeping with the man who killed her brother; this reference is not mentioned in any surviving sources, but it implies that (if Loki is telling the truth) Bragi is responsible for the death of Idun's unknown brother.

The image of an apple granting eternal youth is a common one in mythology around the world; some scholars believe that the apples of Idun were a later addition to the original myth, with imagery borrowed from Greek mythology. In this case, the original Idun herself would have been the source of the gods' eternal youth and health, similar to the way Baldur's mere presence seems to fill those around him with life and joy. Also similarly to Baldur, when Idun is taken away from Asgard, her absence is felt as the gods begin to grow old and weak within hours. It may be that the apples are simply a metaphor for the care she provides to the other gods of Asgard, or that they are a physical manifestation of the power she wields over life.

OPPOSITE: *Idun and the apples*, 1890, by the Irish painter James Penrose; **ABOVE:** Ydun, by Constantin Hansen (1804–1880); **BELOW:** *Ydun*, by Danish sculptor Herman Wilhelm Bissen (1798–1868).

Odin, Hoenir, and Loki set out one day on a journey to Midgard, something they did often, whenever Odin grew tired of his station in Asgard.

IDUN'S APPLES OF YOUTH

They had been wandering for a long time, stopping to help mortals every now and then, when they came to a deserted region with no towns or houses in sight. The trio spotted a herd of oxen in a nearby field and, weary and hungry, they slew one to eat for dinner. Loki the fire god built a large pyre to cook the beast on, and the gods sat down by the fire to wait for the meal to be ready.

Oddly, despite the raging flames, the carcass remained completely raw. Recognizing that some sort of magic was at work, they looked around to see what might be interfering with their cooking and noticed an eagle perched on a tree above them. The bird addressed the traveling gods and admitted that he was the one who had prevented the fire from doing its usual work, but he offered to undo the spell if they would give him as much food as he could eat. The gods agreed, thinking that even such a large bird could not possibly eat an entire oxen. The eagle fanned the flames with his massive wings, and the meat was quickly cooked.

The eagle then prepared to take three quarters of the ox as his share; this enraged Loki, who was almost starving at this point, and he grabbed a large stick nearby and began swinging it at the giant bird, forgetting entirely that the eagle was magical. Immediately, Loki saw that one end of the stake had become firmly attached to the eagle's back and the other to his hands. The eagle took to the air with a laugh, and Loki found himself being dragged over stones and through branches, then high into the air, his arms almost ripped out of their sockets. He pleaded for mercy in vain for hours until the eagle—who revealed himself to be the giant Thiassi–finally agreed to let Loki go on one condition. He made him swear a sacred oath that he would lure Idun out of Asgard so that Thiassi could kidnap her and steal her magical apples.

Finally free, Loki returned to Odin and Hoenir, telling them nothing about the deal he had made. When they returned to Asgard, Loki sought Idun in the forest where she lived. He took her aside and explained, in hushed tones, that he had discovered a tree in Midgard that bore golden apples just like hers. She gladly followed Loki out of Asgard with her basket of apples to examine the tree, but Loki disappeared as soon as they were on their way. Before Idun could react, Thiassi swept out of the sky as an eagle and grabbed her in his talons, lifting her into the sky and carrying her to his home in Jotunheim.

THIS IMAGE: "The eagle reveals himself to be the giant, Thiassi..." *Loki and Thiassi*, by Danish artist Lorenz Frølich; **BELOW:** *Loki and Idun*, by the Swedish artist John Bauer (see pages 124–125); **OPPOSITE:** Idun was known as being very wise, kind, and good, and so had the task of watching over the golden apples. It was these apples that kept the deities of Asgard youthful, and by eating them, they would never grow old. This 1905 illustration shows Idun tending the apples. From *Walhall, die Götterwelt der Germanen*, 1905, by Emil Doepler (see pages 124–125).

In Asgard, it was not long before the effects of the apples began to fade. The gods began to feel the approach of old age, and their youth and beauty began to wane; thus, alarmed, they began to search for the missing goddess. It was discovered that she had last been seen in Loki's company, and soon Loki was forced to admit that he had betrayed her in exchange for his own freedom.

Before the furious gods could administer his punishment, Loki assured them that he would set out to find her at once. Donning Freyja's falcon plumage, he flew off to Thrym-heim, the home of Thiassi; there he found Idun alone, lamenting her exile from Asgard and her beloved Bragi. Quickly Loki transformed Idun into a nut, picked her up, and flew from the window of her tower back towards Asgard.

Meanwhile, the gods had gathered on the ramparts of Asgard to watch Loki's approach. When they saw the massive eagle following close behind him, they quickly began building a massive pyre outside the walls of Asgard, which they set ablaze just as Loki crossed overhead. In his haste, Thiassi was unable to stop, and he flew straight into the wall of fire. His feathers burned to ash, and he fell dead from the sky just as Loki deposited Idun safely within the walls.

SIF

Sif "the golden-haired" is the wife of Thor, the god of thunder. She is a goddess of the harvest, fertility, and prosperity.

There is little representation of Sif in most of the events of Norse mythology, and she is most often referenced as a background character or discussed in reference to Thor and their children. One myth that does feature her directly is Loki's theft of her golden hair and his subsequent trials with the dwarves. Sif was originally known for her long, beautiful, golden hair, which she never cut and which grew almost down to the floor. Her hair was a huge source of pride for the goddess, and something she was rightfully quite vain about. When Loki, in an ill-thought-out prank, cut off all of her hair while she was asleep, this was a dire enough insult that Thor nearly killed him on the spot when he found out. The name Sif "the golden-haired" as a title became much more literal after Loki's attempts to repay her for his theft of her hair: in the same evening that they created Thor's hammer Mjölnir and Odin's spear Gungnir, the dwarves made Sif a brand new head of hair that was literally spun from gold. The new hairpiece shone with light and was even more beautiful than her original hair, which was the only thing that kept Thor from killing Loki for insulting his wife.

Sif also features briefly in the myth of Odin's horse-race with the giant Hrungnir, when Hrungnir demands that Sif and Freyja be given to him as his wives if he wins the race, as well as the story of Loki's flyting, or battle of insults, with the gods. Sif attempts to placate Loki with mead during his verbal tirade, claiming that she alone has done nothing wrong for him to call out; Loki responds by claiming that she once cheated on Thor with him, although he also makes the same claim about most of the goddesses present.

Sif is a goddess of the harvest, fertility, and prosperity, and as there are not many recorded myths featuring Sif in great detail, it is uncertain whether she was more popular during the Viking age. Her golden hair is often interpreted as a symbol of golden wheat and grain, and—as the wife to the god of thunder—she might have been prayed to in order to avert droughts, and bring the rainfall needed for healthy crops. Some scholars believe that Sif as a character was invented as a plot device for the myths she appears in and to give Thor a wife, and that she was never venerated in Old Norse religion in her own right. The name "Sif" translates roughly to "in-law" or "relation through marriage," which also supports this idea.

ABOVE: Sif, from the *Swedish Edda* translation; **LEFT, BELOW:** "In the same evening that they presented Thor's hammer Mjölnir, and Odin's spear Gungnir, the dwarves made Sif a brand new head of hair." From *Journeys Through Bookland*—a reading initiative introducing the world's best literature to children; **BELOW:** How Loki wrought mischief in Asgard, by Willy Pogany; **OPPOSITE:** Loki clips Sif's golden hair. Illustration by Katharine Pyle, 1930.

BRAGI

Bragi is the god of poetry, literature and music. He is usually described as carrying or playing a harp, and is often shown in illustrations side-by-side with his wife, Idun.

He is the son of Odin and either Frigga or a giantess named Gunlod, who once guarded the mead of poetry before Odin stole it. Although Odin had won the mead of poetry for himself, he instead entrusted it into the care of his son. Bragi, who was given great artistry over poetry and performance, used his newfound skills to travel the world, bringing art and music to gods and mortals alike. In some tellings, Bragi was actually born from the mead of poetry itself, similar to the way Kvasir was born from the vase that the Aesir and Vanir gods spat into during their peace treaty. The slain Kvasir's blood is what originally created the mead of poetry that Bragi is entrusted with.

Bragi is the husband of Idun, the goddess of eternal youth, whom he met one day when traveling in the forest, bringing plants and flowers and trees to life with his harp. Idun was delighted by his ability to bring life and joy to the plants and animals around him, and the two quickly fell in love and were married. Some sources say that, before the wedding, Odin carved runes into Bragi's tongue which gave him his renowned mastery over art and poetry.

As a poet, or skald, Bragi was well-loved by the ancient Norse people, and anyone who hoped to be a poet or an artist often made sacrifice to, and honored, the god during feasts and celebrations. Many poets of the time incorporated the word Bragi into their name; however, as the name Bragi can be literally translated to mean "poetry," it may have been more of a title chosen by or given to well-known poets rather than an actual name. In some sources, Bragi is one of the gods who welcomes the spirits of slain heroes to Valhalla once they are brought to Asgard by the Valkyries.

Oddly, despite the fact that skalds were valued members of Norse society, there is some evidence in the original sources of Norse mythology that Bragi did not receive as much respect as the other Aesir gods usually afforded each other. During Loki's verbal battle of insults with the gathered Asgardians, Bragi is one of the gods who he insults the most by refusing to even acknowledge his presence. Loki also calls Bragi a coward, claiming that he hides behind the custom of non-violence adhered to in Asgard. In the same event, Frigga—ostensibly Bragi's mother—says that she wishes she had a son brave enough to challenge Loki in a fight, which may have been intended to shame Bragi for his peaceful ways. Alternatively, as this takes place after the death of Baldur, this may have just been a reminder of Frigga's grief over the loss of her favorite son. Loki also suggests that Bragi is responsible for the death of a brother of Idun, although no surviving source elaborates on this.

THIS PAGE: *Idun and Brage*, 1846, by Swedish painter Nils Blommér; **OPPOSITE:** Bragi, the husband of Idun. He is shown here playing a lyre. From *Walhall, die Götterwelt der Germanen*, 1905, illustration by Emil Doepler (see pages 124–125).

MIMIR

Mimir is an outlier among the giants. Most of the frost giants, even those who are shown to have some measure of wisdom, are described as oafish, cruel, and malevolent; they are generally perceived as the antagonists of Norse mythology. Mimir, on the other hand, is known to be the kindest, gentlest, and wisest being–not just among the giants, but among all living things.

Notably, Mimir's wisdom surpasses even that of Odin himself; Mimir is the guardian of Mímisbrunr ("Mimir's well"), also known as the well of knowledge, and when Odin sacrificed his eye for a single drink from the well and gained all the wisdom of the universe, he was still not as wise as Mimir himself. Mimir's role as the guardian of the well is to determine whether a visitor is worthy enough to make a sacrifice, in order to drink from the well. Odin, it seems, is the only figure in Norse mythology to have been deemed worthy enough, besides Mimir himself. As some myths mention that Mimir regularly drinks from the well, it can be assumed that this is also the source of his unmatched wisdom. Mimir's name literally means reflection, thought, or recollection, in reference to his supernatural wisdom and memory.

Mimir's origins are not stated in perfectly clear terms, but he is believed to be the son of Aegir the sea giant, another giant who stands on good terms with the Aesir gods. Like Aegir, Mimir is treated as an ocean divinity, although his aspect specifically represents the primordial ocean present at the dawn of time rather than the literal ocean that surrounds Midgard. Bestla, the mother of Odin, is sometimes inferred to be the sister of Mimir, which would make Mimir Odin's uncle.

After the war between the Aesir and Vanir tribes, hostages were exchanged between both sides in order to unify the warring clans of gods and provide assurance that they would not enter into conflict again. The Aesir received Njord, Freyja, and Freyr, while the Vanir received Hoenir–Odin's brother—and Mimir to act as chieftain and advisor to the Vanir, respectively. After Mimir's head was cut off and sent back to Asgard, Odin used magic and unknown herbs and potions to preserve Mimir's head, keeping him alive and turning to him for guidance whenever he did not trust his own judgement.

During Ragnarök, Odin returns Mimir to the fountain he once guarded and whispers something unknown to him before riding off to battle. After Ragnarök has come and gone, and the world has been razed in fire and many of the gods have died, the two last humans to emerge from the ashes (Lif and Lifthrasir) will emerge from either a tree or a forest called Hoddmímis holt. This term, which translates to "Mimir's woodland," is believed to be another name for Yggdrasil, implying that the world tree survives the events of Ragnarök and gives shelter to the last of humanity. With this interpretation, it can be inferred that whatever Odin whispered to Mimir before heading to the final battle might have involved the preservation of the tree and of the last two mortals of Midgard.

OPPOSITE: Odin visits Mimir, the kindest, gentlest and wisest being, who is sat under the branches of Yggdrasil, by the side of his well, *Mímisbrunnr*. The *Prose Edda* relates that the water of the well is a great source of wisdom, and here Odin seeks wisdom to make him all-powerful. In exchange, he sacrifices one eye. With him are his ravens Hugin (Thought) and Munin (Memory); **ABOVE:** Here, Mimir's well is interpreted as an ocean. He is believed to be the son of Aegir, the sea giant. The name *Mímir* comes from the ancient Norse, meaning "the rememberer" or "the wise one"; **BELOW:** *Mímir and Baldr Consulting the Norns*, moulded metal frieze, 1821–1822 by H.E. Freund, housed at the Ny Carlsberg Glyptotek, Copenhagen, Denmark.

MIMIR BEHEADED

After the long and terrible war between the Aesir and the Vanir gods, the two clans exchanged hostages to be sure that they would never again fall into such destructive, chaotic conflict.

THIS IMAGE: The three gods Loki, Odin and Hoenir, as narrated in the skaldic poem *Haustlöng*, from an Icelandic 17th century manuscript.

The Aesir gods happily welcomed the sea-god Njord, his daughter Freyja, and his son Freyr into Asgard with open arms. The Vanir twins were beautiful and talented, and they were soon beloved by all of the gods; Freyja taught the Aesir the art of seidr and prophecy, which greatly benefited their lives, while Freyr quickly became known as both a peerless warrior and a beacon of kindness and good cheer.

To the Vanir went Odin's brother, Hoenir, whose traits all made it seem as though he would be a strong leader in Vanaheim. The Vanir were in need of a new leader, and Hoenir's powerful frame, handsome appearance, and noble character made him a perfect fit for the role. Although Hoenir was not the most wise of the gods, Odin also sent Mimir, the wisest of the frost giants—and in fact of all living beings—to be his advisor. The Vanir gods welcomed Mimir and Hoenir gladly and appointed Hoenir to be their leader. Mimir stood at all times at Hoenir's right hand, whispering advice in his ear and guiding him on any important decisions he had to make. With Hoenir's strength and confidence and Mimir's infinite wisdom, when the two worked together they were in perfect harmony—but whenever Hoenir and Mimir were apart, Hoenir's leadership began to crumble.

The Vanir had assumed that Hoenir must have been extremely wise, as he was the brother of Odin, the wisest being in the universe. They did not know that Mimir was even wiser than Odin, nor did they know that it was his guidance that was responsible for all the wise decisions and swift judgments that Hoenir made during his time as their leader.

So, when it came time for Hoenir to answer questions and lead councils without Mimir at his side to guide him, it became quickly apparent that Hoenir—who was not the most intelligent of gods—was near to useless on his own. Whenever Mimir was away, Hoenir would respond to all questions with the words "ask somebody else."

Before long, the Vanir began to suspect that Odin had played a trick on them by sending them his useless brother and some kind of sorcerer as an act of sabotage. Furious at their perceived betrayal, the Vanir gods cut off Mimir's head before he could explain what was happening and sent it back to Odin as a present.

Odin was distraught when he received Mimir's decapitated head, and he was wracked with guilt over sending his longtime friend and advisor to his death. Working quickly, using a combination of embalming herbs, magical runes, and the sorcery that had been taught to him by the recent Vanir additions to Asgard, Odin preserved Mimir's head, keeping him alive without the need of his body. Though he could not return Mimir's head to the rest of his body, Odin kept the wise giant at his side at all times from then on, turning to him whenever he needed advice or could not rely on even his own great wisdom. For many years after his beheading, Mimir was the closest and most trusted advisor to the king of the gods.

ABOVE: *Odin am Brunnen der Weisheit.* A depiction of the Odin drinking from the well of wisdom, by Adolph Lang, 1903; **BELOW:** *Oden vid Mims lik.* Odin stands by Mímir's beheaded body, from a 19th century translation of the *Poetic Edda* by Erik Brate.

VILI AND VE

Vili and Ve are the two brothers of Odin, the king of the gods. All three are the children of the giantess Bestla and the god Borr, who was the son of the first god, Buri. Vili and Ve, alongside Odin, were responsible for slaying Ymir, the first of the frost giants.

TOP: The giant Ymir is torn apart by Odin, Vili and Ve. His butchered body is used to form the world; **ABOVE:** *Ask and Embla* by Robert Engels.

As Ymir was the very first living being created at the dawn of time, the triumph of the three new gods over him cemented their place as the ruling family of all of creation; after Ymir's death, the remaining Jotnar were banished to Jotunheim, and the descendants of the first gods built a paradise for themselves in Asgard, high above the Earth.

Vili and Ve also helped with the construction of the world shortly after the death of Ymir. They helped Odin to butcher the frost giant's corpse and used various parts of his body to build the world as we know it—turning his skull into the sky, his brains into clouds, his eyebrows into the fence that surrounds Midgard, and so on.

Outside of the myths detailing the beginning of time and the creation of the world, Vili and Ve are not commonly attested in Norse mythology. Often, they are mentioned in some sources as traveling alongside Odin, while other sources tell the same myth with Loki and Hoenir in their place. For example, some sources have Vili and Ve at Odin's side when he discovers the trees that he fashions into Ask and Embla, the first of the humans.

During the volley of insults Loki hurls at the Aesir gods in *Lokasenna,* Loki implies that Frigga, Odin's wife, has been cheating on Odin with both of his brothers. This line is a reference to a partially preserved myth in which Odin is away from Asgard on unknown business for a long time. After several months of absence, the gods began to wonder whether he would ever return at all, and his brothers Vili and Ve eventually took up rulership of Asgard in his absence. According to Loki, this assumption of Odin's duties also included sleeping with Frigga, although the claims made in *Lokasenna* are rarely taken at face value. In most retellings of this story, Odin and his brothers remain on good terms, and Odin's return to Asgard is met with a smooth transition of power as he resumes his role as king of Asgard.

As the three brothers share such similar roles when they are first introduced, and as they are not attested as frequently in later sources of Norse mythology, some have argued that the three gods rather represent individual aspects of a single deity. Triple deities are common in many world mythologies, and this is a relatively frequently-used explanation for gods that see little exploration in myths and stories after their introduction. The concept of Vili and Ve as aspects of Odin would explain their only occasional appearances, and—if Loki's claims are correct—would also explain their relationship with Frigga during Odin's unexplained absence.

MAIN IMAGE: Odin and his brothers create the world. (Overlaid on a picture of the polar milky way, over Svalbard in Longyearbyen, Norway.)

Of Odin's many, many children, two were born for the sole purpose of vengeance.

VIDAR AND VALI

The gods Vali and Vidar were born, respectively, to avenge Odin's son Baldur after his death at the hands of Loki, and later to avenge Odin himself after he is killed by Fenrir during Ragnarök. Vidar, who seeks out vengeance upon Fenrir by tearing the wolf's jaws apart and stabbing him in the throat with his father's spear, is not attested in many myths, and the circumstances of his birth are unclear. It can be assumed that, like his brother Vali, Vidar grew to full adulthood moments after he was born so that he might be immediately directed towards his purpose of vengeance.

VIDAR

Vidar, slayer of Fenrir, is also known as the "Silent Aesir" or the "silent one;" after he was born and until the day he slew Fenrir, he never spoke a single word aloud. Little is attested of him in the original source material prior to the battle of Ragnarök; he is mentioned once or twice simply as one of Odin's many sons, but he does not play a significant role in any of the surviving myths. It is likely that as a character Vidar was invented for the sole purpose of avenging Odin, slaying Fenrir, and joining the small tribe of surviving gods who gathered to rebuild the world after the ashes of Ragnarök settled. In in the poem *Grímnismál*, there is one line which describes Vidar in his personal sub-realm within Asgard; here the text mentions that Vidar lives in anticipation of the day he has the honor of avenging his father. This means that, even before Odin's death, Vidar knows that it is his role in life to avenge him. Whether he knows the circumstances of Odin's death in advance or not is unclear.

VALI

Vali, who can be assumed to be the older of the two as he was born to avenge the death of Baldur long before Odin's death, also grew to an adult at full height and strength moments after his birth. Interestingly, Vali's purpose as an avenging god was not to kill Loki—who had actively and maliciously caused Baldur's death—but to kill Hodur, Baldur's blind brother who was used as an unwitting accomplice by Loki. Despite the fact that Hodur felt great shame and grief when he realized that his hand had been used to kill his brother, the fact that it was his hand that struck the killing blow allowed no room for leniency. The fact that Vali was created because it was felt that Hodur had to be killed to pay for Baldur's death gives us some insight into the way Norse culture worked at that time. Clearly, intent did not matter nearly as much as the result; even though Hodur did not know what he was doing and would not have chosen to kill Baldur, he was still responsible enough to warrant his death. Vali also took revenge on Loki, of course; though the fire god could not be killed—either because of his blood-bond with Odin or because of his integral role in the inevitable Ragnarök—Vali devised a fate worse than death for him. Vali bound Loki with the entrails of his own son and hid him deep in a cave, binding a giant snake above him so that burning venom dripped perpetually onto Loki's face. After Ragnarök, Vidar and Vali join the few survivors who come together to rebuild the Earth making a new home for the children of Lif and Lifthrasir so that they can repopulate the world.

TOP: "Víðarr stabbing Fenrir while holding his jaws apart," illustration by W.G. Collingwood, 1908, inspired by the Gosforth Cross, from *The Elder or Poetic Edda*; commonly known as *Sæmund's Edda*. Edited and translated with introduction and notes by Olive Bray, published in 1908; **ABOVE:** *Wali*. Váli travels through a forest, from *Nordisch-germanische Götter und Helden*, 1882, by Wilhelm Wägner. Otto Spamer, Leipzig & Berlin. The illustration is by Carl Emil Doepler (see pages 124–125); **OPPOSITE:** *Vidar och Vale*. (Vidar and Vali.) From Fredrik Sander's 1893 edition of the *Poetic Edda*.

TOP: Heinrich Himmler, who operated the state machinery of Nazi Germany. One of the most feared men in Germany, then later, during WWII, in Occupied Europe; **CENTER:** The *valknut*, one of various viking symbols taken up by the Nazis; **ABOVE:** Nazi recruitment poster flyposted in Norway during WWII: "With the Waffen-SS and the Norwegian Legion against the common enemy..."

NORSE CULTURE AND THE THIRD REICH

Norse culture has been absorbed and repurposed down the centuries, being found in the arts from medieval times onwards—from Shakespeare, to the early 19th century Romantic Movement, and into film in the 20th century. However, the propaganda and mass communication that heralded the rise of the Nazis from the 1920s to 1945 in Germany projected a sinister appropriation of Norse culture—and runic symbolism—to a global audience.

The most blatant use of runic symbolism appeared on the insignia of the uniforms and ceremonial flags of the *Schutzstaffel*—the SS. Originally, the SS was Hitler's security detail, but in 1929 he appointed Heinrich Himmler commander of the SS, and in the early 1930s Himmler began developing it into an *elite corps*, a body which, in the first place recognized Hitler as the embodiment of Germany, and then to also become the complete expression of nationalist race purity—an ideology originally rooted in German mysticism. Himmler was a fanatical advocate of racial purity—but he also entertained ideas which frequently descended into occultism. He adopted the *Hagal* (Ármanen rune) and used it for its symbolic representation of "unshakeable faith" in the Nazi philosophy. It was used in SS weddings, as well as on the SS-Ehrenring (death's head ring) worn by members of the SS.

Most common amongst the Norse symbols appropriated by Himmler was the *valknut*; the winged *othala* rune; and the *sowilo* rune. Much of this development grew out of the 19th century *völkisch* movement, wherein Nazi ideology maintained that Norsemen were genetically superior and "pure" ancestors of the Germanic peoples. The Nazis believed that the Old Norse race was the progenitor for all of human life in Europe, and they attempted to revive and co-opt many aspects of Norse culture into a contemporary context. It should be noted, however, that this idea of the Norse people as a "pure" race—that is, one that remained isolated, and avoided mixing with other races and cultures—has no basis in fact. DNA evidence reveals that the genetic makeup, and social structures, of the Norsemen were varied and diverse, and, given what we know of the viking propensity for trading, raiding, and settling in many European kingdoms, is just about what one would expect.

Although white supremacist groups (having grasped the Nazi mantle) continue to appropriate Norse culture, they are not the only ones for whom these symbols are meaningful. Not every person who displays Norse or viking iconography should be associated with hate groups—for example, many people want to display or invoke their heritage through their body art or jewelry, and in some cases this reconnection with a Scandinavian heritage has caused problems through a clear misreading of the symbolism.

TOP: Nazi poster advertising "SS-Dagen 1943, Oslo"—"SS Day in Oslo," and making explicit the connection of the two nations—"Nazis are vikings"; **ABOVE:** "Nordic Men Fight for Norway"—Waffen SS propaganda poster from 1942 for Nazi-occupied Norway. Again portraying the two nations as one, using the supposed mutual ancestral heritage of the adventurous, and "heroic" Wikings; **TOP LEFT:** One of the most sophisticated and civilized nations on earth is both hypnotized, then coerced, into mass adulation, then complete obedience, on pain of disappearance and death; **LEFT:** The swastika to the left, the Iron Cross to the right, and in the center, the *Wendehorn* symbol. Allegedly symbolizing life, and death, respectively. The term is from Guido von List's *Das Geheimnis der Runen*, where it is not a full member of the Armanen runes, but is mentioned as being "the rune of Freyja, and of childbirth."

4

THE VANIR GODS

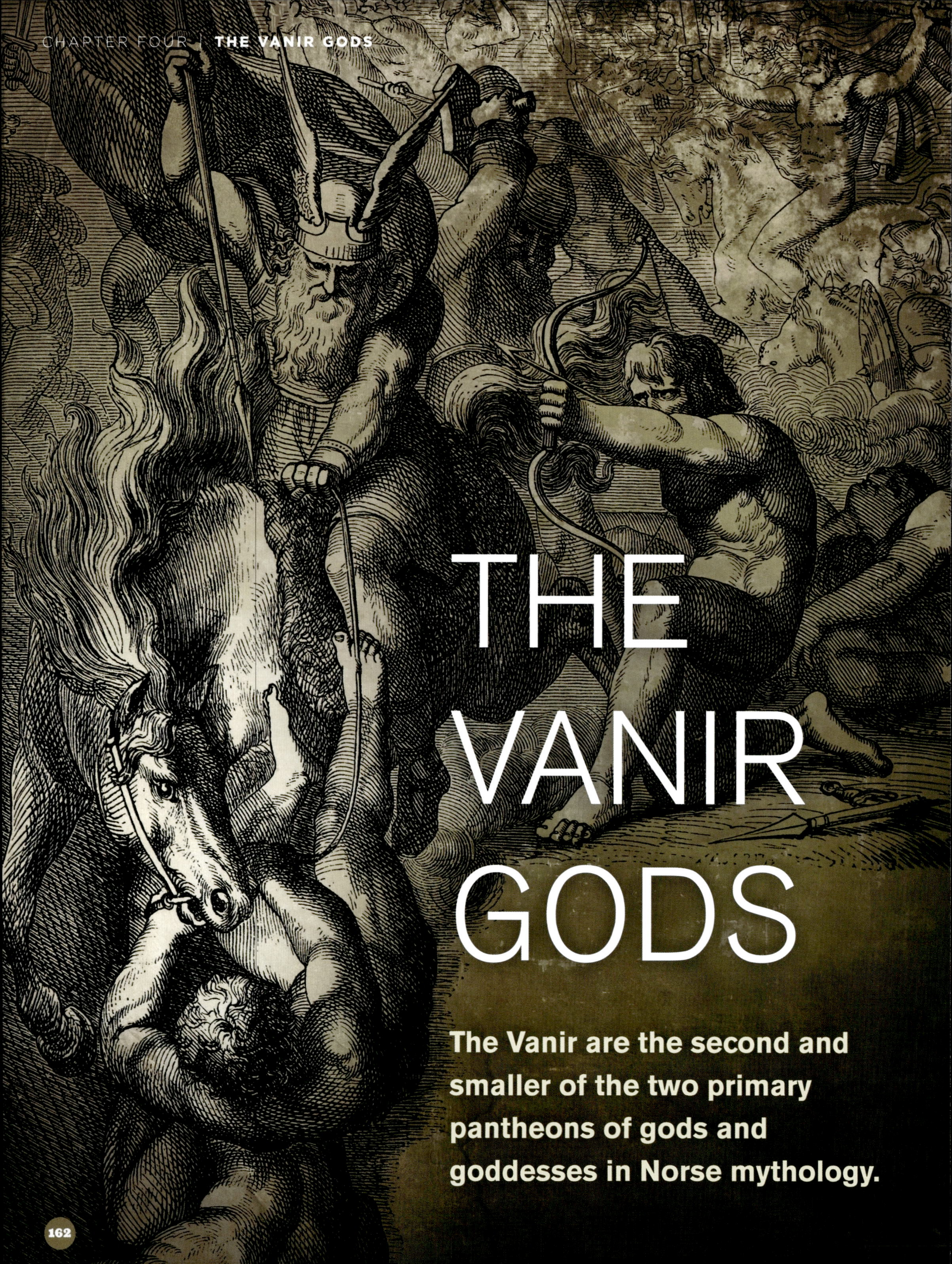

THE VANIR GODS

The Vanir are the second and smaller of the two primary pantheons of gods and goddesses in Norse mythology.

The Aesir, of course, are the larger and most well-known, as almost all of the myths of Norse mythology focus on the gods of Asgard, but the Vanir gods had a distinct presence in old Norse religion as well. Though the source of some of these deities is uncertain, a common theory is that the Vanir gods may have been holdovers from earlier religious beliefs that were later incorporated into the larger body of old Norse religion. Another theory is that they were originally the Norse interpretations of the gods of other nations that the Norsemen visited whilst trading or on raiding voyages. The description of their kingdom of Vanaheim as a far-off realm also implies that the Norsemen could have been referencing a real, physically distant country, rather than a mythological world.

Asgard and Vanaheim were at war for some time early in the chronology of Norse mythology, and as the two tribes were so evenly matched, they came to a stalemate that seemed would never end. Eventually the two clans came together to form a peace treaty, exchanging hostages to live amongst each other to bind the two groups of gods together and avoid future bloodshed. After the Aesir Vanir war, there is little mention of Vanaheim or the other Vanir gods who stayed behind. There is a brief mention of Vanaheim in some sources when describing the events of Ragnarök, as it is sometimes implied that the Vanir sea god Njord returns to Vanaheim rather than fight in the final battle.

In contrast to the Aesir gods, who are generally very organized and law-abiding, the Vanir gods are much more in tune with the natural world, almost primal in their behavior and domains. Most of the Vanir gods are associated with fertility, magic and prophecy, and various aspects of nature. It is believed that the Vanir goddess Freyja most likely brought the practice of seidr to Asgard when she made the journey to Asgard from Vanaheim. In modern depictions, gods such as Freyr and Freyja are often given somewhat more chaotic personalities in accordance with the primal nature of their domains. The Vanir gods are also described as being especially physically beautiful; the twins Freyr and Freyja are often mentioned to be among the fairest of all the gods, and the giantess Skadi accidentally chooses the god Njord over Baldur when choosing a husband, based solely on the appearance of their legs!

OPPOSITE: The war of the Aesir and Vanir gods. wood engraving after drawing, by Karl Ehrenberg, 1887; **TOP LEFT:** An illustration of the Norse god Njörðr (Njord), from a 17th century Icelandic manuscript; **TOP CENTER:** Detail, the Götland Runestone, c. 500–600 AD. The main three figures are identified as Odin, Thor, and Freyr. These three are also the only Norse gods thought to have been actively worshiped during the Viking Age. The runestone is located in the Swedish Museum of National Antiquities, Stockholm; **TOP RIGHT:** Seated on Odin's throne Hliðskjálf, the Vanir god Freyr sits in contemplation, in a 1908 woodcut by Frederic Lawrence; **BELOW:** *Freja Seeking her Husband*, 1852, by the Swedish painter Nils Blommér (1816–1853).

NJORD

Njord is one of the senior Vanir gods. His domain is over wind, the sea, sailors, and fertility; he was associated strongly with all aspects of a hard-working sailor's life, and he was usually depicted as a swarthy, simply-dressed, salt-hardened sailor.

Njord's name was often invoked before any long sea journey or fishing trip, as it was believed that he had the power to soothe a stormy sea, just as he could raise a placid current into a tidal wave at a whim. He was also closely associated with prosperity and wealth, and he was honored by many who were setting out on risky business ventures involving sailing and sea trade.

Though little is depicted of most of the Vanir tribe, either because it is lost to time or because little was ever told about them in the first place, there are quite a few myths that mention Njord at least in passing. He was likely one of the more important members of the Vanir gods as, in exchange for Njord and his two children, Odin sent over his own brother and Mimir himself, the wisest living being.

Like many of the other Vanir gods, Njord was much more wild and primordial than many of the Aesir gods are presented. As the god of the sea, he is depicted as a fierce and emotionally driven character; his personality is a stark reflection of the changeable nature of the sea and the unknown depths beneath. Njord's parentage is unknown, although some have theorized that he was born directly from the sea itself, or perhaps—like Mimir—from the primordial ocean that was present before time began.

Njord was one of the three Vanir gods who were exchanged to Asgard after the peace treaty that followed the Aesir Vanir war. With him Njord brought his two children, the twins Freyr and Freyja, from his first marriage to the goddess Nerthus. Whether Nerthus is his wife, his sister, a consort, or some combination of the three is unclear, as their relationship is never discussed at length. Later, after joining the Aesir gods, Njord marries the giantess Skadi, daughter of Thiassi—although that marriage was exceedingly short lived as the two realized that they could never live together happily.

Some sources imply that Njord is one of the few gods to survive Ragnarök, as rather than fight in the final battle, he returned to Vanaheim to rejoin his original family. Vanaheim is not mentioned explicitly in the events of Ragnarök, though some sources state that all the nine realms are laid to waste. Others, however, discuss only Asgard and Midgard, meaning distant realms such as Vanaheim may have gone unscathed.

OPPOSITE: *Njörðr* (Njord), from Fredrik Sander's 1893 edition of the *Poetic Edda*. Engraving by Carl Fredrik von Saltza (1858–1905); **ABOVE:** Njörðr from *Die Helden und Götter des Nordens, oder Das Buch der sagen*, 1832; **BELOW, LEFT:** "Njörd, Gott (Wane) des Meeres und des Ozeans."

THE MARRIAGE OF NJORD AND SKADI

After the kidnapping and subsequent rescue of the goddess Idun, the Aesir gods returned to Asgard to celebrate their victory and rejoice in the return of the goddess responsible for their everlasting youth and vitality.

They had been feasting for several hours when, without warning, an unwelcome guest burst through the doors of their great hall. The intruder to Asgard was the giantess Skadi, the daughter of Thiassi, who had come to avenge her father's death at the hands of the gods. She wielded a long, gleaming spear and carried a bow and a quiver of arrows over her shoulder, and she brandished her weapons as she strode up and down the long tables demanding retribution. Rather than enter into a battle that would turn the hall into a bloodbath, however, Odin rose from his seat and poured all of his charm and eloquence into appeasing Skadi, slowly calming the giantess down until she was no longer swinging her spear at anyone who came close. Eventually, he convinced her to allow the gods to make up for the injury they had caused her in a way that would not cause further unnecessary bloodshed. Skadi agreed to this, demanding that her deceased father be honored and that her own emotional pain be soothed.

The first of the apologies of the gods was performed by Odin himself, who pulled Thiassi's bright eyes from his head and threw them up into the air, higher than the clouds, higher than anything in Asgard. The eyes

soared up so high that they never came back down, becoming two shining stars in the night sky overhead. Skadi approved of this, for a start, but she was still not satisfied. Next, the gods tried to cheer her up by making her laugh. They tried games, jokes, and stories; they tried to impress her with feats of athleticism and skill; but nothing worked. Eventually Loki, god of mischief and trickery, took it upon himself to entertain the giantess. Loki tied a long rope around the waist of a goat and tied the other end around his testicles; the goat, confused and irritated, began running back and forth around the hall, tugging Loki helplessly behind him as he yelped and flailed about pathetically. Eventually, the goat came to a sharp stop, tripping Loki over its back so that he stumbled forward and collapsed face-first in Skadi's lap. This, finally, drew a laugh from the giantess, and she forgave Loki for his crimes against her family.

Third, as Skadi no longer had her father to provide for her, she demanded to be given a god of her choosing to take as her husband. However, in order to make things fair, it was decided that she could only choose her husband based on the appearance of his legs and feet without being able to see his upper body. Hoping to marry Baldur, the most beautiful and beloved of the gods, Skadi picked the most beautiful pair of legs that she could see. When the cloth that was held in front of the god was removed, however, it was revealed that she had chosen Njord, the Vanir god of the sea; his legs had been toned and sculpted by many years of sailing. Although he was not who she expected, Njord suited Skadi well enough, and they were soon happily married.

After their wedding, however, Skadi and Njord realized that they would soon have to choose one of their homes to live in together. Njord's home was a beautiful seaside estate with bright sun, pristine sand, and an uninterrupted view over the sea for miles from the palace's windows. Skadi's home in Jotunheim was, like all other estates in Jotunheim, a dark, cold, dreary place surrounded by ice and frost and looming black mountains. In the end, they decided to spend a week first in her home in Jotunheim, and then a week in Njord's home by the sea.

Njord, who loved the heat, the sun, and the salty sea air, detested the time he spent in the dark and frigid castle of Jotunheim. Likewise, Skadi missed the peace and solitude of her mountain home, and the heat and bright light of the seaside was unbearable to her. So, after being married for only a fortnight and having found themselves completely incompatible, Skadi and Njord returned to their respective homes, never to see each other again.

OPPOSITE, TOP: *Njörd's desire of the Sea*. Up in the mountains, the god Njörðr is awake, while his wife Skaði sleeps. Njörðr is staring wistfully at the sea. Illustrated by W.G. Collingwood, from *Sæmund's Edda* (*The Elder or Poetic Edda*). Edited and translated with introduction and notes by Olive Bray, 1908; **TOP:** Conversely, Skadi has a longing for the mountains. Again, from *Sæmund's Edda* (*The Elder or Poetic Edda*); **OPPOSITE, BOTTOM:** *Idun & Thiazi* by H. Theaker, 1920. The giant Thiassi, taking the form of an eagle, kidnaps Idun; **THIS PAGE, ABOVE:** Njörðr and Skaði on the way to Njörðr's home Nóatún. Illustration by Friedrich Wilhelm Heine, after the original by Friedrich Wilhelm Engelhard.

FREYR

Freyr is one of the three Vanir gods who left their home to join the Aesir in Asgard after the events of the Aesir Vanir war.

Freyr is the twin brother of Freya, and the son of the sea god Njord; his wife is the frost giant Gerdr, who he went to great lengths and near-desperate measures to woo after falling in love with her at first sight. Despite the fact that he hails from a much lesser-known group of gods, Freyr was an extremely popular and well-worshiped god even among the core pantheon of the Aesir. Like his twin sister Freyja, he is described as incredibly beautiful, talented, and intelligent. He stands among the strongest warriors of Asgard, aided by his magical sword that is enchanted to fight on its own without the aid of a wielder. Freyr is so beloved by the other

gods—and, one can assume, by the Norsemen who worshiped him in their time—that his luminous image nearly rivals that of Baldur, the most beloved of the gods. Early sources, when discussing Freyr, mentioned that he is hated by none and beloved by all. His domain includes a wide range of concepts, all relating to health and prosperity. He is associated generally with fertility, sexual health, bountiful harvests, monetary wealth, and peace. Because of the positive connotations of Freyr's aspects, he was most often honored at celebratory events such as weddings, births, and harvest festivals, rather than before battle or in times of great strife. Freyr is accompanied often by his giant golden boar, Gullinborsti, who was built by the dwarves. Sacrifices of boars were especially common because of their association with Freyr.

Although Freyr is a member of the Aesir and has a home in Asgard, he is usually said to live in Alfheim, the realm of the bright elves. He was given rulership over Alfhim as a teething gift by Odin due to his fair appearance and gentle nature; the gods were so charmed by the young Freyr that they believed him best suited to rule over the similarly beautiful, delicate elves of Alfheim.

Freyr accumulated a number of other wonderful gifts over the course of his life, beyond those afforded to him by his station in Alfheim. He was the master of Skidbladnir, a majestic ship that could fly through the sky as easily as it could sail through the sea, and in a moment the entire ship could fold up into a bag small enough that it could be carried in his pocket. His magic sword was as bright as a sunbeam and scarcely needed a hand to hold it before it cut through any enemy. This sword he gave to his favorite servant, Skirnir, as a reward for his instrumental role in helping Freyr win the hand of the giantess gerda in marriage. During the final battle of Ragnarök, Freyr will come to regret giving away his most powerful weapon as he faces down the fire giant Surtr armed with nothing but a broken antler.

OPPOSITE, MAIN IMAGE: Freyr, Freyja's twin brother, is the god of fruitfulness, crops, sun, and rain. Illustration by Emil Doepler, from *Walhall, die Götterwelt der Germanen*, 1905; **ABOVE, LEFT:** Freyr by Johannes Gehrts; **ABOVE, RIGHT:** *The Rällinge statuette*, believed to depict Freyr, c. 800–900 AD; **BELOW:** Freyr fell in love with Gerd, the beautiful young giantess who was the daughter of the sea giant Gymir. Illustration by Emil Doepler, from *Walhall, die Götterwelt der Germanen*, 1905.

FREYJA

Freyja is the twin sister of Freyr and the daughter of Njord.

Along with her brother and father, Freyja was traded to the Aesir, as friendly hostages after the peace treaty of the Aesir-Vanir war was signed. Freyja is associated most strongly with love, fertility, beauty, and treasure; she is also known for the practice and teaching of seidr, a difficult form of magic practiced almost exclusively by women. It is generally believed that Freyja was the one to introduce the practice of seidr to Asgard and the Aesir gods when she arrived from Vanaheim, and that she perhaps taught the practice of seidr directly to Odin and Frigga. Freyja is usually depicted wearing her sacred necklace or *torc Brisingamen*, which was given to her by the dwarves. The necklace is mentioned often in Norse mythology—often referred to as a necklace of "starry jewels"—but it does not appear to have any magical qualities, unlike most of the gods' prized possessions.

There is a great deal of crossover between the goddesses Freyja and Frigga. They have similar domains, both presiding over sorcery, love, and fertility, and aside from the phonetic similarity of their names and the names of their husbands—Frigga's husband is Odin and Freyja's husband is Odr—some of the earlier source material seems to use the two goddesses as interchangeable characters. Over time, however, the two have become more and more distinct, with Frigga acting as the queen of Asgard while Freyja takes the role of a visitor raised among the Aesir. Many of the more unreserved and adventurous qualities of this shared character are given to Freyja; she is (probably falsely) accused by Loki of having slept with all the gods and all the elves of Asgard and Alfheim, including her brother Freyr, and her temper and use of magic are both much less restrained than those of Frigga.

Freyja also shares a noted similarity with the character Gullveig whose name translates roughly to "gold-drunk." Gullveig, a powerful sorceress with an insatiable love of gold and treasure, once visited Asgard, where she introduced the gods to gold and to the many valuable uses of magic. In the myth of Gullveig, the introduction of sorcery and greed into Asgard caused nothing but strife, and she was exiled after the gods were repeatedly unable to kill her by burning her at the stake. Freyja shares Gullveig's love of treasure and her connection to sorcery, although her presence in Asgard was never revealed the way Gullveig's was.

Some sources note that Odin only rules over half of the Valkyries, whiles Freyja commands the other half. While Odin takes half of those who die honorably in battle to Valhalla to serve as his army of einherjar, the other half of the honored dead are taken to Freyja's hall Folkvangr. While it is never explicitly stated what Freyja and her gathered collection of warrior spirits do during Ragnarök, it can be assumed that she leads her army into battle just as Odin leads his. Another popular interpretation of Freyja's hall, as a counterpoint to Valhalla, is the belief that Freyja specifically collects the spirits of women who died with honor.

MAIN IMAGE: Freyja is the goddess of fertility, love and marriage, and light and peace. Illustration by Emil Doepler, from *Walhall, die Götterwelt der Germanen*, 1905.

TOP: Freyja, Goddess of love and fertility, on her throne, 19th century woodcut; **ABOVE:** The Aesir lift Gullveig over fire. An 1895 illustration by Lorenz Frølich. Gullveig is a powerful sorceress with an insatiable love of gold, and introduces the gods to it, and also the many valuable uses of magic. In the poem *Völuspá*, she comes to the Hall of Odin, where she is speared by the Aesir, burnt three times, and yet is three times reborn. Upon her third rebirth, she begins practicing seiðr and takes the name Heiðr; **BELOW:** Viking pendant representing the goddess Freyja. Around her shoulders is the necklace *Brisingamen*, made for her by the dwarves. The Statens Historiska Museum, Stockholm.

FREYJA'S NECKLACE

ABOVE: *Freya and the Dwarves*, illustration by Harry George Theaker for *Children's Stories from the Northern Legends* by M. Dorothy Belgrave and Hilda Hart, 1920; **BELOW:** *In search of Brisingamen*, illustration by Katharine Pyle, 1930.

One day, as Freyja wandered the world in search of fine works of gold and jewels to add to her collection, she lost track of time. When she finally took stock of her surroundings, she found herself in an unfamiliar location: the sunlight had long since faded, but there was still some light coming from lanterns carried by a group of dwarves who were hard at work in the mouth of a cave nearby, mining and polishing gemstones. Four of them sat in one corner at a low table, putting the sparkling stones together to make a beautiful necklace. Freyja fell in love with the shining necklace of gold and jewels at first sight. She came closer, exclaiming, "How lovely! If only I had that necklace, I would be the most beautiful one at tonight's feast!" And the more she thought about it, the more she wished she could have it.

"Oh, I must have it!" she decided, turning to the four small men. "How much must I pay for your necklace?" she inquired. The dwarves seemed immediately charmed by Freyja's beauty and the delicate tone of her voice, and they answered immediately:

"Oh, if you will only look kindly upon us and be our friend, you may have the necklace as a gift!"

As she took the necklace, however, Freyja thought she heard mocking laughter echoing through the recesses of the cave, as though some voice was whispering that she was a fool to expect something so simple to make her happy. Freyja fled the cave, necklace in hand, and resolved to put the strange laughter out of her mind. When she was finally out in the open air again, Freyja expected her good mood to return. Instead, a strange sense of dread came over her, as if something bad was about to happen. She shook the feeling off, frustrated, and decided to rush straight home to Asgard to show her prize to her husband, Odur.

When she arrived, however, Odur was nowhere to be found. Freyja searched all the rooms in their home in vain; he had vanished, and although Freyja had her beautiful necklace, it was meaningless to her compared to the loss of her beloved husband. Before long, it was time to leave for the night's feast, but Freyja refused to leave without Odur. Instead, she gathered her chariot, drawn by two great cats. "I'll go to the end of the world to find him!" Freyja declared as she set out on her journey.

She went to Midgard first, but no one had seen her husband. Next she traveled beneath the earth, to Niflheim, and even to Jotunheim, the land of giants, but no one had seen or heard of her husband. Freyja wept bitter tears as she searched, and wherever the tears fell and sank into the ground, they turned into gleaming gold.

Freyja refused to give up in her search, and roamed the world without rest. She still wore the beautiful necklace, which she had named Brisingamen. As time passed, the world itself began to pity Freyja; leaves fell from the trees, bright flowers faded, and singing birds flew away, leaving everything bleak and dull.

Eventually, she and her shining necklace were the only points of light and color left in the world. Finally, Odur—who had been lost in a deep, dark forest and could not find his way out—saw the amber glow of her necklace in the distance and ran to her, and the two were reunited. As the couple returned home, their joy was contagious; the world returned to life and color, and the gods of Asgard rejoiced to see Freyja's smile grace them once again.

One late night, not long after their return, all the Aesir were asleep except for the ever-vigilant Heimdall. Heimdall heard soft footsteps, like those of a cat, near Freyja's palace, and went immediately to investigate. When he arrived at the palace, he discovered Loki creeping about outside. Heimdall watched him quietly as he glided into the room where the goddess slept, still wearing her beautiful necklace. Loki had come to steal the necklace, of course, and it was a matter of moments for the trickster god to unclasp the chain and dash away with it, his light footsteps inaudible to anyone but Heimdall. Heimdall gave chase, as he was never willing to let Loki get away with his crimes. When Loki realized he was being followed, he transformed into a small mote of fire; Heimdall turned himself into a shower of rain to put out the fire, and so Loki quickly turned himself into a bear to drink the rain. Then Heimdall turned into a bear as well, and a fierce battle ensued. Heimdall triumphed eventually, then forced the shame-faced Loki to return Freyja's necklace and apologize for his theft.

THIS IMAGE: *Freya*, 1890, by Irish painter James Doyle Penrose (1862-1932). Freyja is the Vanir goddess who teaches the Asgardians, and particularly Odin, the cerebral practice of *Seidr*—prophesising the shape of future events. **LEFT:** *Heimdall returns the necklace Bryfing to Freya*, by Nils Blommer. 1846.

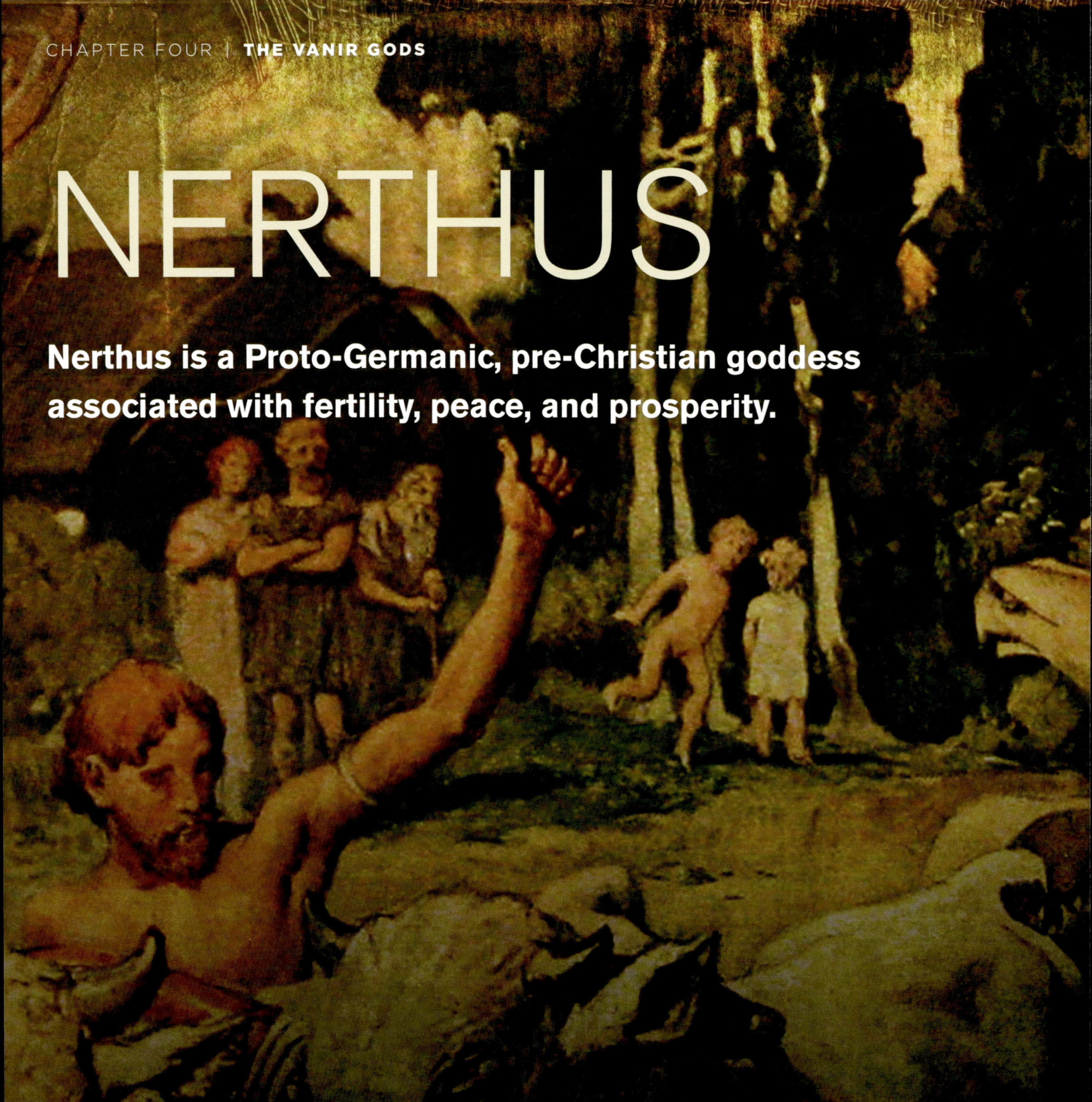

NERTHUS

Nerthus is a Proto-Germanic, pre-Christian goddess associated with fertility, peace, and prosperity.

Nerthus is usually depicted as a god of the Vanir tribe; although the specifics are uncertain, she shares a connection of some kind with the male Vanir god Njord. It is difficult to say definitively in which way she and Njord are paired: some sources imply that Njord and Nerthus are a single, genderless deity, capable of appearing in both male and female form, while others view the two figures as a pair—a husband and wife, perhaps, or siblings, or two unrelated gods intended to act as two sides of the same coin. Nerthus is often mentioned as the mother of the twins Freyr and Frejya; she is also generally associated with nature and the earth, which makes her a suitable foil for Njord due to his association with the sea.

Much of what is known about this goddess was originally recorded by Tacitus, a Roman historian active around the year 100 AD. Tacitus wrote that Nerthus was a deity of

fertility and peace, known for wandering the Earth among mortals, and her cult of worship involved a great deal of ceremony and ritual sacrifice. There is little in the way of description recorded of Nerthus herself, but great detail is paid to the veiled, golden chariot that she travels in. Wherever Nerthus and her chariot go, the people around her are overcome with tranquility and happiness, causing an end to war and conflict wherever she travels. Tacitus also describes a ceremony revolving around Nerthus and her chariot; in this ceremony, several priests escort a cart veiled with a sacred cloth as it is pulled by slaves through the center of a village, allowing Nerthus to experience the company of mortals for a time. After the ceremony, the cart is submerged in a lake by the slaves. As the chariot is too holy for any human to touch, the slaves themselves are then drowned in the lake shortly after.

IMAGE: Spectators watch as the processional wagon of the Germanic goddess Nerthus moves along, inspired by Tacitus' description of the Germanic custom in his first century AD work *Germania*. Illustration by Emil Doepler, from *Walhall, die Götterwelt der Germanen*, 1905.

LEFT: The cover of *Journey Into Mystery* #83, of August 1962 was the first Marvel Comic issue to feature their new superhero: The Mighty Thor, created by writers Stan Lee and Larry Lieber, and drawn by artist Jack Kirby; **RIGHT:** The series was renamed *The Mighty Thor* in March 1966, with issue #126; **BACKGROUND:** Marvel Comics covers and inside pages.

As the stories and characters of Norse mythology have survived over the centuries, they have been recast and retold countless times. In the last few decades, however, there are few more iconic representations of Norse mythology than Marvel's hugely successful *Thor* franchise.

THE MIGHTY THOR

Marvel's version of Thor first debuted in issue #83 of the sci-fi anthology series *Journey into Mystery*, in August 1962, and expanded into a stand-alone series entitled *The Mighty Thor* in March 1966, with issue #126. Later referred to simply as *Thor*, the series depicts Thor and the gods of Asgard in a new light, by casting Thor as a superhero in the Marvel universe, mixing science fiction elements with the mythological aspects of the original source material.

Thor has been one of Marvel's most successful comic book series; it has been running for over sixty years, although it has undergone several changes in terms of art direction, storyline, and staff over the years. The series was originally led by legendary comic creator Stan Lee. Thor and several other recurring characters from the series also feature heavily in many issues of the *Avengers* comics. As of 2022, *Thor* has run for over 700 issues.

The popularity of this comic book also inspired the more recent *Thor* movie franchise, the entries of which have since become a core component of the large Marvel Cinematic Universe. Featuring Chris Hemsworth as Thor and Tom Hiddleston as Loki, these movies (which also connect to the central canon of the *Avengers* movies) have garnered both critical acclaim and a massive fan following. The popularity of this franchise has helped push a notable resurgence of interest in Norse mythology, and many more books, TV shows, movies, and video games based on Norse myths have been produced in recent years. As sensationalized as many stories in comic books and superhero movies are, this franchise has been known to draw surprisingly accurately from many Norse myths, and can be a great way to introduce young people to the subject of Norse mythology in a modern and accessible format. *Thor Ragnarok*, for example, one of the later movies in the franchise, includes the apocalyptic events of Ragnarök, prophesied in Norse mythology. Although the modern depictions of these myths are not exact, one-to-one retellings—few ever are, to be fair—they provide a fresh, compelling take on stories that have been told for over a thousand years.

TOP: A Jack Kirby sketch for *The Mighty Thor* comic book; **ABOVE:** A still from *Thor* (2011), starring Chris Hemsworth as Thor (right), and Tom Hiddleston as Loki. Produced by Marvel Studios and distributed by Paramount Pictures.

5

THE JOTNAR

THE JOTNAR

ABOVE: A stone depicts the giantess Holdrikka, in the open air Museum Kulturen, in Lund, Sweden; **BELOW:** "Die Edda – 1) Ymir, Audhumbla, Buri," one of a set of trading cards from Liebig products "Liebig erzeugnisse: natürliche, eingedickte Fleischbrühe," ("natural, thickened meat broth"), c. 1900; **BOTTOM RIGHT:** An iron shield depicting Thor slaying giants. Sweden, 1890; **OPPOSITE:** As great glacial bergs of ice fall towards *Muspelheim*, the realm of fire, great clouds of primeval steam rise up, only to freeze again into hoarfrost. Eventually a giant figure is formed from the countless layers of ice . . . and the giant Ymir, first of the frost giants, comes to life. Illustration by Emil Doepler, from *Walhall, die Götterwelt der Germanen*.

Although the word *jotunn* (or its plural *jotnar*) is generally translated to mean "giant," or "frost giant," given that they descend from a being who was born whole from primordial frost, the more accurate translation of the word would be "devourer." The term has less to do with their size, though some are certainly physically giant, and more to do with their nature; the frost giants have a voracious, jealous appetite for all the things that they were denied when the gods cast them out into the wastes of Jotunheim. The reason they play the role of the antagonist so frequently in Norse mythology is not necessarily that they are evil by nature. Rather, they are deeply bitter at their lot in life; they live outside the laws and customs of the other "civilized" realms, making their behavior unpredictable; and they have a long-standing blood feud with the Aesir gods, putting them constantly in opposition. Their hatred of the gods is not entirely unjustified, either: after all, the Aesir are responsible for slaying the giants' forefather Ymir and almost wiping their species out of existence in the process; then there is the added insult of the gods building a fence around Midgard to defend against their presence, keeping them trapped in the icy realm of Jotunheim. The giants wage constant war against the gods in retaliation, taking any opportunity to cause them harm or even just inconvenience them however possible. Their schemes rarely amount to much, however, in large part due to the efforts of Thor and his eagerness to do battle with the giants whenever possible.

Though they can be compared to the more uniform tribal groups of the Aesir and the Vanir gods in terms of power and narrative significance, the denizens of Jotunheim are also not one uniform race or species. The term jotunn can be best viewed as a kind of catch-all, rather than a specific classification of traits; Fenrir, for example, is a giant wolf, Jörmungandr is an enormous sea serpent, and Hela is closest in form to a goddess or a human than anything else. These three siblings—the children of Loki—should all be considered jotun, or giants, even though we would not necessarily describe all of them as "giants" in our modern use of the word.

THIS PAGE: *Hel*, an 1889 illustration by Johannes Gehrts. Hel, or Hela, the queen of the dead, presided over her realm of the same name, though somewhat different in conception to the Christian Hell.

HELA

Hela, the goddess of death, is the daughter of Loki and the giantess Angurboda.

She is one of three born to the couple; the others are Fenrir, the giant wolf fated to devour Odin when Ragnarök comes, and Jörmungandr, the world-serpent that wraps its entire body around the realm of Midgard. Of the three, Hela is by far the least malevolent, which is perhaps why she is the most human-like in appearance: She is described as a pale, gloomy woman with sad eyes and a perpetual air of misfortune about her. Half of her body is the color of flesh, while the other half is either blue, grey, or black, depending on the source material. Some more dramatic illustrations feature her non-human side as a rotting corpse, or a skeleton without muscles or organs. It is likely that the more "monstrous" half of Hela's body is intended to signify her role as keeper of the underworld: not quite dead, but banished from the world of the living; not exactly evil, but too strange and dangerous to be allowed to live in Asgard.

When Loki's children were first born, he tried to hide their existence from the rest of the Aesir; though he loved them, he was also ashamed of their monstrous forms, and he was afraid the other gods would kill or exile them if they were discovered. In due time, Odin became aware of the three Jotun Loki had sired, and he had them brought to Asgard to be judged. Jörmungandr and Fenrir were both clearly monstrous, but Hela gave the All-Father more pause; her eyes were full of despair, not malice, and he felt only pity when he looked at her. Though she was a fearsome being, capable of striking a man dead with just a look, Odin could see that she had no control over the way she had been created, and that she took no joy in her powers over death. So, in an attempt to be kind while still keeping Hela safely out of Asgard, Odin made the somber woman the queen of the underworld, granting her a palace where she could comfortably rule all the kingdoms of the dead.

To Hela's domain, Hel, go all the souls who died without honor; the old, the sick, those who fought but did not draw blood, and so on. These she cares for and treats with kindness, allowing them to exist much as they did while they still lived in Midgard. These souls give Hela purpose and some amount of companionship, and their realm is nearest her palace in the center of the underworld. As for the wicked souls who are sent to her—the murderers, thieves, and liars—those are sent far into the dark recesses of the underworld, banished to various forgotten corners to freeze in icy rivers, suffer through caves filled with venomous snakes, and eventually be devoured whole by the great dragon Nidhogg.

On rare occasions, Hela is said to abandon the cold and the dark of her realm to wander Midgard on her pale, three-legged horse, as she sometimes longs for the sunlit world she has been banished from. Death follows her wherever she goes, however, as most mortals would be struck dead by the mere sight of her.

TOP: Heimdall desires Idun's return from the underworld. Hela is on the left. Illustration by Carl Emil Doepler; **ABOVE:** An illustration of Hermod, sometimes called the messenger of the gods, rides to Baldur, in Hel. From an 17th century Icelandic manuscript; **BELOW:** The three children of Loki: the serpent Jörmungandr, the wolf Fenrir, and Hel, or Hela, illustrated by Willy Pogany from *Children of Odin*.

SKADI

Skadi is the daughter of the deceased giant Thiassi, who was slain by the gods of Asgard for his kidnapping of the goddess Idunn.

TOP, MAIN IMAGE: Skaði, from Fredrik Sander's 1893 edition of the *Poetic Edda*. Engraving by Carl Fredrik von Saltza (1858–1905); **ABOVE:** *Skadi Hunting in the Mountains*, from *Asgard Stories: Tales from Norse Mythology*, by Mary H. Foster, 1901.

Skadi is a giantess, although some sources treat her more like a goddess; she attains a higher status among the Aesir through marriage, first to Njord and later to Odin himself. She is commonly associated with bowhunting, skiing, winter, and mountains. She lives in the highest reaches of the mountains, where the snow never melts. After the death of her father, Skadi lives almost entirely alone in the large castle Thiassi owned. She's an avid huntress, and her bow, snowshoes, and skis—a common tool for the Norsemen—are her most often-mentioned possessions.

She was once married to the god Njord. However, their marriage failed shortly after it began, as Njord couldn't stand the cold and desolation of the mountains where Skadi lived while Skadi couldn't stand the light and noise of Njord's seaside home. The marriage was also not entirely intentional: Skadi was only able to view the feet and legs of the men she was to choose from, and though she hoped to find Baldur, she was presented with the swarthy sea-god Njord instead. Much later in life, Skadi and Odin marry and have several children, including at least one future king of Norway.

Skadi is mentioned as the wife of Njord, and one of the goddesses present at Aegir's feast in the prose introduction to the poem *Lokasenna*. Skadi interjects after Loki has a conversation with the god Heimdallr. Skadi tells Loki that he should enjoy his freedom while it lasts; then she threatens him with the fate that both parties seem to understand he will soon meet: to be bound in a cave with sharp rocks at his back and a snake's head dripping poison venom from above. Loki responds that he was instrumental in her father's death, before accusing her of having slept with him—as he accuses most of the goddesses that evening. When Loki is chained in his cave to wait for Ragnarök, Skadi is eager to participate in his punishment; she in turn is the one to hang the venom-dripping snake's head above Loki.

AEGIR AND RAN

Aegir and Ran are two of the most often-mentioned giants in Norse mythology.

They are husband and wife; they dwell in a magnificent hall beneath the ocean, where their walls are studded with thousands of rare shells and pearls as decoration and the floor is pristine white sand. The two have a friendly relationship with the Aesir gods, and the denizens of Asgard are often invited to feasts at Aegir's palace, and vice-versa. Aegir is often depicted as an especially gracious houseguest and host alike, which is somewhat unusual for a giant. It is generally the case that the events of the poem *Lokasenna* take place in Aegir's feasting hall, where Loki arrives uninvited to insult everyone present and stab one of Aegir's servants to death. Aegir has a strong connection to the natural and primordial world, and he is occasionally described not just as a god of the ocean but as the ocean itself, personified in Aegir's form.

His wife, Ran, on the other hand, is a more hostile character; she is also friendly with the Aesir gods, but her usual state is much less warm than Aegir's. If Aegir's domain over the ocean includes its natural aspects, Ran's domain deals more with the interactions between humans and the ocean; she is the goddess of sailing accidents, drowning sailors, those who die at sea, and shipwrecks. Some source material goes further, and implies that Ran actively drags sailors to their death at the bottom of the ocean, rather than performing the more compassionate role of guiding the spirits of dead sailors. Some sources have also posited Ran as a goddess of pirates and Vikings; her connection to violent death at sea seems to track there, as well as the fact that she is often attested to have a deep love for gold and treasure. Sailors who prayed to Ran before setting sail often carried a piece of gold on their person for good luck.

The couple have nine daughters together, who are usually interpreted as being individual spirits of the waves; either they are each a different type or intensity of wave, or they are simply representations of the hidden forces that move the tides in and out.

MAIN PICTURE: Aegir, god of the sea. His wife Ran can be seen beneath the waves. Illustration by Emil Doepler, from *Walhall, die Götterwelt der Germanen*, 1905.

MAIN IMAGE: *Odin fighting with the wolf Fenrir*, by Dorothy Hardy. From *Myths of the Norsemen from the Eddas and Sagas* by Hélène Adeline Guerber, 1909.

FENRIR

Fenrir is a giant, monstrous wolf, large enough to swallow a grown man whole.

Fenrir is the son of Loki, the mischievous fire god, and Angrboda, a giantess of Jotunheim. Loki and Angrboda had three children, making Fenrir the brother of the world serpent Jörmungandr, and the queen of Hel herself. Loki attempted to keep Fenrir's existence a secret, as he did with the other two, but it was not long before Odin discovered their presence in the world and grew concerned. Though Loki allowed Odin to banish Hela and Jörmungandr from Asgard without a fight, for some reason he found himself begging the All-Father to allow Fenrir to stay in Asgard, where they might be able to raise and train him to be good rather than evil. This failed, of course, and the gods were forced to bind Fenrir until the arrival of Ragnarök breaks his shackles.

During Ragnarök, Fenrir will do battle with Odin and the gathered army of *einherjar* behind him; though Odin and his spectral warriors will fight with bravery and ferocity, Fenrir will eventually best him; in some sources Fenrir swallows Odin, while in others the king of the gods is simply torn apart or struck by a mortal blow. After Odin is killed, his son Vidar takes up his fallen spear and takes Odin's place in the battle, tearing Fenrir's jaws apart and finally killing the wolf.

Unlike Jörmungandr, who is more bestial in nature and is never shown to speak, and unlike Hela, whose character is kinder than her nature implies, Fenrir truly seems to be entirely evil. He is shown to be intelligent enough to speak and reason, and he communicates with the gods as they raise him—but he takes more joy in causing pain and fear than anything else, and makes no attempt to hide his bloodlust. When the gods finally attempt to bind Fenrir to keep him from hurting anyone, he bites Tyr's right hand off, when he realizes he cannot break free of his chains.

The great wolves Hati and Skoll are sometimes believed to be the children of Fenrir, though it is difficult to be sure. During the Fimbulwinter that signifies Ragnarök's approach, it is mentioned that Angrboda will be able to feed the wolves Hati and Skol with such an abundance of the bones of murderers and criminals (as crime will be rampant throughout the world), that they will never go hungry.

Fenrir was an important figure in Old Norse religion. Whilst many of the well-known figures of Norse mythology are today attested in only one or two surviving artefacts, images of Fenrir and his deeds can be found etched in a number of carved standing stones throughout Scandinavia.

TOP: Son of Loki, Fenrir is a great wolf. Bound by the gods to prevent him killing anyone, he nevertheless bites off the hand of Tyr, when he attempts to feed him. Illustration by Emil Doepler, from *Walhall, die Götterwelt der Germanen*, 1905; **ABOVE:** An 17th century Icelandic manuscript which depicts the story of Tyr, losing his hand to the monstrous wolf Fenrir.

THE BINDING OF FENRIR

As Fenrir grew among the gods of Asgard, he quickly approached the point at which no god or giant could hope to contest his strength.

TOP: "The gods were so delighted that they began to laugh." *The Binding of Fenrir*, illustration by George Wright, from a children's book illustration, mid-20th century; **ABOVE:** *Tyr feeding Fenrir*, illustration by Huard, from *The Heroes of Asgard: Tales from Scandinavian Mythology* by A. & E. Keary, 1891. Macmillan and Co., London and New York; **RIGHT:** Liebig collectors' card, 1934: Fenrir the wolf is bound by the gods and bites off the right hand of the god Tyr; **OPPOSITE:** *The Binding of Fenrir*, by Dorothy Hardy. From *Myths of the Norsemen from the Eddas and Sagas* by Hélène Adeline Guerber, 1909.

Already the gods were too afraid of the great wolf to approach him with food; only the fearless Tyr was brave enough to feed Fenrir, though it went unappreciated. Odin worried that the wolf would soon hurt someone. Finally, one night after the wolf had returned to his lair, Odin called a meeting of the gods. He told them of his fears, saying they must find some plan for guarding themselves and their home against this monster. They could not kill him, however, as they had sworn an oath to never shed blood within the walls of Asgard. There was silence for a long moment before Thor stood, declaring that he would use Mjölnir to forge a mighty chain to bind Fenrir. The gods cheered, sure of Thor's success, and the god of thunder seized his hammer and strode off to his forge. There he worked all night, and the sound of Mjölnir hammering at the anvil echoed through all of Asgard.

The next night, Thor brought forth his new-made chain and approached Fenrir. To the gods' surprise, the proud wolf willingly let himself be bound with the chain; but all at once Fenrir gave one bound forward, broke the great chain as though it were made of paper, and walked off to his lair as if nothing had happened. Thor, not discouraged in the slightest, declared that he would make another chain, this one far stronger than the first. Again he set to work, and for three nights and three days Thor worked tirelessly at his forge without resting.

The new chain was so heavy that even the mighty Thor could hardly lift it. This time Fenrir was not so willing to be bound; but the gods talked of his great strength and told him they were sure he would easily break this chain as well. After a while he agreed to let them put it around his neck, and, just as before, he tore through the enormous chain without any effort at all. The Aesir met again that night in Odin's palace, and this time Thor sat in sullen silence. Instead Freyr, the king of the elves, spoke first. "Since we cannot make a chain strong enough to bind Fenrir, let us go to the dwarves and ask them to make us a magic chain instead."

The dwarves, an untrustworthy lot, were afraid of Odin and dared not disobey him directly. After two days and two nights of work, a messenger returned to Asgard holding a small, fine, chain, which the dwarves had named Gleipnir. "This may seem to you to be small and weak; but it is a most wonderful piece of work," he said. "This chain can never be broken; and if you can once put it on Fenrir, he will never be able to throw it off."

Odin feared that Fenrir would not let them bind him a third time, so he proposed they treat this last attempt as a contest of strength. As they all gathered around Fenrir, Freyr brought out Gleipnir, and asked them all to try to break it. Thor and Tyr tried in vain, and Thor said, "I do not believe anyone but Fenrir can break it—and maybe even he cannot do it."

Fenrir did not want to be bound again; the chain was so thin that he thought it must be magical to be so strong—and Fenrir did not trust magic. But he was very proud of his strength, and, for fear of being called a coward, said at last he would participate. His one condition was to hold the right hand of one of the gods in his teeth while they bound him, as insurance that they were not using magic to trick him.

When the gods heard this, they looked at each other, and all but one of them drew back. Only the brave Tyr stepped forward, quietly putting his hand into Fenrir's mouth. The other gods then wrapped the chain around Fenrir and fastened it to a huge boulder. Fenrir leapt and struggled against the chain to no avail, only drawing it tighter with each attempt. The Aesir cheered at their victory, but joy soon turned to sorrow when they saw that the brave Tyr had lost his right hand; the dreadful wolf had shut his teeth together in his rage when he found he could not get free.

THIS PAGE: Thor and the jötunn Hymir at sea, where Thor gets Jörmungandr on the hook; from an Icelandic 17th century manuscript.

JÖRMUNGANDR

Jörmungandr, also known as the world serpent or the Midgard serpent, is a colossal sea-serpent who lives in the deepest recesses of the ocean surrounding Midgard.

The sea-serpent is one of the three monstrous children of Loki and Angrboda, all of whom Odin exiled or bound to keep them from causing chaos and destruction. When Odin first saw the serpent Loki had sired, he did not hesitate to pick the creature up and hurl it out of Asgard and into the ocean—but Jörmungandr took to his new environment well, and before long he began to grow to impossible proportions; within months he was large enough to wrap his entire body all the way around the world of Midgard and bite down on his tail, becoming a physical barrier between the world of men and Jotunheim.

When Ragnarök comes, Jörmungandr will cause a series of cataclysmic events by releasing his tail from his mouth and writhing up out of the ocean and onto dry land. His escape to the surface world will cause huge tidal waves and earthquakes, and huge areas of land will be flooded. As he roams across the world to meet with his brother Fenrir, the sickly venom that spews from Jörmungandr's throat will poison the air and the ground for miles in all directions, killing any plants, animals and men who come too close.

Thor and Jörmungandr have a long-standing rivalry. Though the world serpent is not usually attested to be especially intelligent—he does not speak or plot but instead acts on violent instinct—he has a specific hatred for the god of thunder, who once managed to hook him on the end of a fishing line using an ox's head as bait. Thor would have slain Jörmungandr then, had the giant Hymir not cut the line in fear.

During Thor and Loki's journey to Utgard in Jotunheim, one of the trials of strength Thor faces is to lift an impossibly heavy cat off the ground. Thor succeeds only in raising one of the cat's paws into the air—and it is revealed later that the cat was the magically-disguised Jörmungandr, and that Thor had lifted the serpent almost entirely into the air without realizing it.

When Thor and Jörmungandr do battle again at Ragnarök, Thor will finally slay the world serpent, but the deluge of venom that floods from the monster's corpse will strike Thor dead in turn.

The image of a snake eating its own tail, known as an *ouroboros*, is frequently seen in cultures all over the world. The ouroboros tends to symbolize cycles of life, death, and rebirth—such as the cycle of Ragnarök in Norse mythology, which will continue to repeat for eternity. Similar symbols and myths can be found in the ancient cultures of China, Egypt, Greece, and South America, as well as in belief systems like Gnosticism and esotericism.

ABOVE: The ouroboros or uroboros is an ancient symbol depicting a serpent or dragon eating its own tail. The ouroboros entered Western tradition via ancient Egyptian iconography and the Greek magical tradition. It was adopted as a symbol in Gnosticism and Hermeticism and most notably in alchemy; **BELOW:** A scene from Ragnarök, the final battle between Thor and Jörmungandr. Illustration by Emil Doepler, from *Walhall, die Götterwelt der Germanen*, 1905.

NIDHOGG

THIS PAGE: Nidhogg gnaws at the world tree. Woodcarving relief by Dagfin Werenskiold, on the exterior facade of Oslo City hall.

Nidhogg, whose name translates roughly to "curse-striker" or "he who strikes with malice," is the largest and most hateful of all the dragons mentioned in Norse mythology.

Nidhogg lives at the base of the world tree, beneath its roots that reach down to Helheim. There he spends almost all of his time chewing on the strongest roots of Yggdrasil, trying to tear down the world tree. On occasion, the dragon pauses in his attack on the tree to devour the bones and souls of those who were sent to hell after committing terrible crimes in life. It is doubtful that Nidhogg is intentionally helping the goddess Hela punish these souls for the things they've done; it's more likely that the dragon simply eats whatever is put in front of him.

Nidhogg is a perfect example of blind, chaotic evil, which is a surprisingly uncommon concept in Norse mythology, where even the cruelest villains are usually acting with some level of intelligence and purpose. Nidhogg's destruction of the tree is directly self-destructive, as not only does the tree stand directly over Nidhogg's head and would crush him if it were to fall, it also supports all nine realms; if Yggdrasil collapsed, all of creation would follow. It is also a particularly cruel act on the dragon's part, as Yggdrasil has been attested to feel the pain of all the creatures it supports, that are constantly gnawing at its branches and leaves for sustenance; this is a sacrifice Yggdrasil willingly makes to sustain life, but Nidhogg gains nothing from his destruction of the world tree's roots.

Nidhogg is surrounded by a countless number of smaller lizards, snakes, serpents, and lesser dragons, all of whom join him in their constant devouring of the roots of Yggdrasil. The only other living beings he interacts with, for the most part, are the great eagle at the very top of the world tree, and the squirrel Ratatoskr, who ferries insulting messages between the two. Though the dragon and the eagle will never meet, they hate each other more than any two enemies in any of the Norse myths—aided in part by Ratatoskr's editorializing of their messages.

When the sun and the moon are eaten by Skoll and Hati during Ragnarök, Nidhogg will finally succeed in gnawing through one of Yggdrasil's roots, which will cause the whole cosmos to shake. Nidhogg is expected to survive the events of Ragnarök; after the world is reborn, he will remain in his place under Yggdrasil to drink the rivers of blood that will seep down through the earth from the battlefield above.

TOP, INSET: Metalwork depicting Nidhogg, the Norse dragon; **ABOVE:** The world tree Yggdrasil, with the assorted animals that live in it and on it; **LEFT:** Unfortunates in Hel wade through venom, dripping from the serpents above, in Náströnd ("Corpse Shore") as attested to, in *Völuspá*. Náströnd is a region in Hel where Nidhogg lives and chews on corpses. It is the afterlife for those guilty of murder, adultery, and oath-breaking, considered the worst possible crimes. Probable preparatory drawing for woodcut.

SKOLL AND HATI

In their constant efforts to undo the work of the Asgard gods, the giants of Jotunheim had set a pair of giant, vicious wolves in chase from the moment they first saw the sun and moon race across the sky.

MAIN IMAGE: *The Wolves Pursuing Sol and Mani* by John Charles Dollman, 1909; **BELOW RIGHT:** *Far Away and Long Ago*, by WillyPogany. Sköll chases Sól, the personified sun, and his brother Hati Hróðvitnisson chases Máni, the personified moon. From *The Children of Odin* by Padraic Colum, 1920. New York: The Macmillan Company.

The wolves, who were named Skoll and Hati, had no purpose but to chase down the gleaming chariots of Sol and Mani, the sun and the moon. Skoll's target was the sun, while Hati hunted the moon, and for countless years they were never quite fast enough to drag their prey from the sky. They, like many of the other giants, were desperate to rid the world of light and warmth, things they had long been denied in their icy, barren home of Jotunheim.

In some iterations of the Skoll/Hati myth, it is Fenrir who is prophesied to devour the sun and plunge the world into darkness. Though it is not stated explicitly, a popular theory is that Skoll and Hati are relatives or children of Fenrir. Angrboda, Fenrir's giantess mother is prophesied to nurture and feed the two voracious wolves during the long period of cold and hunger that is the Fimbulwinter, implying that she has some maternal or familial care for them. During the Fimbulwinter, there will be such an unending amount of wanton violence, betrayal, and crime throughout Midgard that Angrboda will have no shortage of the wolves' favorite food: the bones of murderers and thieves.

When Ragnarök begins in earnest, Skoll and Hati will finally overtake their prey. The death of Baldur and the misery of the Fimbulwinter combined will render Sol and Mani and their horses too weak to keep up their constant gallop across the sky, whilst those same aspects of darkness and despair only make the two wolves stronger and faster. When they finally draw level with the sun and the moon, Skoll will attack first, crushing the sun in his jagged teeth. Hati will drag the moon out of the sky and tear it apart on the earth, and as the blood of the two celestial gods floods Midgard, all the stars in the sky will begin to die. This will continue the chain reaction that leads to the events of Ragnarök—the breaking of bonds, the rising of the seas, and the inevitable destruction of the world itself.

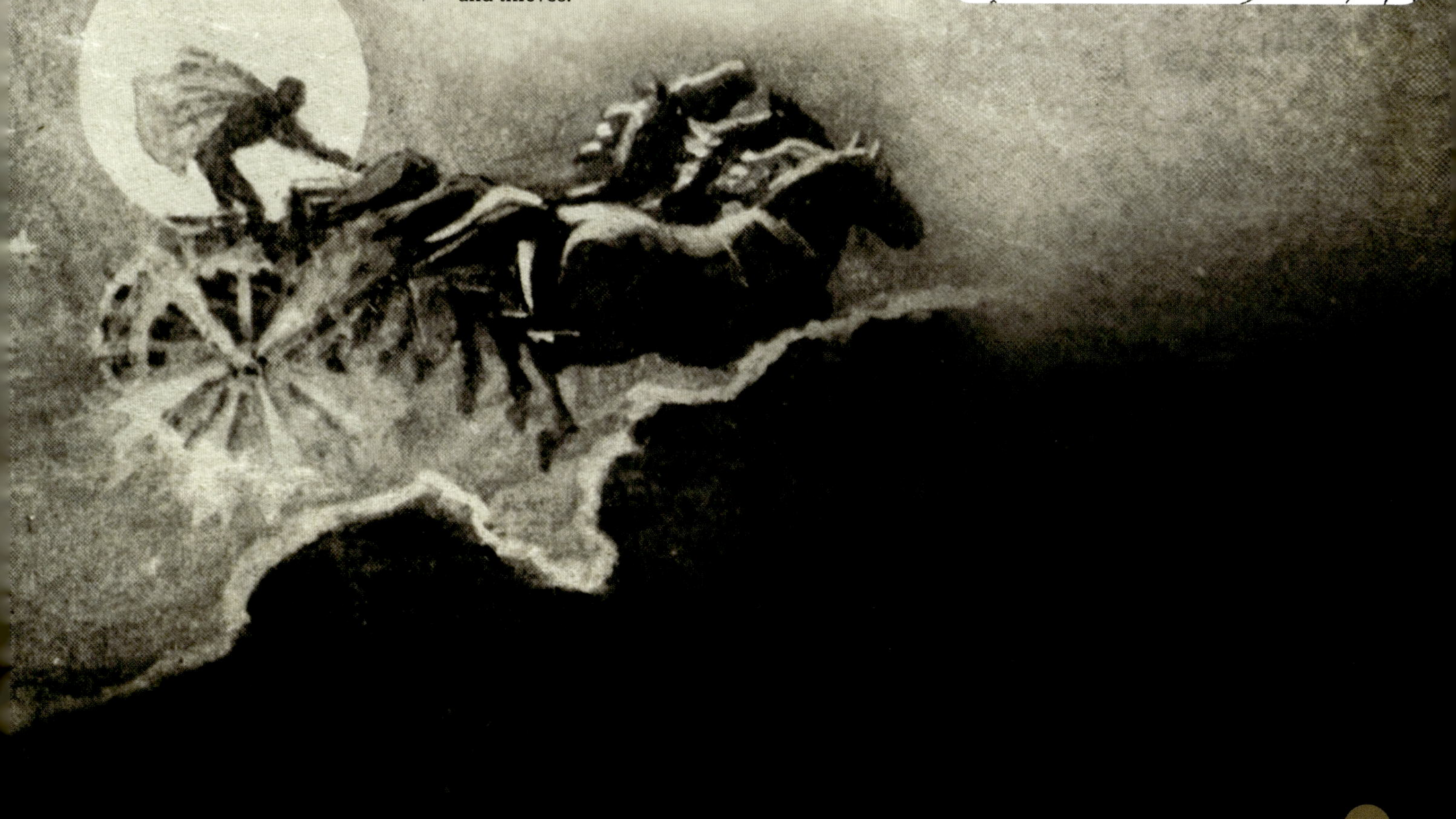

SURTR

Surtr, or Surt, is the fire giant who guards, and likely rules, the primordial realm of fire known as Muspelheim.

Little is ever spoken of Surtr outside of the myths that detail the very beginning of creation and the events of Ragnarök that undo it all. As for the eons of time between these two points, Surtr never leaves his station outside the gates of Muspelheim. For similar reasons, little is known of Muspelheim itself, beyond its role in the beginning and end of the world. Surtr is one of a number of fire giants who do not appear elsewhere in Norse mythology. Although they are opposite the frost giants thematically—fire versus ice, and so on—they are allied against the gods of Asgard and the men of Midgard. When Ragnarök comes, Surtr will finally abandon his post, and he will lead a number of fire giants known as the Sons of Muspell through a rift between the worlds into Midgard, where they will lay waste to all life on earth.

Surtr wields a sword of fire and is usually depicted as standing much taller than any of the other gods or giants; he is able to level mountains and cast the entire world in fire with a single swing of his blade. In the final battle of Ragnarök, Surtr and Freyr will fight; although Freyr will fight nobly and hold the fire giant at bay for as long as possible, he will do so without the use of his magic sword and eventually fall to Surtr. When Freyr dies, there is no one left to stop the fire giant from destroying the world.

Surtr uses his flaming sword to burn everything down, annihilating all remaining life on the battlefield (including himself and the forces of Jotunheim) until there is nothing but ash. According to some sources, he destroys all the kingdoms of hell and even obliterates the dead spirits who linger there. The heat of the flames that he covers the earth in is so intense that the seas themselves boil, killing all sea life as well as all plant, animal, and human life. Similar to a forest recovering after a wildfire, however, a new earth eventually rises from the ashes, and the boiling seas become cold again, allowing life to return and creating a new, young earth that will thrive . . . until Ragnarök occurs again.

Unlike most of the other forces at play in Ragnarok's final battle, it is unclear what Surtr's motivations are for going to battle against the Aesir gods. We can see why the giants of Jotunheim and Loki and his children despise the gods, but there has been no interaction between the Asgardians and the fire giants of Muspelheim. It is possible that they are simply single-purpose beings who live for nothing more than the eventual destruction of the world in order for it to be reborn again, or that they are simply motivated by hatred and violence and are drawn to the battle of Ragnarök for no other reason than to join in the chaos.

TOP: Surtr, from *Danmarks, Norges og Sverigs Historie, populært fremstillet efter de bedste trykte Kilder*, by N. Bache. From the British Library; **ABOVE:** Surtr (left) and Freyr (right), by the Danish artist Lorenz Frølich; **BELOW:** *Surtr Hurls Fire*, relief sculpture by German artist Ernst Alpers, 1867; **OPPOSITE, MAIN IMAGE:** *The Giant with the Flaming Sword*, by John Charles Dollman, 1909. From *Myths of the Norsemen from the Eddas and Sagas*. London: Harrap.

6

MONSTERS AND OTHER CREATURES

MAIN IMAGE: Kraken attacking a ship during a storm, c. 1700.

After the gods killed Ymir and began constructing the earth from his remains, they began to notice tiny creatures thriving like maggots in the unused remnants of the first giant's flesh.

DWARVES

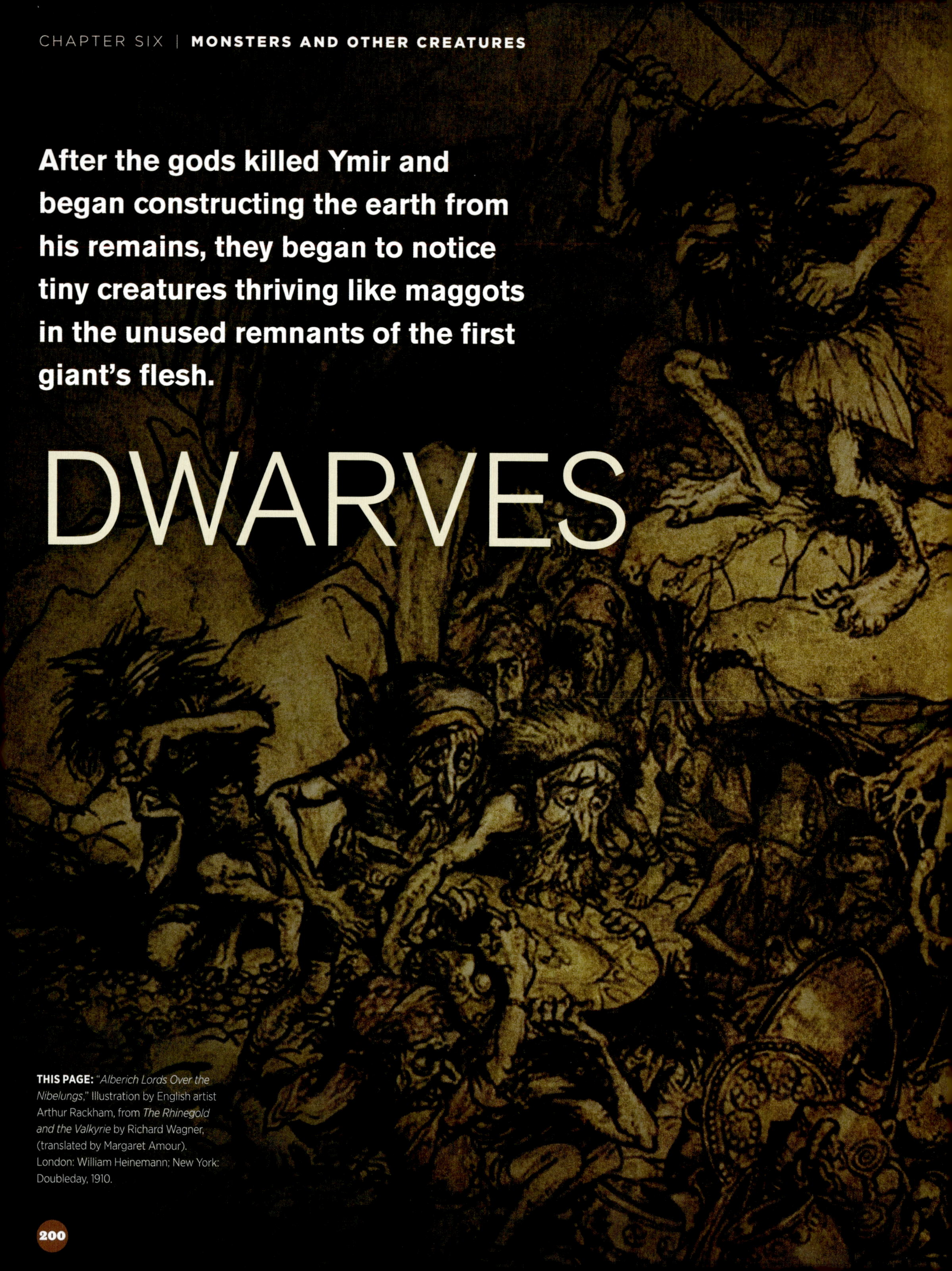

THIS PAGE: "*Alberich Lords Over the Nibelungs*," Illustration by English artist Arthur Rackham, from *The Rhinegold and the Valkyrie* by Richard Wagner, (translated by Margaret Amour). London: William Heinemann; New York: Doubleday, 1910.

When the gods examined these creatures, they discovered that they were not insects but small, sentient beings who had not yet been given physical form; curious, the gods bestowed physical form and intelligence on them, and the tiny creatures grew into what were later known as the elves. They were generally divided into two classes. Those who were beautiful, kind, and wise, whom the gods called the light elves, were sent to Alfheim. Those who were ugly, cruel, and treacherous, whom the gods called dark elves, or dwarves, were sent to Svartalfheim.

The subterranean realm of Svartalfheim was located deep beneath the earth, accessible only through winding systems of caves and tunnels, so that no God or mortal would have to look upon their hideous faces or be threatened by their malicious nature. Should the dwarves ever return to the surface world without permission, they would be turned immediately to stone under the light of the sun, meaning they could only surface in darkness, without the express permission of the gods.

However, because the dwarves were valuable for their unmatched skill in mining, metalworking, and the crafting of magical items, they were not entirely separated from all other life; many gods and men would visit the dwarves in their underground cave systems to commission the creation of magical items, seek their wisdom on certain niche issues, and ask for assistance dealing with cursed and enchanted trinkets. The dwarves were known for their love of precious metals, jewels, treasure, and magical items. Because they spent all of their time underground, mining and forging unique and wondrous artefacts, they quickly became the most adept smiths, jewelers, and craftsmen of all living things.

As is the case with a number of the gods' enemies, it could be argued that their treacherous nature and maliciousness towards the gods is not an innate aspect of the dwarves' character, but rather a response to the way they were treated by the gods. Just as the frost giants were cast out into Jotunheim for the crimes of their ancestors, the dwarves were banished deep into the earth as their physical appearance assumed an evil nature.

The dwarves also had some magical abilities of their own that even the gods did not possess. According to various sources, they were capable of concealing themselves through invisibility or changing their shape to hide among the rocks and stones, a skill they used often to escape danger and trick trespassers in Svartalfheim into danger. They were also able to transport themselves instantly from one place to another without effort, allowing them to appear without warning in places where they may or may not be welcome. Many people believed that echoes in caves, valleys, and cliffsides were actually dwarves' voices, mimicking the voices of travelers in order to mock and mislead them.

Amongst the many wonderful things made by dwarves, several feature centrally in well-known Norse myths. The dwarves were responsible for creating Mjölnir, the mighty hammer of Thor; Gleipnir, the chain that bound Fenrir the great wolf; Skidbladnir, the ship that can sail through the sky and fold up small enough to fit in a pocket; Gungnir, the magical sphere of Odin; Brisingamen, Freya's beautiful necklace; and the golden-spun hair of Sif, the wife of Thor.

TOP LEFT: *Svartalfheim.* From *The Temple: Mythologies of the Most Exquisite Cultural Peoples up to Christianity*, by Johannes Minckwitz. Alfred Oehmigke, Leipzig, 1880; **TOP RIGHT:** *The Third Gift, An Enormous Hammer*, by American writer and artist Elmer Boyd Smith (1860–1943). The dwarven Sons of Ivaldi forge the hammer Mjölnir for Thor, while Loki looks on. On the table before them sits their other creations: the multiplying ring Draupnir, the boar Gullinbursti, the ship Skiðblaðnir, the spear Gungnir, and golden hair for the goddess Sif; **ABOVE:** An illustration of two dwarves for *Völuspá*.

Of the maggot-like creatures that bred from the discarded flesh of Ymir, the first of the frost giants, not all were perceived to be as ugly and malicious as the dwarves.

LIGHT ELVES

Many of those small creatures were born to be beautiful, kind, and gentle; these the gods called the light elves. The light elves, often referred to simply as "elves" in contrast to the dark elves being named "dwarves," were sent to live in the sunlit, airy plains of Alfheim, high in the branches of Yggdrasil. Although the realm of Alfheim is not attested frequently in surviving sources of Norse mythology, it is often depicted as a kind of heaven or paradise. The elves are such unquestionably good creatures in most depictions of Norse mythology that the realm they live in follows suit; Alfheim is generally shown to be home to vibrant flowers, butterflies, and natural beauty. Light elves have often been compared or conflated with the fairies or *fae folk* of Celtic mythology due to their delicate appearance, mysterious nature, and otherworldly abilities. The fairies of Celtic mythology, however, are a much more capricious species, and many of the myths that they feature in involve the attempts of humans to either appease, trick, or escape the ire of the fae folk. Norse elves have also been compared to the angels of Christianity over the years, especially during the conversion of ancient Scandinavia into Christianity after the end of the Viking age.

The light elves of Norse mythology were ruled over by Freyr, the Vanir god who was generally perceived as being among the fairest and kindest of the gods—perhaps second only to Baldur himself. Freyr was given his rulership over Alfheim as an infant or a young child, as the gods immediately recognized that he would be best suited to govern a realm of similarly kind, beautiful creatures. Some sources refer to the Vanir gods themselves as elves, which does correlate with the description of many of the Vanir gods as beautiful beings who are more in touch with nature and magic than most of the Aesir gods. The elves are also often associated with a number of minor deities, nature spirits and other beings that exist vaguely between the realm of human and god; their vaguely-defined nature means elves are often used as a kind of catch-all for any non-malevolent non-human creatures.

There was also some overlap between Norse ancestor worship and their belief in the existence of the race of elves. Some may have believed that humans could become light elves after their death, as a kind of ascension from the mortal world into a higher form, while others believed that Alfheim could serve as an afterlife where one could go after death if they lived a glorious and respectable enough life. There are some minor mentions of relationships between elves and humans, resulting in half-elf, half-human children. It is unclear whether the elves were ever worshiped as such in the way that the gods were, or whether they were merely respected and perhaps feared as mysterious supernatural beings.

MAIN IMAGE: *Älvalek* (*Dancing Fairies*), 1866, by the Swedish artist August Malmström (1829–1901); **TOP:** *Fairy in Irises*, Watercolor, 1888, by American artist Dora Wheeler Keith; **ABOVE:** The god Freyr, riding his boar, Gullinbursti. Illustration by Ludwig Pietsch, from *Manual of Mythology: Greek and Roman, Norse, and Old German, Hindu and Egyptian Mythology*, by Alexander Murray, 1874. London, Asher and Co.

Of Odin's many abilities and magical possessions, there were few things he was more proud of than Sleipnir.

SLEIPNIR
ODIN'S EIGHT-LEGGED HORSE

As Odin was the king of the gods of Asgard, Sleipnir was a king among horses; he was the fastest and strongest of any horse who ever lived, and he was able to ride through the sky and across water just as easily as he could across land. His unique eight-legged form is likely due to his parentage, as he has some Jotun blood in his veins. The three best known children of Loki are Hela, Fenrir, and Jormunganr, the three monstrous offspring of Loki and the giantess Angrboda, who all play an instrumental role in the coming of Ragnarök and the twilight of the gods. Sleipnir, however, is another of Loki's children, one who does not bear their propensity towards violence. Sleipnir is the son of Loki and the horse Svadilfari, who belonged to the giant who built the great walls surrounding Asgard.

When the gods hired the mysterious giant—who had disguised his true identity—to construct the walls of Asgard, Loki convinced them to offer the builder a contract that he would never be able to complete in time so that they could avoid paying him. When the deadline for the construction project drew close and it became clear that the giant was going to complete the walls in time—which would mean that the gods would have to allow him to take Freya as his wife, as well as ownership of the sun and moon—Loki was then forced to find a way to get out of the deal he had convinced them to make. Loki's solution was to distract the horse Svadilfari, who was a key component in helping the giant drag the heavy stones from a quarry to Asgard so that he could build them into the walls. Loki transformed into a horse himself and led the horse Svadilfari away into the woods, and the two did not return until after the deadline had already come and gone the next day. Much later, Loki—still in the form of a mare—gave birth to a horse who was named Sleipnir. As all of Loki's children had some monstrous quality to set them apart, Sleipnir had eight legs; this clearly worked in his favor, however, making him the fastest and most enduring of all horses.

Sleipnir features in numerous myths, most of which mention him as the primary mode of transportation for Odin, although he is sometimes lent out to the other gods in times of great need. When Odin first mastered the runes, he carved magic runes into the teeth of Sleipnir as well as into the shaft of his spear, granting them additional magical abilities and protections. The horse features primarily in the myth of Thor and Hrungnir, which begins with Odin and Hrungnir entering a race to see which of their horses—Sleipnir or Gullfaxi—is the fastest. Sleipnir defeats Gullfaxi in the race, proving him the fastest horse among both the gods and the frost giants.

OPPOSITE: "Raging, Wotan / Rides to the rock!," Illustration by English artist Arthur Rackham, from *The Rhinegold and the Valkyrie* by Richard Wagner, (translated by Margaret Amour). London: William Heinemann; New York: Doubleday, 1910; **TOP:** *Loki and Svadilfari* by Dorothy Hardy, from *Myths of the Norsemen from the Eddas and Sagas;* **ABOVE:** Odin riding his 8-legged horse, Sleipnir, while holding his enchanted spear Gungnir; **BELOW LEFT:** *Odin and Sleipnir*, by John Bauer.

HULDRA

TOP: *Huldra's Nymphs* by Bernard Evans Ward (1857–1933); **ABOVE:** A huldra meets a man in the forest.

The huldra is a beautiful, elf-like female forest spirit depicted in Norse mythology.

Some sources describe a single being named "Huldra," while others depict the huldra as a species of supernatural creature. Huldra appear at first glance as an especially attractive human woman, although their true nature can be determined if the traveler they approach notices their animal tail—usually that of a cow or fox—or their back, which has the appearance of a hollowed-out tree. Huldra tend to appear from the darkness of the forest and approach human men traveling alone, who they will attempt to lure off the path and into the forest. Their precise goals are not consistently stated; in many myths, huldra share similarities with other supernatural creatures such as mermaids or sirens, who take the form of beautiful women in the hopes of luring human men to their deaths. Some myths state that the goal of a huldra is to trick or force a human man into marrying her, at which point she will lose her inhuman qualities, become fully human, and in some sources also gain supernatural physical strength.

Other myths, however, imply that the huldra are kind, gentle creatures who will be helpful and friendly as long as humans behave as such to them. They are mentioned to be particularly friendly to charcoal makers; in exchange for food and a place by the fire, a huldra will watch over the kiln so that the human charcoal burner can sleep.

A male huldra is known as a huldrekall.

KRAKEN

The Kraken is an enormous sea monster, first depicted in Norse mythology, that has since expanded to appear in the stories and folklore of cultures all over the world.

Kraken—generally assumed to be a species, rather than a single unique creature—were said to grow to colossal sizes, often as large as a mile in length, and are usually depicted as large enough to pick up an entire sailing ship with one tentacle and swallow it whole. The Kraken were believed to be real, extant threats to anyone who went out on a long sailing mission overseas, especially into uncharted waters. It is believed that the original inspiration for the Kraken myth was likely a sighting of a giant squid, a species of deep-sea squid, which can grow up to 40 feet in length and certainly would have seemed like a giant sea monster to the ancient Norsemen. Kraken were usually depicted as a giant squid or octopus, although some sources have also described them as being vaguely crablike with pincers or armored chitin to protect them. Many myths describe Kraken so large that they could be mistaken for an entire island, allowing human sailors to land and climb onto their backs only to submerge and drown them all at once. Some of the first depictions of the Kraken come from the *Orvar-Oddr* saga, a collection of stories detailing the adventures of a legendary hero named Oddr. The Kraken has often been conflated with the *hafgufa*, or "sea-reek," a similar sea monster of Norse mythology; whether they were the same creature or two distinct species is a matter of debate.

TOP: *Octopus vulgaris*, 1896, by Comingio Merculiano (1845–1915); **ABOVE:** *St. Brendan and the Whale*, from a 15th-century manuscript. Hafgufa is a legendary massive sea monster. When the creature remains stationary it's mistaken for an island; **BELOW, LEFT:** A ship is ensnared by a "kraken." Engraving by W.H. Lizars (1788–1859).

THE NORNS

The Norns, or Fates, are the only beings over whom the gods held no authority.

They are often depicted as three sisters, sometimes as descendants of the giant Norvi. Though they are free to roam the realms as they wish, the Norns usually shelter in the roots of the great ash Yggdrasil, near the Urdar fountain. Although there are many Norns, some named and some not, the three Norns, Urd, Verdandi, and Skuld are the most well-known. Urd and Verdandi are considered to kind and benevolent, while the third, Skuld, relentlessly undoes their work and often tears it angrily to shreds, scattering the remnants to the winds.

The Norns understand the destiny of every living thing, even of the Aesir themselves, and they alone know the truth of every aspect of creation. At the birth of every child the Norns are present to determine its fate, and no human or god lives one day longer than the Norns grant him. They do not necessarily control fate itself, however; the tapestries and webs that the Norns weave are of a design they do not choose, and their role is to read and interpret the patterns that emerge when they are finished.

The Norns often feature in Norse myths as oracles or seers; Odin regularly consults with the Norns that gather around Yggdrasil's roots to glean some knowledge of the future from them, though he is almost always unhappy with what he learns. The Norns are often unwilling to divulge everything they know, although it has been shown that knowledge of the future does not allow one to alter the course of events—as with Odin's attempts to avert Ragnarök. The Norns are also responsible for watering and caring for the world tree, as well as (in some sources) growing the golden apples carried by the goddess Idun.

RATATOSKR

The squirrel Ratatoskr, whose name translates roughly to "drill-tooth," is both a pest and a vital component of Yggdrasil's ecosystem.

Ratatoskr scampers perpetually up and down the trunk of the world tree, back and forth across its branches, and in and out of every hollow, knot, and tangle of roots, all across the great ash tree. The squirrel serves the valuable purpose of carrying messages between the many denizens of the tree, as he moves much faster across Yggdrasil's surface than any other creature could hope to. He spends most of his time, however, carrying and embellishing increasingly inflammatory messages between the great eagle that roosts in the highest branches of the tree and the dragon Nidhogg that gnaws perpetually at Yggdrasil's roots, forever hoping to start a proper fight between the two. Ratatoskr is known as a font of unreliable gossip and hearsay, though his time spent all over the world tree does give him the occasional rare insight to share with visitors. As is the case for most of the creatures that live in and on the world tree, Ratatoskr often chews on the leaves and bark of the tree for sustenance. Ratatoskr is one of several creatures who are depicted as less-than-welcome guests among Yggdrasil's branches; his role is primarily one of stirring up malice and antagonizing the other creatures of the world tree, which depicts him as a destabilizing force in what might otherwise be a harmonious ecosystem. His gnawing on the bark of Yggdrasil, weakening the structure as a whole, can be interpreted the same way.

ABOVE: Ratatoskr in Yggdrasil. From the 17th century Icelandic manuscript. The Árni Magnússon Institute, Iceland; **MAIN IMAGE, LEFT:** The Nornic trio of Urðr, Verðandi, and Skuld, beneath Yggdrasil, the World Tree. On the trunk of the tree is the squirrel Ratatoskr. Illustration by Ludwig Burger.

HUGIN AND MUNIN

The two ravens Hugin (Thought) and Munin (Memory) are Odin's closest companions; they can almost always be found perched upon Odin's shoulders as he sits upon his high throne above Asgard

ABOVE: Swedish postage stamp, with runes running down the left vertical, Odin on Sleipnir, one of his two wolves, and his two ravens, Hugin and Munin; **MAIN IMAGE, TOP:** "The Ravens of Wotan," 1911, by Arthur Rackham; **RIGHT:** *Wotan*, marble statue by Rudolf Maison (1854–1904).

The ravens act as Odin's eyes and ears out in the nine realms of the cosmos, and he sends them out into the world every morning, anxiously watching for their return at nightfall when they whisper the news of everything they have seen and heard into his ears. This, combined with his high throne that gives him an unmatched vantage point over all of creation, is how Odin is able to know almost everything that happens outside of Asgard. The two ravens have come to Odin's aid many times throughout the canon of Norse mythology; for instance, when the giant Gunlod was tasked with the protection of the mead of inspiration—something Odin desperately wanted in his endless quest for knowledge—it was Hugin and Munin who led Odin to the cave where the mead of inspiration was hidden. Today, Ravens are still closely associated with the values the Norsemen placed in them—wisdom, the occult, and a general sense of foreboding. Ravens are mischievous and highly intelligent birds, qualities Odin has been shown to value a great deal; this may also partially explain why this specific bird was chosen to depict Odin's familiars.

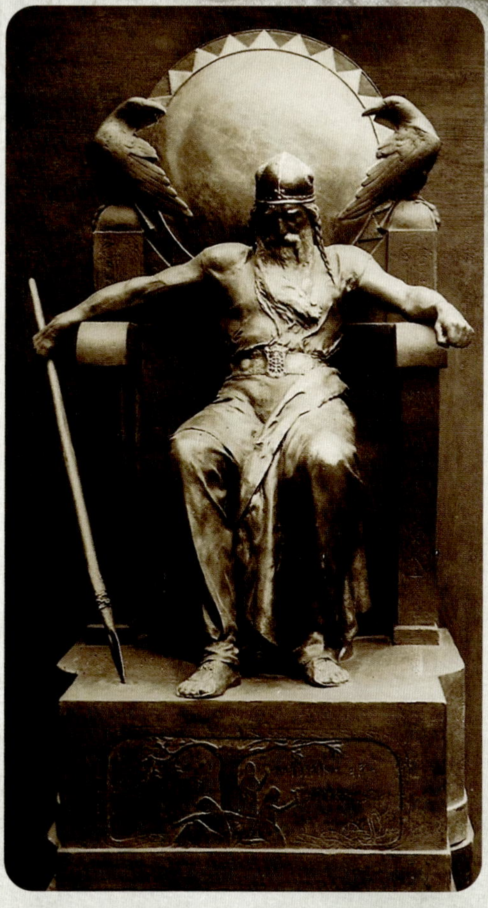

TROLLS

Trolls in Norse mythology are stocky, physically powerful creatures.

Their great physical strength often results in gods and mortals hiring Trolls to construct buildings and bridges, although those who attempt to cheat a troll out of their payment will usually regret it. The dwarves of Svartalfheim are also occasionally referred to as trolls, depending on the source material. Troll women are said to have the power to change themselves into *Maras*, or nightmares, and use that power to torment anyone they please in their sleep; but if the victim succeeds in covering up the hole through which a Mara entered his house, she will be trapped inside.

One notable myth focuses on the story of Helva, daughter of the Lord of Nesvek, who was being courted by a poor man named Esbern Snare. Their relationship was rejected by her proud father with the words: "When you have built a beautiful church at Kallundborg, then will I allow you to marry Helva." Esbern, although of low birth, was just as proud as Helva's father, and was determined to marry Helva. So off he strode to find a troll in Ullshoi Hill, and made a deal with him. The troll would build a church for Esbern, on completion of which Esbern was to guess the troll builder's name—or forfeit his own eyes and heart.

The troll worked night and day, and as the building took shape, Esbern Snare grew more and more desperate. He listened at the crevices of the hill by night; he watched during the day; he grew pale and thin with anxiety; he even asked the elves to aid him. All the same, nothing helped him uncover the name of the troll. Soon the church was complete but for a single pillar, and worn out by despair, Esbern sank to the floor with exhaustion, still hearing the troll hammering the last stones in the quarry underground. "Fool that I am," he said bitterly, "I have built my own tomb."

Then, louder than the sound of the troll's hammering, Esbern heard the sound of a troll-wife singing to her baby, telling the child that soon its father "Fine" would return bringing a mortal's eyes and heart to eat.

Sure of his victory, the troll hurried to Kallundborg with the last stone. "Too late, Fine!" cried Esbern, and at the word, the troll vanished with his stone; the church was finished, and Esbern and Helva were finally free to be happily wed.

TOP: *In the Christmas Night*, John Bauer, 1913; **ABOVE:** The church "Vor Frue Kirke" in Kalundborg, West Zealand, Denmark; **BELOW:** Statue of Danish nobleman Esbern Snare.

THE VALKYRIES

The Norse believed that whenever conflict was impending, Odin sent out his special attendants, the Valkyries, who were tasked with selecting the most noble and valiant of fallen warriors after the battle.

MAIN IMAGE, LEFT: Among the clouds, and upon a white horse, a valkyrie rides with the corpse of a man. Flanked by Odin's ravens, two others ride behind her, one raising a spear. Illustration by Emil Doepler, from *Walhall, die Götterwelt der Germanen*, 1905; **ABOVE:** *Brünnhild* by Gaston Bussière, 1897; **BELOW RIGHT:** Three valkyries bring the body of a slain warrior to Valhalla, where they are met by Heimdallr. Illustration by the Danish artist Lorenz Frølich, 1906.

Those souls chosen by the Valkyries would be carried to Asgard over the rainbow bridge, the Bifröst, into Valhalla, where they would fight eternally at Odin's side until the coming of Ragnarok. The Valkyries are pictured most often as young and beautiful warrior maidens, with dazzling white cloaks of swan-feathers and flowing golden hair. They wear helmets and armor of silver or gold, and ride their pristine white steeds through battle without any trace of fear. The flying horses of the Valkyries are held in almost as high honor and regard as the Valkyries themselves. Some other depictions eschew the horses entirely, however, in favor of giving the Valkyries wings themselves.

The mission of the Valkyries is not only to the battlefields of earth; they often ride over the sea, snatching the dying Vikings from their sinking dragon-ships. Sometimes they stand upon the strand to beckon to drowning warriors, a sign that though the coming struggle will be their last, that they will die with glory and honor.

The numbers of the Valkyries differ greatly according to various sources, ranging from three to sixteen; most authorities, however, name only nine. The Valkyries are often also considered minor goddesses of the air and the wind; they are also occasionally conflated with the Norns. In some tellings, the goddess Freyja and the Norn Skuld lead them into the fray when they appear during a battle; in others, Skuld is one of the Valkyries herself.

The Valkyries also have important duties in Valhalla, where, having laid aside their armor and clad themselves in pure white robes, they pour out mead for the Einheriar, the honored Fallen warriors. The god Tyr is also considered in many myths to have a troupe of Valkyries, if not all of them, at his command, and it was sometimes thought that Tyr was the one who personally selected the warriors to be brought to Valhalla and who chose which battlefields to search for honorably-slain souls.

One myth tells of three of the Valkyries, Olrun, Alvit, and Svanhvit, who were swimming in a lake when suddenly the three brothers Egil, Slagfinn, and Völund the smith stumbled across them. The men stole their swan-feathered cloaks, forcing the Valkyries to remain on earth among the mortals and become their wives. The Valkyries remained trapped with their husbands for nine years before recovering their cloaks and escaping, leaving the men to wander in search of them forever. There are many other tales of swan maidens or Valkyries who were said to have consorted with mortals; The most popular of all is that of Brünhild, the wife of Sigurd, a descendant of Sigmund and one of the most renowned of the Norse heroes.

7

OTHER MYTHS

A "lay," or "lai," is a lyrical, narrative poem that deals with tales of adventure and romance.

THE LAY OF RIGER

Under the alias Riger, Heimdall left his place in Asgard one day to wander the earth, as the gods often did.

He had not gone far before he came to a ramshackle hut on the seashore, where he found Ai and Edda, a poor but kind couple who hospitably invited him to share their meager meal of porridge. Riger gladly accepted this invitation, and he remained with the couple three whole days, teaching them many things during that time. At the end of his stay he bid the couple farewell and left to resume his journey. Some months after his departure, Edda bore a hardy, thick-set baby boy, whom she called Thrall. Thrall soon showed uncommon physical strength and a great aptitude for all hard work and manual labor. When Thrall grew to be a man he was wed to Thyr, an equally sturdily-built girl with sunburnt hands and flat feet, who, like her husband, labored early and late. Many children were born to this couple, and from them descended all the serfs and thralls of the land.

After leaving the poor hut on the barren sea coast, Riger pushed inland, where before long he came to cultivated fields and a well-kept farmhouse. Entering this comfortable dwelling, he found an old couple named Afi and Amma, who hospitably invited him to sit down with them and share the plain but bountiful fare which was prepared for their evening meal. Riger accepted the invitation and he remained three days with his hosts, imparting all manner of useful knowledge to them. After his departure from their house, Amma gave birth to a blue-eyed, stocky boy, whom she called Karl. As he grew up he exhibited great skill in agricultural pursuits, and in due course he married a beautiful and hard-working wife named Snor, who bore him many children, from whom descend all the farmers and builders of the land.

Leaving the house of this second couple, Riger continued his journey until he came to a hill, upon which was perched a stately castle. Here he was received by a couple named Fadir and Modir, who received him cordially and set before him rare meats and rich wines. Riger stayed for three days with this couple and taught them what he could, afterwards finally returning to his own palace atop the Bifröst, to resume his post as guardian of rainbow bridge. Before long the lady of the castle bore a handsome, slenderly built son, whom she called Jarl. This child quickly showed a great taste for the hunt and all manner of martial exercises, learned to understand runes at a young age, and lived to perform great deeds of valor which made his name distinguished and added glory to his family line. As an adult, Jarl married Erna, an aristocratic, delicate maiden, who ruled his household wisely and bore him many children, all destined to rule. The youngest of his sons, Konur, became the first king of Denmark.

OPPOSITE, TOP: *Rig in Great-grandfather's Cottage*, an illustration from *Rígsþula*; **OPPOSITE, BOTTOM:** *Heimdall as Rig*, by Lorenz Frølich; **ABOVE:** *Heimdall Instructs Jarl*, by Lorenz Frølich; **BELOW:** *Heimdall visits Fadir and Modir*, by Lorenz Frølich.

The god Freyr always grew restless in the winter, with few plants to tend to, and little work to be done outdoors.

SKIRNIR'S JOURNEY

TOP: Skírnir. An illustration from Fredrik Sander's 1893 Swedish edition of the *Poetic Edda*; **ABOVE:** Seated on Odin's throne Hliðskjálf, Freyr sits in contemplation of the great panorama of earth and sky, in a 1908 woodcut by Frederic Lawrence; **RIGHT:** *The Lovesickness of Freyr*, a woodcut by W.G. Collingwood, 1908.

So, one day when Odin was away on a journey, Freyr wondered whether there was any spot in Asgard from which he could look down and see what was going on in the world, and quickly became curious to see where Odin had gone. Freyr wandered restlessly about from one marble hall to another, slowly getting nearer each moment to Odin's great gold throne, until at last he stood directly before it. Unable to resist any longer, Freyr boldly stepped into Odin's sacred seat. He gave a gasp of wonder as his eyes travelled quickly over the panorama of earth and sky that lay spread out before him.

He did not care to rest his gaze very long on frozen Jötunheim, for there was nothing in that dreary country to attract the beauty-loving Freyr; but as he turned to look at a tall old castle standing on the top of one of the wind-swept hills, he saw the door suddenly open. Soon, a giantess appeared on the threshold, and Freyr gazed upon her with surprise and delight, for she seemed too beautiful to belong to the monstrous race of giants. She was Gerd, the daughter of Gymer. Never before had he seen any woman whom he wished to marry; but here in the land of the frost giants he had found her all the same. When she returned inside, and out of view, Freyr's heart almost broke. He descended slowly and sadly from Odin's throne, more restless and unhappy than before. He longed for another sight of the giant's daughter.

One day his trusted servant Skirnir asked him why he looked so sad; so Freyr told him of his love for Gerd and of how he had watched her from Odin's throne. Then Skirnir offered to make the journey into Jötunheim at once, to do his best to woo the giant's daughter for his master. So Freyr gave him his swiftest horse, filled his hands with rich gifts, and finally girded upon Skirnir his own sword, which he promised to give to the servant if the mission should be successful.

As fast as the faithful horse could carry him, Skirnir hurried toward Jotunheim; it was not long before he arrived at the foot of the castle where the giant Gymer lived with his beautiful daughter. As he neared the gates, two enormous dogs sprang at him, barking furiously. Unable to approach, Skirnir called out loudly to the giantess until the hills echoed. Angry, and yet curious to see who stood so boldly outside the castle, Gerd threw open the great hall doors; at the sight of her the two fierce dogs stopped howling and lay quiet at her feet. Gerd allowed him to enter, and when they were seated by a great fire in the hall, Skirnir told the maiden how Freyr had seen her from Odin's seat and now loved her with a passion that would surely kill the once-joyous god unless she agreed to become his wife. Gerd listened coldly to his words, and his impassioned pleading left her unmoved. When Skirnir spoke of taking her at once with him to Asgard, she cried angrily, "Go back to your master and tell him that though he should die for love of me, Gymer's daughter will never be wed to the enemy of her race."

Then Skirnir brought out a wonderful ring and many costly gems—the gifts of Freyr—and offered them to Gerd; but she haughtily refused to touch them. Failing in this, Skirnir drew his sword—the shining blade which he hoped to win for himself with the success of his mission—and flashing this before the maiden's eyes he swore by the spear of Odin that he would kill her if she would not consent to wed with Freyr. But Gerd only laughed at his threats and looked unmoved at the glistening steel.

As neither gold nor threats could move the beautiful Gerd to listen to his master's request, Skirnir grew more and more frustrated. Speaking words of magic, he laid a terrible curse upon Gerd for her coldness to the unhappy Freyr. The curse promised that the sun would never shine on her again, that she would be burdened with sickness and pain, and that she would never bear children, all as punishment for spurning his master's love. At first Gerd paid no heed to these fearful words; but soon they seemed to weave a sort of spell about her. She trembled, and her beautiful face grew pale with fear.

Feeling rather guilty, Skirnir gently told her again how wonderful his master was, and how the curse would be fulfilled if she hardened her heart against Freyr. And as she listened to the servant's eager words of praise, Gerd's heart was touched; finally, she gave Skirnir her promise to become Freyr's wife in nine days. The nine days of waiting seemed very long to the impatient Freyr, but at last the time came. Freyr went joyfully to their meeting place, and finally there stood Gerd, even more beautiful than he remembered.

ABOVE: *Skyrnir and Gerda*, an illustration by Harry George Theaker from *Children's Stories from the Northern Legends* by M. Dorothy Belgrave and Hilda Hart, 1920.

THE LAY OF GRIMNIR

Odin often wandered Midgard in disguise, and he was fond of meddling in the affairs of mortals. Once, he became especially interested in the development of two young princes named Geirrod and Agnar.

Odin and his wife Frigga grew so fond of the two boys that they disguised themselves as an old mortal couple and went to live upon a desert island which lay far out at sea. One day, Odin conjured a storm while the boys were out fishing, and the winds blew their little boat away from the shore until it reached their island. The boys were received kindly by Odin and Frigga, who cared for them all winter and taught them everything they could. The hot-headed Geirrod was Odin's favorite, and he taught Geirrod to fight and swim. Frigga loved the gentle Agnar, the older boy, who would sit by her side and rest his head on her knee while she told him tales of Asgard, the home of the gods.

Eventually, Odin put the two boys aboard a boat and instructed them to sail back to their father. The moment the boat touched the shore,

ABOVE: *Odin and Frigga*. From *Walhall, die Götterwelt der Germanen*, 1905, illustration by Emil Doepler (see pages 124–125); **RIGHT:** *Odin in Torment*: As Odin is tortured by Geirroð, he is handed a full horn from which to drink by Agnar, as described in *Grímnismál*.

however, Geirrod sprang out and pushed the boat back out to sea with all his might. Geirrod believed his brother was too weak to inherit their father's throne, and he had decided to remove Agnar from the line of succession. Odin was on his way to Asgard, and thus he did not see the boat carrying Agnar away to the edge of the world.

Eventually, when Geirrod had sat for some time on his long-dead father's throne, Odin finally observed him again from his high throne in Asgard. He was pleased to see how strong Gierrod had become, and said as much to Frigga, laughing that the younger brother had claimed the throne. Frigga argued that Geirrod had grown to be a cruel, inhospitable, unfit king. Odin decided to prove Geirrod's worth. Donning his broad hat and blue-grey cloak, he disguised himself as an old man and set out for Geirrod's castle to beg for food and shelter. As soon as he left, however, Frigga sent a messenger to the king, telling him to beware of a suspicious old man in a cloak who planned to bewitch the king. She was sure she was right, but still wanted to take no chances.

It came as a surprise to Odin then, when, instead of being offered a seat at the table and a bed for the night when he arrived at the castle, he was seized by the beard and dragged roughly into the hall. "Where do you come from, and what is your name, you miserable old man?" asked the cruel king.

"My name is Grimnir," answered Odin, now on his guard, and refused to say anything further.

His silence infuriated Geirrod. Finding it impossible to make the old man speak, Geirrod had him chained to a pillar between two giant fires; for eight days and nights Odin was imprisoned, starved, and burned. One night, when the guards were sleeping, a servant quietly offered Odin a drink of cold water, and Odin recognized him as Agnar, rightful heir to the throne.

The next evening at dinner, Odin began to sing. He sang that Geirrod, who had so long enjoyed the favor of the gods, was finally about to receive punishment for his misdeeds. As his voice echoed through the hall, the chains fell from his hands and the flames died away, and Odin was finally revealed in all the might and majesty of a god. Panicked, Geirrod stood and drew his sword—but he stumbled in his haste, fell on his own blade, and died in disgrace. With Geirrod dead, Odin turned to Agnar and commanded him to take his rightful place upon his father's throne. In return for Agnar's kind act, Odin promised him prosperity and happiness for the rest of his life.

ABOVE: "No one gave him a thought of pity, save little Agnar." Odin, disguised as Grímnir, is offered a drink by Geirröd's brother Agnar, as described in *Grímnismál*. Illustration by George Wright, 1908.

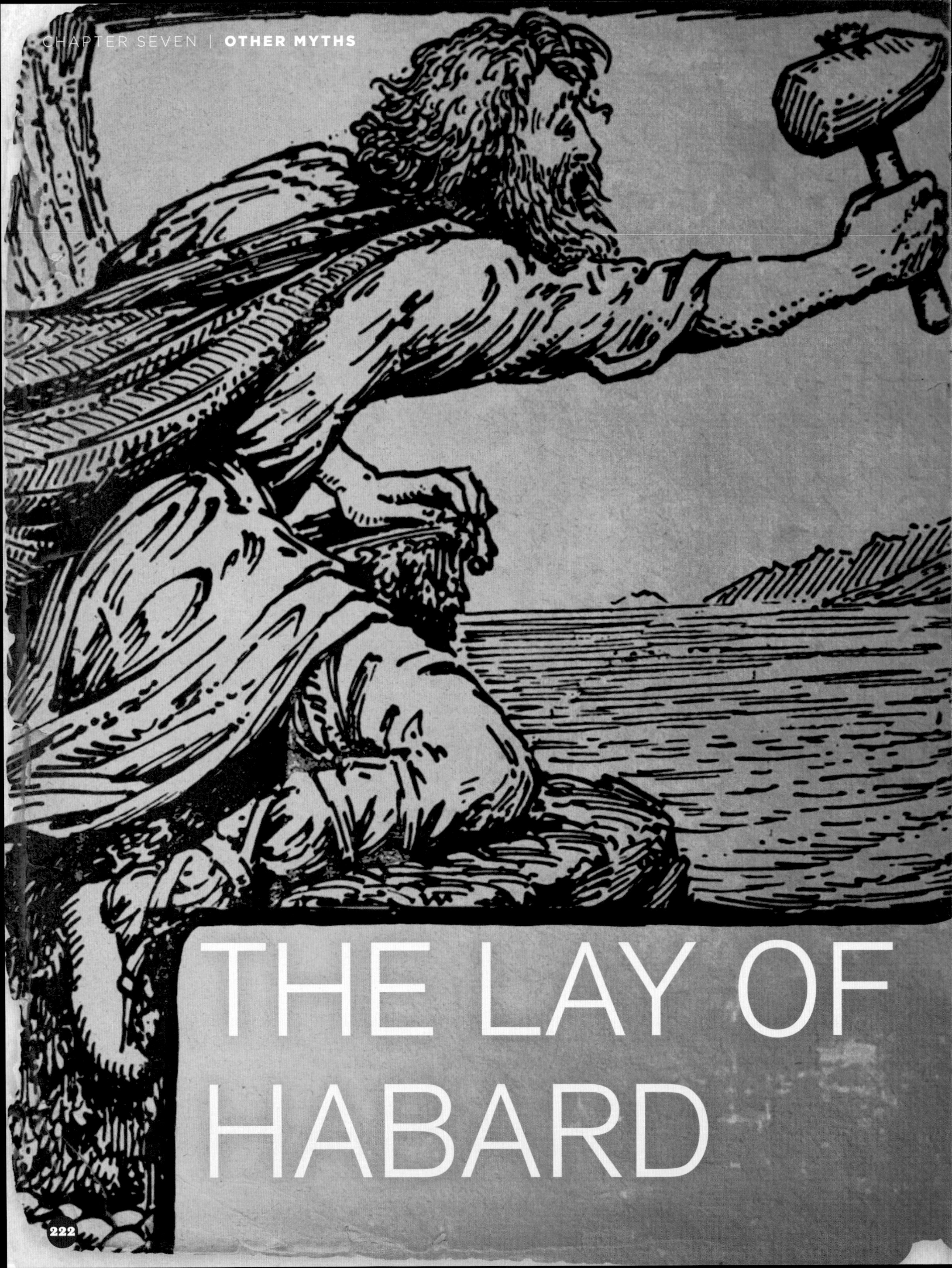

THE LAY OF HABARD

One day, while on his way home from one of his many adventures, Thor came across a river that blocked his path back to Asgard.

BOTH PICTURES: Opposite: Thor threatens Greybeard; Above: Greybeard mocks Thor. Illustrations by W.G. Collingwood, from *The Elder or Poetic Edda*, or *Sæmund's Edda*. Edited and translated with introduction and notes by Olive Bray, 1908.

ABOVE: *Thor and Harbard*, an illustration by Franz Stassen in *Die Edda: Germanische Götter- und Heldensagen (Germanic sagas of gods and heroes)* by Hans von Wolzogen, 1920. Thor, holding Mjölnir, has a duel of wits with the ferryman Harbard. Insults are traded back and forth across the river, and Thor quickly loses his temper.

As he looked up and down the length of the water for a place to cross safely, he saw an old ferryman standing on the other side of the river next to his boat. Perhaps because he was tired from traveling, or perhaps because of his outsized pride as the god of thunder, Thor called out at once to the ferryman, insulting him even as he asked to be ferried across the water.

"Who is that frail old man," he called, "who stands across the water?"

This, of course, the old man took offense to. "Who is that oafish peasant yelling across the river?" asked the ferryman in response.

Thor, slightly cowed and still wishing to cross the river, responded more politely after this first volley; he offered to pay the old man with food and provisions from the basket he carried on his back, as he had fish and porridge to spare after his long journey. The old man, however, was still offended.

"Bragging about your food, are you?" he asked, laughing. "You must not know what waits for you at home—your mother is dead, I believe, and only misery is in your future."

Thor, who was a rather simple man at times and often failed to see immediately when he was being mocked or lied to, was aghast; it was not until the old man carried on with his insults that Thor began to understand, and he was quickly flooded with indignant rage.

"Further still," the old man continued, "you look too poor even for a peasant; your clothes are ragged, and I doubt you own any property at all. You must be a beggar, then, not even a worthy peasant—and I will not ferry a beggar across the river."

"Look, just bring the boat over, don't be scared," demanded Thor. "Anyway, whose ferry is that? Because I am sure it does not belong to you."

"Hildolf owns this ferry," said the old man smugly, naming a local chieftain, "and he has tasked me to ferry only worthy men; no thieves, no beggars. So, who are you, beggar? Tell me your name if you want to cross."

"I am Thor," said Thor, "son of Odin, brother of Meili, father of Magni—I am the strongest god of Asgard. Now, who are you?"

"I am Harbard," said the old man. "Harbard the grey-beard, and rarely do I hide my name."

"You must be an outlaw," said Thor, "Or you would never hide your name at all."

By now, the two were standing on either side of the river and shouting at each other, deeply embroiled in their *flyting*, a contest of insults. The sun began to drop down beneath the horizon as they stood there, ankle deep in cold water. Thor boasted of his many victories against the giants, naming the strongest to fall before him; Harbard boasted of his seduction of countless women and his own exploits in battle, calling Thor a coward, despite his claims. Harbard was just in the middle of telling Thor that his wife, Sif, was certainly cheating on him at home, when Thor finally remembered he was supposed to be making his way home.

"Damn you, old man," Thor cried, "You've delayed me for hours! Now, are you going to ferry me across the water, or will you make an enemy of Thor, son of Odin?"

"No," said the old man, grinning wider than ever. The setting sun illuminated his face under his wide-brimmed hat, and his one eye sparkled shrewdly. "I will not aid you in your journey, Thor, son of Odin, father of Magni."

Thor stood there on the riverbank for a moment, gripping Mjölnir tight in one massive fist, but he had finally realized that here at last was a trial he could not overcome with raw strength alone. Humbled by the one-eyed old man across the water, and still not quite quick enough to recognize who Harbard might truly be, Thor relented and asked politely for directions back to Asgard. The old man finally pointed out the path Thor could take back to Asgard. Still grinning, he sent the god of thunder on his way, reminding him to greet his mother Frigg when he finally got home.

BELOW: *Odin the Wanderer*, by Georg von Rosen, 1886.

There was once a young prince named Svipdag. He was raised in a castle by his father and his stepmother, who resented Svipdag and his claim to the throne. Svipdag's birth mother had died not long after he was born, and though his father had remarried, he had never sired another son.

THE LAY OF SVIPDAG

MAIN IMAGE: *Svipdag*, watercolor illustration byJohn Bauer, from *Our Fathers' Godsaga* by Viktor Rydberg, 1911.

The queen could not bear to see Svipdag's face around the palace every day. So, as she could not kill the young man or have him banished, she began making increasingly bold, dangerous requests of Svipdag, sending him out on long journeys and quests. Svipdag, who did his best to live up to his stepmother's demands and did not understand her hatred for him, did as she asked each time; he returned successful but exhausted after each quest, only to be given another the very next day. Finally, Svipdag's stepmother gave him a quest that she was certain would lead to his death—or at least one he would never return from. She asked Svipdag to seek out and marry Menglod, a beautiful but entirely unapproachable goddess. Menglod lived in a great hall named Gastropnir, the walls of which were surrounded by strong stone and walls of roaring flames, and the gates of her home were guarded by the giant Fjolsivd and his two giant hounds.

This time, even Svipdag knew that he had been given an impossible task, and he mourned the fact that his stepmother would make such cruel demands of him. Still, he refused to fail her, and he set out from the castle at dawn the next day. He headed first for Helheim, the realm of the dead. There, using magic that he had learned on his many journeys, Svipdag summoned the shade of his long-dead mother, the witch Groa. Groa was delighted to meet her son after so long, and—proud of the man he had become and fearful of the impossible quest he had been given—she quickly agreed to help him on his journey. Using the last of the magic available to her since her death, Groa cast nine spells on her son to protect and aid him. The protective spells warded Svipdag from sickness, cold, the curses of Christians, and violent weather; they ensured that rivers would part for him, enemies would want nothing but peace with him, and he would never lose his way. The final spell flooded Svipdag's mind with wisdom, granting him all the knowledge and wit needed to protect himself on his journey.

Svipdag thanked his mother for her blessings and released her from his summons, allowing her to rest once more with the knowledge that her son would be safe. Then he set out for Gastropnir, the impassable stronghold where Menglod lived. He navigated his way through raging rivers, precarious mountain peaks, and roaming bands of warriors—any of which would have been his death were it not for his mother's protective magic.

When he finally came to the estate of Gastropnir, the first walls of flame parted for him just as the rivers had on his journey; he approached the gates unscathed, though he was exhausted from several days of hard travel. Finally, he stood at the feet of the enormous castle—but one more obstacle stood in his way. Fjolsivd, the enormous giant who guarded the gates, loomed tall over Svipdag, bounded on either side by his giant, red-eyed hellhounds.

TOP: *Freya-Menglad*, engraving by Jenny Nyström/Gunnar Forssell, from Fredrik Sander's 1893 edition of the *Poetic Edda*; **BELOW:** *Groa Awake Mother* by John Bauer, 1911.

ABOVE: Menglod/Freyja and Svipdag. Illustration by John Bauer.

"What do you want?" demanded the giant, his voice booming as he glared down at the young prince. "Why are you here? What are you doing out of your home? Are you a child, lost in the woods?"

Svipdag was so startled by the barrage of questions that he forgot to introduce himself properly to the giant watchman.

"Who are you?" he replied instead, "To interrogate me without so much as a greeting?"

"I am Fjolsvid the wise, the guardian of this fortress," replied the giant, "and you will never enter here. I have no food for you, no seat for you, no welcome to offer you. You are lucky that my hounds have not already devoured you." The hellhounds at Fjolsvid's sides growled a little, but they seemed to regard Svipdag with curiosity more than their usual violent hunger.

Svipdag, however, was determined, and he refused to turn back after coming so far. He explained to the giant that he was there to seek the hand of Menglod, the beautiful goddess who lived within the high walls of the fortress, and that he would not leave without seeing her.

Fjolsvid grew irate as Svipdag ignored his threats, and instead began asking the young man question after question, testing his knowledge and making him list every one of his ancestors. Svipdag's mind was strengthened tenfold by his mother's magic, however, and he answered each question without hesitation, following every time with one of his own. He asked Fjolsvid for hidden truths about the creation of the cosmos, the nature of the world, and the future, all of which the giant answered with ease. The interrogation went on for hours.

Finally, Svipdag asked: "Is there no one at all who you would allow to enter the castle and ask for Menglod's hand in marriage?"

"No one," replied the giant, "Save for the one man destined to be Menglod's true love. That man is named Svipdag, and he alone is fated to marry her."

At this, Svipdag cried out; partially with joy, as he finally saw the end of his quest in sight, and partially with dismay, as he had foolishly wasted hours and hours arguing with the giant without ever bothering to give his name.

"Well, open the gates, then,' he said, "because I am Svipdag!"

At this, Fjolsvid's hounds leapt up, finally recognizing the one man they had been ordered to allow entry and *not* tear to pieces. They licked at Svipdag's face like newborn puppies, providing all the proof Fjolsvid needed of the prince's identity. Fjolsvid turned and threw the gates open with such force that they fell from their hinges; he was eager to see the goddess he cared for finally happily married.

Svipdag made his way into the fortress and entered the great hall, where he finally found Menglod waiting for him. She was as beautiful as he had heard, standing tall and imposing at the head of the long table, and he knew at once that he loved her—but she looked at him with eyes as hard and cold as ice as he approached.

Countless men had visited the fortress and claimed to be her destined husband, after all, and she was wary.

Menglod turned first to address Fjolsvid, her voice as cold as her stare. "If this man is yet another liar, I will have your eyes gouged out by the ravens and hang you from the gallows. Now—what is your name, and where have you come from?"

To this final test, Svipdag replied: "I am Svipdag, son of Groa and Solbjart. I have traveled countless miles through rivers and across mountains, through fire and bitter cold, to reach your side."

Finally Menglod smiled, knowing that Svipdag was telling the truth, and she strode forward to take his hand. "My wishes have been granted at last," she said, her voice and her eyes no longer like ice. "I have waited for years to meet you, to leave this place, and I will not wait a moment longer. We will live out our lives together, side by side, and I will never be locked away again."

ABOVE: Menglöð surrounded by nine maidens, by Lorenz Frølich, from *Fjölsvinnsmál*, 1893; **BELOW:** *Day-spring finds Menglöd*. Svipdagr and Menglöð hug.

VIKINGS ON FILM

***THE VIKINGS* (1958)**
***VIKINGS* (2013-2020)**
***THE LAST KINGDOM* (2015-2022)**

ABOVE: After the battle—Ragnar (Travis Fimmel, right), and his son Bjorn (Alexander Ludwig) in *Vikings*; **TOP:** Ragnar and a war party go on the attack in season two of *Vikings*; **OPPOSITE, LEFT:** A dramatic shot of the Heimdall-like hornsman atop the viking settlement's watchtower, alerting the tribe to the return of their chieftain, Ragnar, and his warriors, after a successful raid, in *The Vikings* movie of 1958. The great horn call melody is the central *leitmotif* of the movie's soundtrack, composed by acclaimed Italian composer Mario Mascimbene.

"All things begin and end as stories."

Ragnar Lothbrok, *Vikings*

The 1958 Hollywood movie *The Vikings*, and 2013's *Vikings* television films share a common source—the 13th century legendary saga *The Tale of Ragnar Lodbrok*. This in itself is an early written form of stories told and re-told in the viking oral tradition. Like Homer's *Iliad* and *Odyssey* in ancient Greece, the medieval *Ragnar saga* is set in the distant misty past of hundreds of years before. It tells of Ragnar Lodbrok and his many adventures (including the slaying of a dragon), his crossing of the sea and incursions into the British Isles, and his eventual capture and execution (cast into a snake pit) by the Northumbrian King Aella (an historical figure). Further sagas tell of the great viking army assembled to invade Britain and gain revenge for this heinous act—a key event which altered the course of British history.

2015's *The Last Kingdom* is set in ninth century Britain (after the great viking army has invaded), and adapted from Bernard Cornwell's novels *The Saxon Stories*. The central character is *Uhtred of Bebbanburg*—born a Saxon ælder, but taken as a child into the viking tribe of *Earl Ragnar*. He grows into a great warrior, but becomes, by various turns of fate, "the Daneslayer" and "oath-man" of Saxon king Alfred (known in British history as "Alfred the Great," another authentic figure from history), whose burning desire is to unite the various smaller kingdoms into one nation—England. Uhtred leads the Saxons to a great victory over the vikings at the Battle of Ethandun—a real historical event which took place sometime in May 878 AD. The plot weaves the character of Uhtred into known historical events—and, tongue-in-cheek, his fictionality is cleverly referenced in a dialogue aside, when Alfred says: "Uhtred is my sword of Wessex, and he has changed the course of our history—but as a Dane he will never be mentioned in my manuscripts. *Therefore, in the future, he will appear never to have existed...*"

The Vikings stars Kirk Douglas, Tony Curtis, Janet Leigh and Ernest Borgnine—all heavyweights of 1950s Hollywood—and was shot by Jack Cardiff in the spectacular Maurangerfjorden, Norway. 2013's *Vikings* was

filmed predominantly in Ireland—production beginning in July 2012 at Ashford Studios, south of Dublin. Key "Norse" backgrounds were filmed in Hellesylt, Norway, and Gullfoss, Iceland. The cinematographer on season one was John Bartley, with the first nine episodes being directed by Johan Renck, Ciaran Donnelly and Ken Girotti, respectively. In the story, *Ragnar Lothbrok* is shown how to navigate across the sea, and the viking raid on Holy Island in 793 AD is bloodily recreated. The Norse cosmogony and beliefs driving the lives of Ragnar's tribe gradually unfold across the series—*Yggdrasil*, the World Tree (see pages 42–49); *Ragnarök*, the end of the world (see pages 242–249); and, in episode 8, the disturbing concept of willing human sacrifice.

The soundtracks to *Vikings* and *The Last Kingdom* soar dramatically across ambient soundscapes—from primitive drones, pagan drums and plaintive chants, to the arresting title tracks—whilst the music for *The Vikings* was written by Italian composer Mario Mascimbene. The movie's haunting *leitmotif* is a melodic horn call, first heard as Ragnar's longship arrives, powering up the Fjord, and blown to alert the village by the Heimdall-like watchman high on his tower—it's a genuinely uplifting movie moment. *The Vikings*, though, is now some sixty-three years old, and with *The Last Kingdom* and *Vikings* appearing only recently, you would expect different attitudes to be struck. In *The Vikings*, all the female characters are subservient to men—even big star Janet Leigh has ridiculously few lines. That women occupied a more significant role in viking society than they did in Christian communities (see pages 18–19) is well observed in both of the two more recent productions: In *Vikings*, Ragnar's wife, *Lagertha*, is a shieldmaiden who takes no prisoners. *The Last Kingdom* features several strong women: *Brida*—a Saxon girl taken, along with Uhtred, by the vikings, but who grows up alongside him, and becomes leader of her own viking army; *Hild*, a Saxon nun-turned-warrior; *Skade*, a seductive but ruthless viking seer who throws curses and takes sadistic pleasure in killing; and *Aethelfled*, warrior first lady of Mercia—king Alfred's daughter, and another real figure from history. (A statue of her stands in the West Midlands town of Tamworth—in the 8th century, a key settlement of the Mercian kingdom.)

Various ruthless viking chiefs populate *The Last Kingdom*, but the characters which really leave a bad taste are the Christian bishops. Most are portrayed as devious, hypocritical, and arrogant, interested only in maintaining their exalted status in the community.

In *The Last Kingdom*, place name titles introducing a scene appear onscreen first in their original Old English/Old Norse incarnations, before dissolving into their modern equivalents. It's fascinating to imagine cities such as Loidis (Leeds) and Dunholm (Durham) as early English settlements, surrounded by virgin countryside! Ironically, though, *The Last Kingdom* was predominantly filmed on the Korda studios estate outside Budapest, Hungary.

Despite its great acting, tremendous locations and consistent "screen presence," Kirk Douglas's *The Vikings* is more a product of its time, and today looks quaintly like a reflection of US gender values of the 1950s. *The Last Kingdom* and *Vikings* both look and feel far more "authentic"—rough, raw, bloody, savage, and naturalistic—though in the end, all three demonstrate the enduring pulling power of great storytelling.

TOP TO BOTTOM: Kirk Douglas, the lead actor of *The Vikings*, 1958. He plays Einar, the son of Ragnar Lodbrok; Travis Fimmel as Ragnar Lothbrok, in *Vikings*; Lagertha, played by Katheryn Winnick, a viking shieldmaiden and first wife of Ragnar Lothbrok; *The Last Kingdom* lead character Uhtred of Bebbanburg, played by Alexander Dreymon; Emily Cox playing Brida in *The Last Kingdom*.

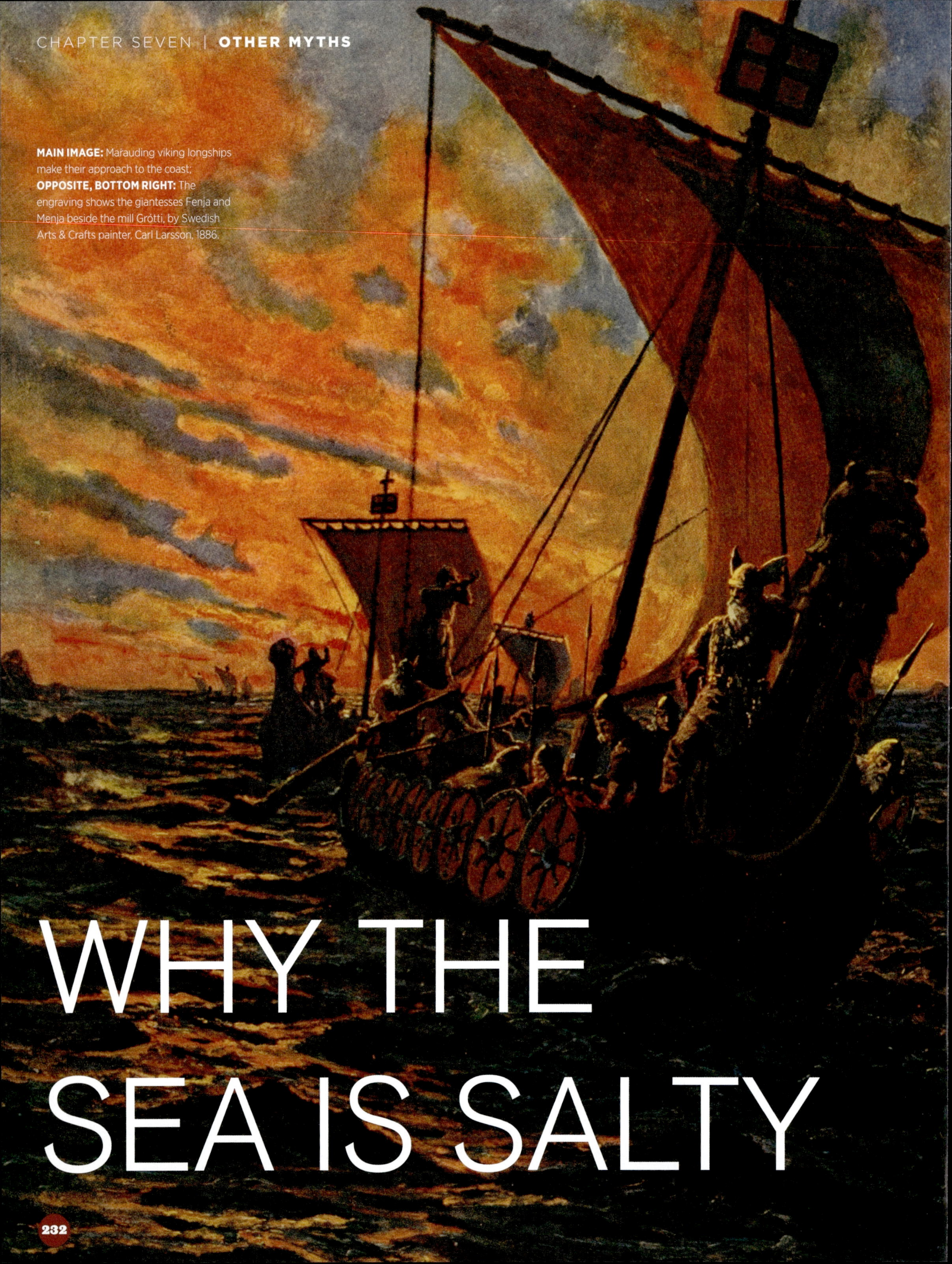

MAIN IMAGE: Marauding viking longships make their approach to the coast;
OPPOSITE, BOTTOM RIGHT: The engraving shows the giantesses Fenja and Menja beside the mill Grótti, by Swedish Arts & Crafts painter, Carl Larsson, 1886.

WHY THE SEA IS SALTY

Frodi, the son of Freyr, ruled for a time as the king of Denmark. Once, Frodi received a set of two enchanted grindstones, called Grotti, which were so massive that none of Frodi's servants or warriors could hope to operate them.

The grindstones were enchanted to provide anything the owner desired, from nothing but the labor of the one turning the stone—and Frodi was eager to see them at work. He eventually decided to go and purchase the two giantesses Menia and Fenia as slaves to work the grindstones, as they were more than powerful enough to manage the heavy stones. On his return home, Frodi led his new servants to the mill and instructed them turn the grindstones and grind out gold, peace, and prosperity. They set to work without complaint, and instantly the stones began producing whatever he asked for. The two women worked ceaselessly for hours on end until the king's coffers were overflowing with gold, and prosperity and peace flooded throughout the land. Soon hunger was a thing of the past, crime was forgotten, and all was well in the kingdom.

But when Menia and Fenia asked to rest for a moment, having clearly completed their task, Frodi commanded them to keep working; his greed had overtaken him. He forced them to continue working without rest, grinding the heavy stones for hours; the only moments of reprieve were when Frodi asked them to sing for him instead, as any requests made of the grindstones had to be delivered in verse. The giantesses grew sick of this treatment before long and decided to take revenge.

One night while Frodi slept, they changed their song, and, instead of prosperity and peace, they grimly began to produce a massive army from the stones. Before the sun rose, a horde of Viking longships had arrived on the shore, and Frodi was slain before he even rose from his bed. The Vikings made quick work of looting everything of value from Frodi's estate before vanishing into the night once more, pushing their ships silently back into the water.

The leader of the Viking raiding party took the grindstones and the two giantesses with him as he boarded his ship and set sail. He requested that they grind salt for him to trade at the next port, and they got to work at once, happy to be free of Frodi. However, it quickly became clear that this man, too, would allow them no rest while they produced salt from the magic stones. Furious and exhausted, Menia and Fenia ground more and more salt, far more than the ship could carry, ignoring the leader's pleas to stop. Soon the salt weighed the ship down, bowing the wooden boards, and the entire vessel and all its crew were dragged down into the sea. The salt that the stones had produced in such enormous quantities dissolved into the water, spreading out further and further until the entire sea was saturated with salt—as it has been ever since.

TOP: The cover of Asbjornsen and Moe's *Norske folkeeventyr* 5th edition, 1874. The book includes this tale of *Why the Sea is Salty*.

One day before dawn, the goddess Freyja set out along the Bifröst, riding a giant boar as her mount. She made her way down to a dark, damp cave, from which she could hear guttural snores echoing from miles away. As she arrived, she called out into the cave from the opening, unwilling to go any further into the dripping darkness.

THE LAY OF HYNDLA

"Hyndla!" She cried out, dismounting the boar and yelling into the cavern. "Hyndla, dear, please wake up, I have need of your services."

The snoring stopped, but it was a long time before Freyja saw anyone emerge from the cave. Finally, Hyndla emerged. Hyndla was a witch, seer, and hermit who held great contempt for almost all living things, save for Freyja, who she tolerated with the barest amount of civility.

"What do you want?" she demanded, too tired and irritable to bother treating the goddess with any reverence. Freyja, who was used to this from the bitter, cave-dwelling woman, responded calmly.

"We must journey to Valhalla together, my friend, to win a gift from Odin. You ride one of your wolves, and I will ride my noble boar, and we will travel there together."

Hyndla, who had been eyeing the boar suspiciously, finally laughed with sudden realization. "You lie to me, Freyja," she said, pointing at the boar. "You ride Ottar, your favorite mortal man, along the road in the form of a boar. Why, I have no idea—but do not lie to me."

Freyja laughed, a little nervously. "You must be joking—Ottar, my mortal favorite, transformed into a boar? Ridiculous. Now, come with me to Valhalla, and we can talk on the way."

It took many long hours of debate before Freyja finally convinced Hyndla to leave her cave and travel to Asgard with her; when they set out, the sun was high overhead. Hyndla rode a giant wolf, while Frejya rode her oddly intelligent boar. As they rode, Freyja made casual mention of a competition between two mortals that was to take place at Valhalla that day, where two men would name all their noble ancestors to see who was more worthy of a gift from Odin. The contest would be between Agantyr, a mortal man, and Ottar, her favorite mortal. Hyndla looked across at the unsubtle Freyja in silence, raising an eyebrow, then glanced down again at the boar.

"Look," said Freyja, exasperated, "Ottar is deserving of some favor. He built an alter to me, and he has sacrificed countless oxen in my name! It is only fitting that he win this contest. Now, tell me about the ancestry of these two men—who are the noble ancestors of Ottar?"

Rolling her eyes at the farce, Hyndla relented. She looked down at the boar and addressed him directly, ignoring Freyja's protests that he was certainly just a boar, and began listing all of Ottar's ancestors one at a time. It took hours, and by the time she finished, they were at the gates of Asgard. Freyja had a look of some concern on her face; for all her faith in her favorite mortal follower, she doubted Ottar would be able to remember all the gods, goddesses, and mortal kings Hyndla had named. Pushing her luck with the increasingly frustrated witch, Freyja begged for a potion to help Ottar remember the entire list.

"Fine," Hyndla finally said with a shrug, producing a small bottle from her robes. "Here—a potion to grant your "boar" perfect memory. It is cursed, however, because you have irritated me, and will surely kill him."

Freyja laughed with delight and took the potion. "Thank you, Hyndla," she called out as the witch headed home on her wolf. She knew it would be no work at all to turn the curse into a blessing, and that Ottar—who now stood at her side, human once more—would surely win the contest.

OPPOSITE: *Freyja awakes Hyndla.* An illustration to *Hyndluljóð*. Illustrated by W.G. Collingwood. From *The Elder or Poetic Edda* (or *Sæmund's Edda*). Edited and translated with introduction and notes by Olive Bray, 1908; **OPPOSITE, BACKGROUND:** Detail from *The Rhine's Fair Children*, Arthur Rackham, 1910; **ABOVE:** The goddess Freyja is nuzzled by her boar Hildisvíni while gesturing to Hyndla, from *Hyndluljóð*. By Lorenz Frølich, 1895; **BELOW:** *The Ancestry of Ottar*, by W.G. Collingwood, 1908.

OTTER'S RANSOM

MAIN IMAGE: *Andwari's Fluch* (*Andwari's Curse*). Andwari (left) curses the ring Loki is holding, as he marches off with it and the treasure. Illustration by Emil Doepler, from *Walhall, die Götterwelt der Germanen*, 1905 (see pages 124–125); **OPPOSITE, BOTTOM RIGHT:** Detail of an illustration of two dwarves for *Völuspá*, 1895.

One day, Odin, Loki, and Hoenir were out wandering the realm of Midgard once again. They were walking along the edge of a river when they spotted a young otter eating a freshly-caught salmon just a short distance away. Loki, who was both very hungry and very bored, picked up a stone and threw it straight at the otter's head, killing it in a single blow. Loki boasted and crowed about this impressive bit of hunting as he skinned the otter; he had caught both an otter and a salmon for the price of a single stone. Loki stowed his prizes in a bag, and the gods continued on their way.

Eventually, the gods arrived at a house near the river, which happened to be the home of a powerful magician named Hreidmar. The magician and his two sons Fafnir and Regin welcomed the gods into their home gladly, and Odin was pleased to inform them that they could pay for the hospitality by sharing the food they had just caught. Hreidmar and his sons flew into a rage, however, when Loki revealed the otter's remains. In a voice like thunder, Hreidmar informed Loki that he was holding the remains of the magician's third son, Otter, who was a shapeshifter; Otter had been fishing in his animal form when Loki slew him.

TOP: The three gods Loki, Odin and Hoenir, as narrated in the skaldic poem *Haustlöng*, from an Icelandic 17th century manuscript; **ABOVE:** Ótr on the Ramsund carving in Södermanland, c. 1030 AD; **TOP RIGHT:** *Fafnir the Dragon*. Siegfried stands over the body of Fafnir the dragon, from *The Story of Siegfried*, by James Baldwin, 1882. New York, Charles Scribner's Sons. Illustration by Howard Pyle. Note the runes etched into Siegfried's sword; **OPPOSITE:** "In dragon's form Fafner now watches the hoard." illustration by Arthur Rackham. From *Siegfried and the Twilight of the Gods*, 1911.

Enraged, Hreidmar and his sons set upon the gods; they used all the magic at their disposal to strip the trio of their magical weapons and armor, bring them to the ground, and bind them hand and foot. Odin, Loki, and Hoenir were now the captives of three mortal men. Hreidmar stood above the captured trio and raised his hands, gathering all of his magic to strike them dead and avenge his son. Odin spoke up, then, his voice steady despite his seemingly impending doom. He offered to pay Hreidmar a ransom for Otter's death, promising to pay whatever price the magician demanded.

Hreidmar paused at this. It was true that a ransom payment would be more practical than extracting his vengeance from their blood. So, finally, he nodded and gestured to his surviving sons to lay Otter's pelt out before the hearth.

"You will cover every hair of this pelt with gold. Only then will your debt be repaid." Hreidmar stooped to cut their bindings, letting the gods stand once more. They agreed to the terms at once, and Odin—after whispering instructions in Loki's ear—sent the trickster god out on his own to recover the payment.

Taking his time, Loki made his way down into the earth towards Svartalfheim, the realm of the dwarves, carrying a magical net in one hand. He delved deeper and deeper into the caves and tunnels until he came to a large underground pool in the center of a cavern. He snuck silently up to the edge of the water, then hurled the net into the pool, snaring a huge, thrashing pike. As he dragged the fish onto the shore, the struggling creature transformed into a sullen dwarf by the name of Andvari. Loki held the dwarf tight as he struggled to break free, but the magical net kept him from breaking free.

Andvari, even more than most elves, was a known hoarder of treasure of all kinds, and Loki knew that the dwarf held more than enough gold to complete the ransom. Still, Loki demanded every last coin of Andvari's gold in exchange for setting him free, and the dwarf was helpless but to comply. Cursing all the while, Andvari led Loki into a hidden cave near the pool and set about gathering up the huge pile of gold coins, bars, trinkets, and jewelry

in a large sack. Loki hefted the sack over one shoulder and found that even he struggled to carry its weight—it was certainly more than they needed. So, of course, Loki pointed at the gold ring on Andvari's finger and demanded that he add it to the pile as well. Andvari begged, pleaded, and cursed Loki not to take his last piece of gold, but Loki paid him no heed and pulled the ring from the dwarf's finger himself. As he turned to leave the cave, Loki heard Andvari's voice call out behind him:

"A curse on that ring and that gold, may they destroy whoever comes to own them!"

For reasons Andvari could not understand, Loki only laughed as he exited the cave with the cursed gold over his shoulder.

Back at Hreidmar's house, Loki dumped the gold on the floor with a smug, crooked grin. Hoenir set about the task of piling the gold onto the pelt, while Odin examined the twisted gold ring. Enthralled by its beauty, Odin slipped it onto his own finger; then the three gods got to work spreading the enormous pile over Otter's pelt. Somehow, despite the sack that had held the gold being much larger than the pelt, the gold only barely covered the pelt; Hreidmar watched hawkishly as they worked, and when they had used every last coin, he declared that a single hair on the pelt was still exposed.

"Ah," said Loki, grinning wider, and gestured for the ring on Odin's finger. "But we have one last piece." he paused as Odin pulled the ring off and placed it on the pelt, completing the layer of gold and passing the whole of Andvari's hoard into Hreidmar's possession. Odin straightened, and he too wore a shrewd smile, his one eye shining with much of the same mischief that Loki's own eyes often held. "Now the ransom has been paid, and the gold belongs to you." He and Hoenir turned to leave, strolling out into the night. Loki, who had lingered behind, paused at the threshold to look back at Hreidmar, still wearing that crooked grin. "Oh! But there was one more thing. When I took this gold from the hoard of the dwarf Andvari, he had this to say: '*A curse on that ring and that gold, may they destroy whoever comes to own them.*'" Loki shrugged, and before Hreidmar or his sons could respond, he too vanished into the darkness, leaving the words of the curse hanging in the air behind him.

The curse took effect quickly. The gold created a rift of greed, jealousy, and distrust between the brothers and their father, and Regin and Fafnir soon murdered Hreidmar to hasten their inheritance. Fafnir then stole the entire hoard for himself, however, and fled with it deep into the woods. There, over several years, the corrupting gold transformed him into a dragon.

Regin, on the other hand, became a blacksmith for a local king; he hoarded no wealth and had no family of his own, but eventually adopted a boy named Sigurd who had been sired by the king's unwed son. Regin raised Sigurd on stories of the dragon Fafnir and his hoard of gold, urging him to slay the beast. He forged the magical sword Gram for the boy when he came of age, and Sigurd went into the woods at once to complete his quest. He slew Fafnir with ease, but he decided to eat a piece of the dragon's heart before claiming the hoard of gold. Eating the flesh of a dragon granted Sigurd great wisdom; he sensed suddenly that his father Regin had followed him to the cave, and he knew that Regin meant to kill him and reclaim the gold. As Regin entered the cave and drew his knife, Sigurd ran him through with Gram, killing him and finally ending the curse of Andvari's hoard.

THE LAY OF ALVIS

MAIN IMAGE: *All-wise answers Thor.* Thor holds his daughter Þrúðr while conversing with the dwarf Alvíss. Illustrated by W.G. Collingwood, 1908. From *The Elder or Poetic Edda* (or *Sæmund's Edda*). Edited and translated with introduction and notes by Olive Bray; **TOP RIGHT:** The dwarf Alvíss puts a ring around the arm of Þrúðr, who looks on him smiling. Illustration by Lorenz Frølich.

Thor was twice married; first to the giantess Iarnsaxa (meaning "iron stone"), who bore him two sons, Magni and Modi. Both Magni and Modi were destined to survive their father after his death at Ragnarök, the twilight of the gods, to rule over the new world which would eventually rise from the ashes left behind.

His second wife was Sif, the golden-haired, who bore him two daughter, Lorride and Thrud. Thrud, the younger daughter, grew into a powerful young giantess who quickly became renowned for her size and strength. In her adulthood—in a classic example of opposites attracting—Thrud was courted by the dwarf Alvis, and she returned his affections in kind. One evening, when this suitor—who, being a dwarf, could not face the light of day—presented himself in Asgard to officially ask the gods for her hand, the assembled gods did not refuse their consent. After all, Thrud was happy with Alvis, even if he was a lesser being than the Aesir. They had scarcely given their approval, however, when Thor, who had been absent on a long journey, suddenly appeared. Thor looked down at Alvis with contempt for his size and species and declared that the dwarf would have to prove that his knowledge atoned for his small stature before he could win his bride. If Alvis was not physically powerful, Thor explained, he must at least possess great wisdom. This, however, was not Thor's true intent. For all the skill and knowledge of the dwarfs, and for all Thrud and Alvis seemed happy to be together, Thor could not stomach the idea of his daughter being married to a species he deemed so inferior to the gods.

To test Alvis's mental powers, Thor then questioned him in the languages of the Aesir, Vanir, elves, and dwarfs. Alvis answered Thor's intensive lines of questioning gracefully even as Thor dragged the test out longer and longer, until eventually the sun began to rise. Then, the first beam of light broke over the horizon and struck the dwarf, instantly turning the poor suitor to stone. There he stood from that day onward, both as an enduring example of the gods' power and to serve as a warning to all other beings who might dare to test it.

BOTTOM LEFT: Otto Schenk's interpretation of Asgard and Bifröst, in Wagner's *Das Rheingold*; **ABOVE:** *Sun Shines in the Hall.* The dwarf Alvíss is turned to stone by the first rays of morning sunlight. Thor and Þrúðr hold hands and look on. Illustrated by W.G. Collingwood, 1908. From *The Elder or Poetic Edda* (or *Sæmund's Edda*). Edited and translated with introduction and notes by Olive Bray.

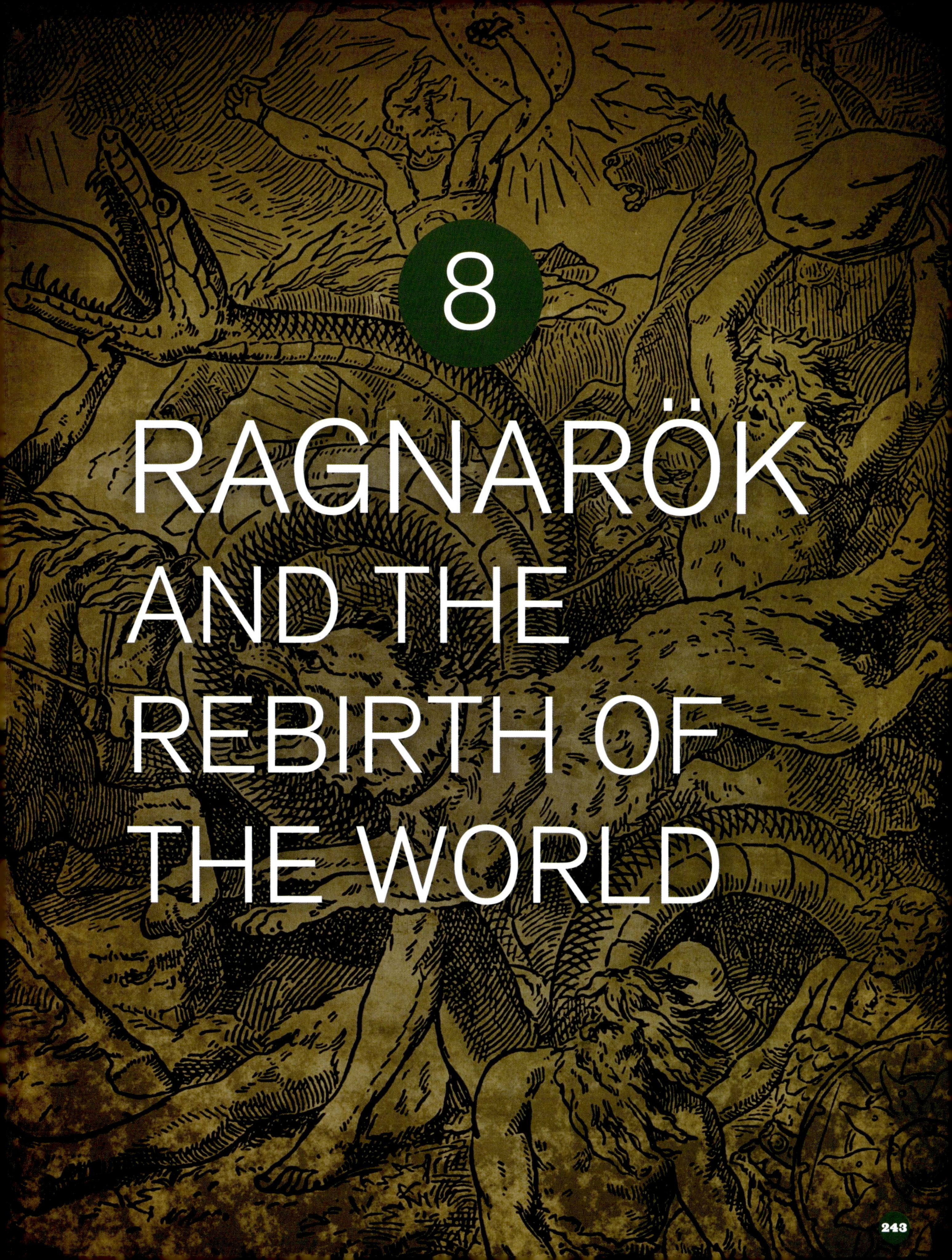

8

RAGNARÖK AND THE REBIRTH OF THE WORLD

Ragnarök, the twilight of the gods, is the prophesied end of the world as written in Old Norse religion.

RAGNARÖK AND THE REBIRTH OF THE WORLD

THIS IMAGE: "Der Asen Untergang" ("The Downfall of the Aesir"). The heavens split and the "Sons of Múspell" ride forth upon the Aesir at Ragnarök. Illustration by Karl Ehrenberg, from *Nordisch-germanische Götter und Helden* by Wilhelm Wägner, 1882. Otto Spamer, Leipzig & Berlin.

It was believed that the gods, though long-lasting and immensely powerful, were not truly immortal; the gods were born, just like humans, and so it seemed inevitable that they must also eventually die. Ragnarök as a myth encapsulates the concept of inevitable doom and regeneration that was so prevalent in Norse culture, as well as the grim determination required to go fearlessly into certain death. The rebirth of the world—new life, new gods, new realms to replace the ones burned by the fires of Surtr—presents a glimmer of hope at the very end of everything, lightening the dread of an apocalypse that the Norsemen truly believed would come to pass.

Odin and Frigg, with their great wisdom and skill in prophecy, knew of Ragnarök long before it came to pass, although it is uncertain how much of this information they shared with the rest of the Aesir. Despite the fact that they knew no prophecy could be avoided, Odin and Frigg both made many attempts to avert the fate of the gods. Odin in particular felt hugely responsible for the safety of the Aesir, as even those who were not his direct descendants still trusted in and relied on him as the All-Father, the king of Asgard. This was one of the core reasons behind Odin's perpetual quest for knowledge, wisdom, and arcane secrets; he had a burning need to lead the Aesir well, to guide them to the right choices, and to keep them safe. The prophecy of Ragnarök only intensified that, and Odin set his considerable powers towards finding some way to prevent or at least postpone the twilight of the gods.

The most notable of these attempts is the gathering of the einherjar in Valhalla. Though Valhalla is generally perceived to be an afterlife for the warriors of Earth—a reward for those who are deemed the most fearless and who gained the most glory in life—the true purpose of the enormous army of fallen warriors that Odin amassed in Valhalla was self-preservation. The spectral forces of Valhalla were hand-selected to fight at Odin's side during the final battle of Ragnarok, to hopefully sway the battle in favor of the gods. The enormous wall that was built around Asgard was another attempt to survive Ragnarök, though the final battle is fought outside the city. The binding of the children of Loki—Fenrir, Jörmungandr, and Hela—was yet another attempt to keep Ragnarök at bay.

Frigg, as well, attempted to avert the prophecy, particularly with regards to the death of Baldur, her favorite son. Baldur's death marks the first sign of the approach of Ragnarök, according to the prophecy, and it is the only event that has already taken place. In the telling of the events of Ragnarök, Baldur has already died, and the world as we know it exists in the moments between his death and the beginning of the apocalypse. When Loki engineered Baldur's death, the loss and grief Frigg felt were compounded by the realization that the end of the world had just begun—and her failed attempts to save him proved once more that there was no way to prevent it.

Baldur, the shining, beautiful god of light, represents everything good in the world. When he dies, all the light, warmth, and joy fades from Asgard and Midgard. The sun still shines, but the world is colder, darker, less vibrant. In Baldur's absence, evil and malice are free to spread through the world. Eventually, some time after Baldur's death, the precursor signs of Ragnarök begin.

TOP: Asgard burns. A scene from the climax of Ragnarök, after Surtr has engulfed the world with fire. Illustration by Emil Doepler, from *Walhall, die Götterwelt der Germanen*, 1905 (see pages 124–125); **ABOVE:** Detail of the north portal of the 12th-century Urnes stave church. Many stave churches have been dated back to the 9th and 10th centuries. The Urnes church's depictions of snakes and dragons are thought to represent Ragnarök; **BELOW:** *Ragnarok: the End of the World.* Liebig Products collectors' card, 1934.

ABOVE: *Beginn des Weltunterganges.* (Beginning of the end of the world). Loki breaks free from his fetters at the beginning of Ragnarök and faces the snake that has tormented him. Illustration by Ernst Hermann Walther; **BOTTOM RIGHT:** Naglfar and Fenrir on the Tullstorp Runestone in Scania, Sweden; **OPPOSITE, TOP:** *Kampf der untergehenden Götter*, (*Battle of the Doomed Gods*), illustration by F.W. Heine. Ragnarök begins—Odin rides into battle, aiming his spear towards the gaping mouth of the wolf Fenrir. Thor defends against the serpent Jörmungandr, while wielding his hammer Mjölnir, Freyr and Surtr fight, and an immense battle goes on around and atop Bifröst behind them; **OPPOSITE, BOTTOM:** "Then the awful fight began," by George Wright.

THE EVENTS OF RAGNARÖK

First will come an age of ice and darkness. This first stage will be called the Fimbulwinter: a long, freezing cold winter that deadens the earth and covers the land and snow and ice. The winter will last three long years with no summer or spring, and everywhere in Midgard and Asgard alike will be rendered frozen and bleak. The arrival of the Fimbulwinter marks the day when the gods will know, beyond a shadow of a doubt, that Ragnarök has finally come.

During this long period of darkness and cold, the humans of Midgard will begin to turn cold in equal measure. Driven by hunger, misery, and resentment, the humans will turn on each other. The Fimbulwinter opens the path for an age of senseless violence and unending war. The world of midgard will be ravaged by crime and hatred, and wanton bloodshed will become commonplace. Brothers will kill brothers, fathers will kill sons, and all family bonds and friendships will be broken.

Weakened by the darkness, the cold, and the depravity that the world of Midgard beneath them has spiraled into, the sun and moon in their shining chariots will slow in their perpetual race across the sky. Finally, after eons of fruitless hunting the sun and moon, the great wolves Skoll and Hati will finally catch their prey. Skoll will crush the sun between his teeth, Hati will drag the moon from the sky, the stars will vanish from the sky, and Midgard will be flooded in a sea of celestial blood. With the wolves finally fed, the world will be plunged into deep, endless darkness.

The earth itself will begin to shudder. Trees will sway and fall, mountains will crumble; the seas will rise, and every bond and binding and shackle will break. Loki and his children will be freed: Loki will emerge from his cave to join the frost giants in their war against the gods, Fenrir's magical bindings will snap, and Jörmungandr will writhe from the ocean onto dry land. Fenrir and Jörmungandr will charge across Midgard side by side, Fenrir breathing out flames and Jörmungandr spewing rivers of venom. The dread ship Naglfar, made of dead men's nails, will break free of its grave deep under the sea; With the frost giant Hymir at its helm, the Naglfar will carry all the frost giants towards the field of Vigrid. Loki will sail for Vigrid in his own ship, carrying with him all the dishonored and resentful souls of hell: the murderers, the liars, the thieves.

The sky will split open, and Surtr the fire giant and the Sons of Muspell will finally break free of the flaming abyss of Muspelheim, tearing their way into the world of Midgard.

The fire giants will ride through the sky and across the Bifröst towards Asgard, shattering the Rainbow Bridge behind them. The fire giants, the frost giants, Loki and his horde of dishonored dead, and all the evil things in the world will gather on the green field of Vigrid, their ranks stretching hundreds of miles in every direction.

At the very first omen of Ragnarök's arrival, Heimdall in his high tower will blow the Gjallarhorn, sounding the call that the end of the world has begun. The gods will wake, and make ready for war, gathering at the gates of Asgard. Odin and his eight-legged horse Sleipnir will ride out to Mimir's well of knowledge one last time, where Odin and Mimir will exchange final, secret words that will never be known. Yggdrasil, the great world tree that holds up the cosmos, will groan and creak; its branches will shake, and every being in all the realms will be filled with fear.

The gods will arm themselves and march towards Vigrid with Odin leading his host of fallen warriors at the front. Odin will wear his gold helmet and carry his magic spear, Thor will wield Mjölnir; but for all their preparation, the gods will be forced to enter the final battle at a disadvantage. Odin has only one eye; Tyr has only one hand; and Freyr, having given away his magical sword, has only an antler to fight with. Their forces will be diminished by the death of Baldur and Hodur, and Loki—who was once one of them—will abandon Asgard to fight on the side of the giants.

Then, finally, the battle of Ragnarök will begin. Odin and his 800-strong army of einherjar will face down the great wolf Fenrir; they will fight more valiantly than any man or god has ever fought or ever will, but it will not be enough. Odin and his army of spirits will fight alone: Thor and the world serpent crash into each other on one side, and Tyr and the vicious hellhound Garmr wrestle on the other. In the center of the battlefield, Freyr will do battle with Surtr and his flaming sword, keeping the leader of the fire giants at bay with only an antler for a weapon.

Odin will be the first to fall in battle. Fenrir, though grievously wounded, will defeat the king of the gods, and Odin will be torn apart after the last of the einherjar fall around him. Odin's son Vidar will take up his father's spear and hurl himself at the wolf in blind rage and despair. Vidar will leap into Fenrir's mouth, stand on his giant teeth, and tear Fenrir's jaws apart with his bare hands before plunging Odin's spear into the wolf's throat.

The ground will shake as Thor and the world serpent do battle. Though Thor will strike Jörmungandr dead with his mighty hammer, the serpent's dying torrent of spewed venom will drench the god of Thunder, half drowning him in poison. Thor will walk only nine steps from the corpse of the world serpent before he too falls to the ground, dead. Thor's sons, Magni and Modi, will pick up Mjölnir and carry it from the battlefield.

Tyr and Garmr will grapple in the mud, tearing into each other recklessly until both lie dead. Loki and Heimdall will face each other and finally settle their longstanding animosity, Heimdall with his sword and Loki with his knife. Heimdall will strike Loki dead, but only after Loki deals him an equally fatal blow.

Finally, Freyr, unarmed and unafraid, will fall in battle to Surtr. Surtr will swing his flaming sword wide and cast fire across the sky, setting the entire world aflame. The fire will consume all living things, the seas will boil, and the gods, the giants, and all the evil gathered on the plane of Vigrid will be turned to ash. In the silence that follows the Earth will sink into the boiling sea.

TOP, MAIN IMAGE: *Odin und Fenriswolf, Freyr und Surt.* Illustration by Emil Doepler, from *Walhall, die Götterwelt der Germanen*, 1905 (see pages 124–125); **MIDDLE:** *Surtr and Freyr*, by the Danish artist Lorenz Frølich; **BOTTOM:** Thor fights Jörmungandr, the World Serpent, in the apocalyptic final battle of Ragnarök.

After some time—days, years, maybe centuries—the Earth will rise anew from the sea. The new Earth will be green again, a vibrant field will spread out from where Asgard once stood, and trees and flowers will grow once more. The gods of light and darkness, Baldur and Hodur, will return from the ruins of Hel to begin rebuilding the world. Hoenir, too, will return alive, as will Odin's sons Vidar and Vali and Thor's sons Modi and Magni. The daughter of Sol, the sun, will take her mother's place in the sky. The surviving gods will gather, mourn their tremendous losses, and then—eventually—begin to rebuild. Finally, from the roots of Yggdrasil beneath Mimir's well, two lone surviving humans will emerge. The couple, Lif and Lifthrasir, will live in harmony with the new earth; they will be unharmed by fire and eat only dew, and from them will come a new line of humans to rebuild the Earth. In time, the ruins of the world that came before will be buried and forgotten, and the cycle of life, death, and rebirth will begin again.

LEFT AND BELOW: *Das Goldene Zeitalter* (*The Golden Age*). Norse mythology says that a Golden Age will follow Ragnarök. Illustration by Emil Doepler, from *Walhall, die Götterwelt der Germanen*, 1905 (see pages 124–125); **ABOVE:** *Lif and Lifthrasir*. After the apocalypse of Ragnarök, two new humans, Lif and Lifthrasir, emerge in the aftermath and repopulate the earth. Illustration by Lorenz Frølich.

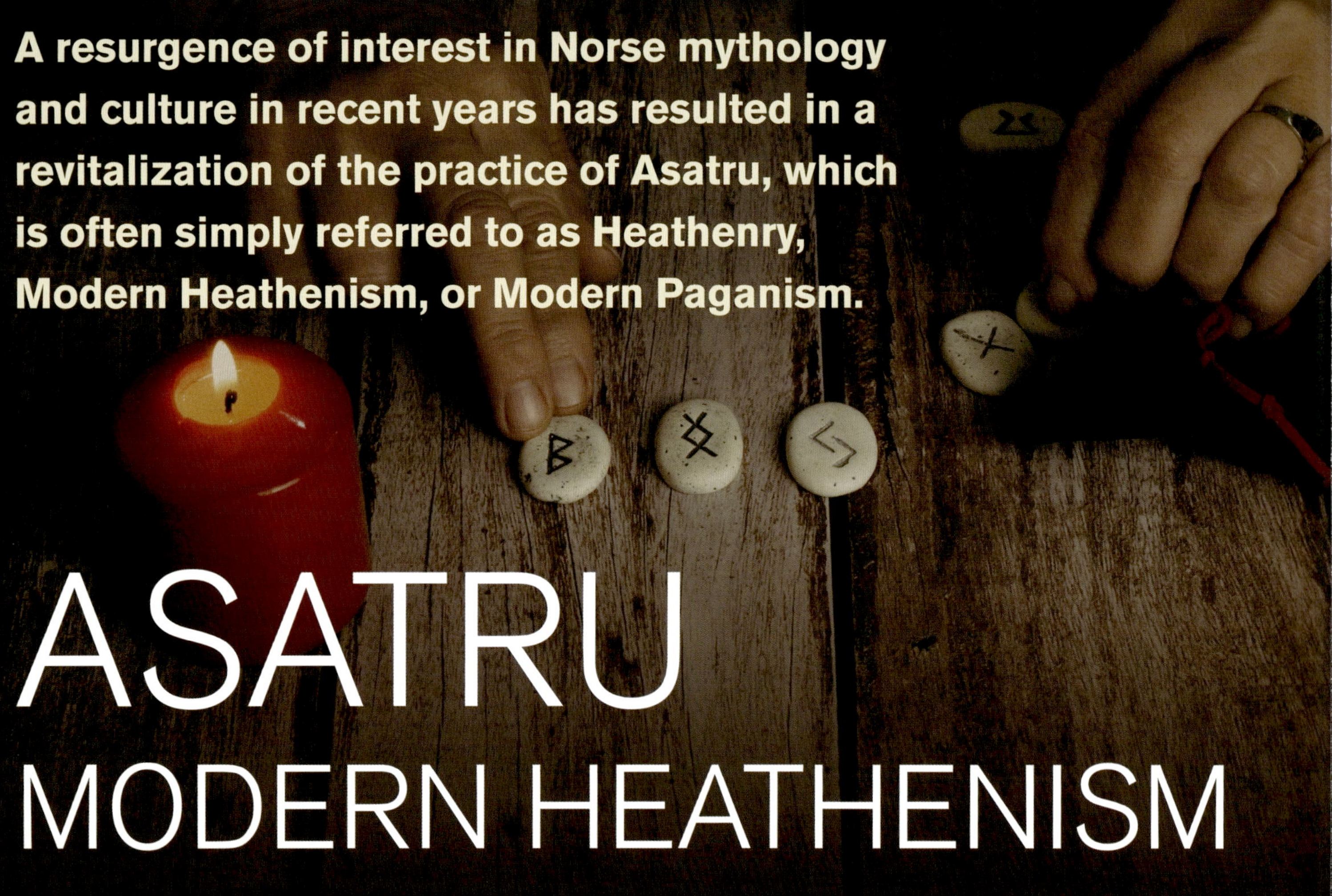

A resurgence of interest in Norse mythology and culture in recent years has resulted in a revitalization of the practice of Asatru, which is often simply referred to as Heathenry, Modern Heathenism, or Modern Paganism.

ASATRU
MODERN HEATHENISM

Asatru incorporates the belief systems and practices of old Norse religion into modern life, often with particular focus on the rituals and ceremonies practiced by the Norsemen. Asatru first developed in the late 19th century. The *völkisch* movement led by the Nazi party in the early 20th century caused a schism in the Heathen community: Heathenry today is divided sharply between the *universalists*, who believe that Heathenry should be open to people of any ethnicity, and the *folkish*, who adhere to the racist ideology of the völkisch movement.

The term Asatru literally means "Aesir belief," referring to those who venerate the Aesir gods. This is the most common variety of Modern Heathenism, although there are some groups who instead venerate the Vanir gods, deities from other cultures, or even the Jotunn. As with the original Old Norse religion, the concepts of personal honor and the value of one's word are core aspects of Asatru. Emphasis is placed heavily on one's deeds and actions in life, and sworn oaths are treated with great reverence in adherence to the original values of ancient Norse culture. Similar to the practices of the old Norse religion, Heathenry has no unified theology. Instead, it is generally the case that each individual or small group worships the way they see fit, focusing on the particular aspects of Old Norse religion that are most valuable or significant to them. This allows for some inconsistencies when looking at Heathenry as a whole, but it also means that each individual's relationship to their belief system is personal and intentional.

One popular aspect of Modern Heathenism is a focus on ritual magic, particularly the practices of *seidr, galdr,* and rune divination. A common practice involves the creation of runic sigils, which are magical symbols designed to represent a specific intent based on the runes used and the configuration they are arranged in. Sigils are usually made by writing a word or phrase in Elder Futhark runes, then condensing and overlapping the runes into a single design. These are then often carved into objects to be carried as talismans or worn as jewelry. Rune casting—analyzing the arrangement and meaning of a randomly-drawn selection of runes—is used to interpret the past, present, or future, similar to the practice of Tarot reading. Many early forms of rune-based magic can be found in *grimoires* (spell books) such as the *Galdrabók*, a 16th century Icelandic text featuring 47 sigils, spells, and incantations.

Norse runes and sigils have also become very popular in the world of body art in recent years. Tattoos that feature specific runes, runic phrases, or sigils—often intended to grant protection, luck, or peace of mind—are common even among non-Heathens. Some of the most commonly-used sigils in Asatru body art are the helm of awe, which invokes bravery and protection in battle; the web of wyrd, which represents fate; and the vegvisir, which guides and protects travelers safely home.

OPPOSITE, TOP: A woman uses rune stones, with black symbols, for fortune telling; **OPPOSITE, BOTTOM LEFT:** *The Northern Gods Descending* by W.G. Collingwood, 1890; **TOP, LEFT:** A man with a Helm of Awe tattoo; **ABOVE:** The sigils of, from the top: the Helm of Awe; the Web of Wyrd; and the Vegvisir; **FAR LEFT:** The völvas, pagan priestesses who specialize in chanting *galdrs*; **LEFT:** A page from the *Galdrabók*, an Icelandic grimoire (book of magic). It contains magical drawings, spells and the use of herbs. The *Galdrabók* manuscripts are 17th century, though the genesis of the spells probably pre-dates the Viking Age (c. 800–1100 AD); **BOTTOM LEFT:** Detail from an Old Norse wedding. Hands hold the Oath Ring, and a wedding couple swear an oath of allegiance.

INDEX

CREDITS

The majority of the images in this book are in the public domain, but in all cases are courtesy of: **The Metropolitan Museum of Art, New York City; Shutterstock; Wikipedia;** and **Wikimedia Commons; Alamy; Adobe Stock; Fine Art Images; Arni Magnusson Institute, Iceland; Mary Evans Picture Library; Vikings Brand; Educational Publication Company; The Statens Historiska Museum, Stockholm; The British Library.** Contact Moseley Road Inc. for errors or omissions.